Country Women
Cope with Hard Times

WOMEN'S DIARIES AND LETTERS OF THE SOUTH
Carol Bleser, Series Editor

Country Women Cope with Hard Times

A Collection of Oral Histories

Edited by Melissa Walker

University of South Carolina Press

© 2004 University of South Carolina

Published in Columbia, South Carolina, by the
University of South Carolina Press

Manufactured in the United States of America

08 07 06 05 04   5 4 3 2 1

Library of Congress Cataloging-in-Publication Data

Country women cope with hard times : a collection of oral histories / edited by
Melissa Walker.
    p. cm. — (Women's diaries and letters of the South)
Includes bibliographical references.
  ISBN 1-57003-524-5 (cloth : alk. paper)
  1. Rural women—South Carolina—Diaries. 2. Rural women—Tennessee—
Diaries. 3. Rural women—South Carolina—Correspondence. 4. Rural women
—Tennessee—Correspondence. 5. Depressions—1929—South Carolina.
6. Depressions—1929—Tennessee. 7. South Carolina—Rural conditions.
8. Tennessee—Rural conditions. 9. Oral history. I. Walker, Melissa, 1962–
II. Series.

HQ1438.S6 C68 2004
305.4'092'2757—dc22   2003020071

Dedicated to the honor of my grandmother
Evelyn Petree Lewellyn
And in memory of my grandmother
Maude Lambert Walker

CONTENTS

Illustrations

County Women Cope with Hard Times: A Collection of Oral Histories is the twentieth volume in what had been the Women's Diaries and Letters of the Nineteenth-Century South series. This series has been redefined and is now titled Women's Diaries and Letters of the South, enabling us to include some remarkably fine works from the twentieth century. This series includes a number of never-before-published diaries, some collections of unpublished correspondence, and a few reprints of published diaries—a potpourri of nineteenth-century and, now, twentieth-century southern women's writings.

The series enables women to speak for themselves, providing readers with a rarely opened window into southern society before, during, and after the American Civil War and into the twentieth century. The significance of these letters and journals lies not only in the personal revelations and the writing talent of these women authors but also in the range and versatility of the documents' contents. Taken together, these publications will tell us much about the heyday and the fall of the Cotton Kingdom, the mature years of the "peculiar institution," the war years, the adjustment of the South to a new social order following the defeat of the Confederacy, and the New South of the twentieth century. Through these writings, the reader will also be presented with firsthand accounts of everyday life and social events, courtships and marriages, family life and travels, religion and education, and the life-and-death matters that made up the ordinary and extraordinary world of the American South.

The rise of oral history as a scholarly discipline in the twentieth century offers opportunities for historians and, indeed, book publishers to include the lives of Americans who have left few or no written records. Professor Walker and others have found a way to capture the immediacy of their subjects' experiences and to preserve them as part of the historical record. An important theme of Walker's *Country Women Cope with Hard Times* is her examination, by way of the life stories she presents, of the great transition that took place in the American South as farming for a living was replaced by an economy based upon industry and commerce. These women, born between 1890 and 1940 in eastern Tennessee and western South Carolina, grew up on farms, in labor camps, and in remote towns during an era when the region's agricultural system changed dramatically. Their recollections paint a vivid picture of rural life in the first half of the twentieth century for a class of women underrepresented in the historical canon. Their life stories reveal the effects upon two generations of southerners of the industrialization of their region and the reintegration of the South into the national and world economy. While they recollect hard times—drought, low crop prices, and the uncertainties of tenant farming—they also talk of good times and the communities of church and kinfolks that they sustained as wives, mothers, and independent women. In some ways these women recount the last stages of darning and restitching the fabric of the nation that was torn apart by the American Civil War.

Carol Bleser

Acknowledgments

Any collection of stories is a collaborative work, and I am grateful to many people who made this collection possible. First, I am deeply appreciative of the women who shared their life stories with me. All the women here shared their stories with a generosity of spirit I hope to emulate, and I thank them for their time and their openness.

I also appreciate the help of all those who pointed me to oral history subjects, including Ann Ross Bright, who gave up several days of her busy summer in 1994 to arrange interviews and to accompany me while I spoke with members of her community. Margaret Proffitt suggested several wonderful Blount County, Tennessee, narrators, as did my parents. Frances Amidon suggested that I interview Virginia Harris and Dorothy Skinner. Mike Corbin shared his notes on peach farming and directed me to Ruth Hatchette McBrayer. Sheila Oliver read about my book in her local newspaper and contacted me to suggest that I interview her parents, Mary and Eldred Quinn. The ever alert Alumnae Office staff at Converse College shared Elizabeth Adamitis's correspondence about her mother, an action that ultimately led me to meet Mrs. Adamitis and spend time with her in her beloved Sevier County in Tennessee.

I thank Carol Bleser for suggesting that I edit some of my oral history interviews for a collection in order to make these wonderful stories available to a wider audience. I appreciate her encouragement and guidance throughout this process. I appreciate the support and advice of Alex Moore, my editor at the University of South Carolina Press, and the suggestions of two anonymous readers of the original book proposal. Their ideas have strengthened this book and made it more useful for readers.

I am especially grateful to colleagues who read portions or all of the manuscript. Thanks to Cathy Jones West, Laura Feitzinger Brown, and Suzanne Schuweiler-Daab for their most helpful comments on the afterword. I also appreciate psychologist Monica McCoy's careful reading of the afterword, especially the section on memory. She saved me from some embarrassing errors and shared additional scholarship on memory that has strengthened the afterword. Thanks to my colleague John Theilmann for reading the entire manuscript and making some important suggestions.

I owe a very special thanks to Rebecca Sharpless. Colleague and friend, she made time to read the manuscript during an extremely busy and stressful period in her own life. Her careful reading saved me from some careless errors, and her cogent comments on the introduction and the afterword improved both immensely. Rebecca's respectful approach to oral history interviewing and the use of oral history in scholarship is a guiding example to me, and I am grateful for her help and her friendship.

As always, I thank my colleagues at Converse College for their support and encouragement of my scholarship and particularly for their interest in my efforts to preserve the life stories of ordinary southerners. I especially thank my department chair, Joe Dunn, for his encouragement (indeed prodding) of my writing and for his efforts to provide me with a flexible teaching schedule that enables me to carve out time to work on my scholarly projects. I thank the Converse Faculty Development Committee for summer research grants that have supported some of this research.

Thanks to my parents, Guy and Rachel Walker, and to my husband, Chuck Reback, for their abiding love and support. They are my biggest cheerleaders.

This book is dedicated to the honor of my maternal grandmother, Evelyn Petree Lewellyn, and in memory of my paternal grandmother, Maude Lambert Walker. They are two rural southern women whose lives continue to provide lessons that guide my own.

INTRODUCTION

Farm Women and Their Stories

> Stories . . . are the tale, the people who tell them, the words they are made of, the knot of memory and imagination that turns material facts into cultural meanings. Stories . . . communicate what history means to human beings.
>
> Alessandro Portelli

I have listened to stories about hard times on the farm for my whole life. Growing up on an east Tennessee dairy farm in the heart of what was then a thoroughly rural community, I spent many hours listening to the older people around me describe those challenging early-twentieth-century farm years. I heard my grandparents and their friends lament drought years, early freezes, and low livestock and crop prices. They told vivid stories about farmhouses burning, children falling out of cherry trees, and colorful hired hands. Even my parents' generation got in on the act, comparing new farming disasters to the year the hail destroyed the wheat crop and measuring new ideas to improve profitability against the years "we grew tomatoes."

Given the way that these stories molded my consciousness—the way they provided me with a way of understanding my family's past—I guess it is no surprise that I have centered my academic studies on the stories that people tell about farm life. I turned to historians' accounts of life on the land in the early-twentieth-century South to place the stories I heard in a larger context, first writing an undergraduate thesis on the impact of the Tennessee Valley Authority on agriculture. I wrote my doctoral dissertation on the impact of twentieth-century transformations of southern agriculture on the region's women. Although government records and other documents provided plenty of details about the nature of the transformation, these written sources provided few clues to what women themselves were thinking and feeling. To understand women's responses to the changes sweeping their lives, I turned again to the stories the old farm people told.

Alessandro Portelli is right that stories "communicate what history means to human beings." Stories are powerful tools for understanding the ways ordinary people interpret the larger events shaping their lives. People tell stories to make sense of the world around them; in the words of historian Rhys

Isaac, the story is "a developed form of narrative that pervasively orders our worlds." He goes on to explain that

> Stories generate and sustain most of our knowledge of human affairs through their terse presentation, review, and evaluation of particular actions, great and small. In telling, interpreting, and commenting on our own and others' actions, we gain our most valued knowledge of ourselves and others. In establishing a sense of person and a sense of self, stories do essential cultural work.[1]

Isaac points to another function of stories: people use stories to express their sense of who they are—their identity. By telling a life story, an individual not only talks about the activities that filled her days, but she can also assert to a listener her values, hopes and dreams, disappointments and setbacks— all the facets that make an individual unique. People tell stories as a means of sustaining their personal identities—their sense of uniqueness.[2]

Finally, people use stories to educate others about the past—their personal past and the way the larger historical past affected ordinary people. In the process they communicate ideas about how people *should* live their lives and about the range of possibilities for human beings in any given setting. As Tim O'Brien has observed, "Stories are for joining the past to the future. Stories are for those late hours in the night when you can't remember how you got from where you were to where you are. Stories are for eternity, when memory is erased, when there is nothing to remember except the story."[3]

First and foremost, then, this is a book of stories. It is an edited collection of oral histories from women who lived in rural South Carolina and Tennessee in the first half of the twentieth century. The stories that these women tell provide readers with insights into the ways ordinary women experienced economic hardship, agricultural transformation, and the joys and challenges of rural life. By reading their stories, we get a sense of the things these women thought were important and the lessons they wanted to pass on to the next generation. They share vivid memories of the transformations that gripped the rural South during the early and mid twentieth century.

Reconstructing the lives of elite women who kept diaries and wrote letters has always been easier than studying ordinary women who left few written records. Women whose lives were filled with an endless round of physical labor rarely enjoyed the leisure or, often, the education to create written documents. As a result, historians have had to look for other methods to help us reconstruct the lives of ordinary people, and we turned to stories. In the past thirty years, social historians have developed oral history as a tool to aid in understanding the lives of ordinary Americans—as a way to give voice to the voiceless. Although there are limitations and challenges to using oral history as a source of evidence—limitations and challenges discussed in the afterword—oral history narratives are a rich source of information and understanding about the past as lived by the average southern farm woman early in this century.

A Note on Method

Most of these interviews were completed between 1992 and 1998 for use in my dissertation and subsequent book, *All We Knew Was to Farm: Rural Women in the Upcountry South, 1919–1941* (Baltimore: Johns Hopkins University Press, 2000). *All We Knew Was to Farm* is a monograph that examines how women in the hill and mountain areas of the rural South coped with the Great Depression, rural industrialization, shifts in the structure of the agricultural economy, and increasing government intervention in daily rural life. I have since completed more interviews as part of my ongoing research on rural southern life between the two world wars.[4]

Given my roots in east Tennessee, I began my research there. I used my own and my parents' contacts in farming communities and agricultural organizations to locate about thirty subjects. I also sent author's queries to local newspapers, requesting that people who were interested in talking with me about early-twentieth-century farm life contact me. This proved to be my least successful method of locating oral history subjects; although most newspapers printed the queries, I located only three interviewees this way. For later interviews, I turned to referrals from local county extension agents, community leaders, and other sources to locate people who might be willing to talk with me. Usually I had one face-to-face interview with the subject. Most interviews lasted between one and two hours. I structured the interviews loosely, beginning by telling the subjects the nature of my project and asking them to tell me what they remembered about rural life in the early twentieth century. The subjects largely shaped their own interviews. Most people began telling their stories in childhood, but others began at other points in their lives. I followed up on their recollections with additional questions and asked specific questions they had not addressed before we concluded.

I then transcribed each interview as accurately as possible. I did not try to replicate the subjects' regional accents and dialects. Rather, I transcribed the interviews into Standard English. For example, I did not drop the *g* off of a word ending in *ing* regardless of how the subject may have pronounced it. On the other hand, in the transcripts, I left grammatical errors, stuttering, and digressions intact.

Once the interview was transcribed, I sent each person I interviewed a copy of her transcript and asked her to make corrections. I also sent each subject a family history questionnaire that asked her to trace her own ancestors and descendents two generations in each direction. Additionally, I often appended a list of additional questions. Most subjects responded by completing the family history form and answering my questions in writing. A few indicated corrections to the transcript on a separate sheet; a few others annotated the interview transcripts to provide additional information and/or to make corrections. Some made no changes at all.

The transcripts were useful to me as a researcher, but they would not appeal to the average reader. Transcripts are often disjointed, repetitive, and confusing. As with all personal conversations, oral history narrators jump from one topic to another and back, free-associate, mumble, and use hand gestures to transmit meaning. Many of these idiosyncrasies are indicated in the transcript, but they are confusing and difficult to follow, particularly if one cannot compare the transcript with the tape recording. As a result, turning oral interviews into a book required extensive editing for clarity and readability. I began by selecting the most vivid interviews—those that provide the clearest picture of rural women's lives in the interwar years. Using standards established by earlier oral historians, I turned question-and-answer interview transcripts into narrative accounts.[5] I began the editing process by reordering the material so that it formed a coherent narrative, but I tried very hard to preserve the connections made by the narrator. For that reason, sometimes a narrator will return to a subject she has discussed early in the narrative because it connects with a topic she brings up later. I eliminated stuttering, false starts, unnecessarily repetitious information, and distracting asides as well as my own questions and statements as the interviewer. I often needed to add transitions and parenthetical information to improve the flow and clarity; these additions are indicated in brackets. Where annotation was necessary to identify people or places, define unfamiliar terms, or explain obscure references, I did so in a footnote or in brackets. As in the transcripts, I left grammatical errors intact, but I did not try to replicate regional accents. My goal was to preserve the unique voices of these women while making their stories lively and accessible for the general reader.

A brief biographical sketch of the narrator precedes each interview. Using the family history questionnaire each woman completed, as well as information from my notes gathered before or after the formal interview, I provide the reader with an overview of each woman's life. This sketch also includes some background information on the narrator's family and community, explains unusual details from each woman's life, and describes the environment in which the narrator lived, the setting of the interview, and the corrections the interview subject made to the original transcript.

Organizing these narratives proved challenging. I could not organize them thematically, since most of the women talked about the same major themes. I finally grouped them geographically, beginning with the women who lived in the east Tennessee mountains, followed by women from the Tennessee foothills. Then I moved to the South Carolina upcountry, concluding with a single interview from the South Carolina piedmont. Within these categories, interviews are arranged in a roughly chronological order based on the narrator's birth year.

RACE AND CLASS IN THE UPCOUNTRY

These interviews are not intended to provide a cross section of upcountry southern life. Because most tenant-farming families left the land by mid century, I found it difficult to locate narrators with tenant-farming backgrounds, though there are a few here. Most of these narrators were themselves landowners or were the daughters of landowners, making them more prosperous than many upcountry southerners. As a result of their higher socioeconomic status, a disproportionate number of the women whose stories are told here enjoyed high school or college educations. Indeed several became schoolteachers. Several women spent time moving back and forth between town and country (see below).

The interviews are also not representative with respect to race. Racial segregation was a way of life in the upcountry South, and the Jim Crow system shaped the lives of black and white women. Yet the African American farm population of the upcountry was small compared to the rest of the South. For example, only 4 percent of east Tennessee and 25 percent of upstate South Carolina farmers were African American in 1920. In the 1930s and 1940s, African Americans found themselves lured off the land by job opportunities elsewhere and pushed off the land by mechanization and by government policies that favored large landowners over small landowners and tenants.

I have written at length about the lives of African American farm women elsewhere, but readers will not find interviews with them here. Locating African American women with farm backgrounds proved difficult. For the most part, their families left the land years ago, particularly in east Tennessee and upstate South Carolina. For this reason, I was able to identify few African American women to interview either through my personal networks or through the author's queries that were printed in local newspapers. I did conduct three interviews with African Americans, but for various reasons they were not suitable for inclusion in this collection. Two were simply not as rich in detail as the interviews I have included, while the third narrator left the farm at the age of six and focused her interview on recalling the farm life of her great-grandmother. To reconstruct the lives of African American farm women, I relied on various government records, manuscript sources, and oral history interviews conducted by other scholars and archived for general use. For these reasons, all of the women whose stories are included in this collection are white.[6]

The Rural Upcountry, 1900–1945

The women whose stories are found in this book lived in east Tennessee and upstate South Carolina, and they were born between 1890 and 1940. At first blush, the two regions may seem an odd pairing. East Tennessee is often associated with the hill people of Appalachia, while South Carolina is seen as plantation country. And to some extent, the choice of these two regions for my research was an accident of geography. The initial research was conducted in my hometown and surrounding counties of east Tennessee. Later I moved to upstate South Carolina, and I found it convenient to conduct research there.

But upon closer examination, the two regions are not so different. The agricultural patterns in each region were similar. In both east Tennessee and upstate South Carolina, most early-twentieth-century farmers practiced diversified general farming. Farm families in both areas were likely to combine subsistence strategies with involvement in the market economy. They produced a variety of crops, garden produce, and livestock for family use and also one or more crops for sale on the market. In east Tennessee, farmers usually produced tobacco, corn, or perhaps livestock for sale, while in upstate South Carolina the cash crop was more likely to be cotton or peaches. Some farmers in both areas devoted most of their time to subsistence production; others devoted most of their time to cash crops. Three socioeconomic groups farmed in both regions: prosperous landowners, marginal landowners, and tenants with various arrangements. Both regions also offered some off-farm employment alternatives to rural people. East Tennessee farmers could often go to work for timber and mining companies who extracted the area's natural resources, while upstate South Carolina farmers often turned to jobs in the region's textile mills to supplement their farm incomes.[7]

Farmers in both areas operated within the context of a complex credit system known as the crop-lien system, which had evolved in the years after the Civil War. Strapped for cash with which to pay laborers in the wake of emancipation, landowners contracted with landless agricultural workers to work their land. The arrangements varied from landowner to landowner and from one region to another, but in general landowners provided tenants with land and a house in exchange for cash rent or for a share of the crop. The latter arrangement became known as sharecropping. Cash renters paid a fixed rent for their land, bought their own seed and equipment, and usually owned their own tools and work stock. In addition to a house, they usually received a garden plot and sometimes worked for cash wages on the landowner's farm. Cash renters kept all the profits from their crops, and they were free to move to a new farm at will (although they usually waited until after the harvest since they could not move the crops in which they had invested so much labor and money). Sharecroppers enjoyed less independence than cash renters. Often landowners provided more than land and housing. Some landlords furnished tenants with seed and fertilizer necessary for making a crop. Landlords provided tools and mules to the poorest tenants. The more goods the landlord provided, the more of the crop to which he was entitled. In most areas, tenants who provided their own tools and work stock paid the landlord "on thirds and fourths," that is, with one-third of the corn crop and one-fourth of a cotton or tobacco crop. A sharecropper who provided nothing but his own labor and the labor of his family gave the landowner half of his crop. This arrangement was known as "farming on halves."[8]

The crop-lien system, which originally evolved as an ingenious solution to landowners' lack of cash to pay wages and sharecroppers' desire to farm while maintaining some autonomy in their day-to-day work lives, soon became an insidious trap for many landless southerners. Unable to pay their living expenses throughout the year, many tenants turned to "furnishing merchants," often also landlords, who offered them goods on credit. Tenants charged food, clothing, and even medical bills at the local store in anticipation of a good return from their crops in the fall. The tenants' share of the coming year's crop was used to secure the debt. This arrangement left sharecroppers vulnerable to abuse and exploitation and compromised their independence. Unfortunately, tenants often did not always raise successful crops. A drought or a hailstorm could destroy a crop. A year of low farm commodity prices could mean that the crop did not bring enough money to cover the debt. Furnishing merchants also charged outrageous prices. Since tenants were usually uneducated and often illiterate, rarely able to keep track of their own accounts, they often fell victim to dishonest landlords who did not pay them the market price for their crops or overcharged them for supplies. African American sharecroppers were at a double disadvantage, as they risked violent retaliation if they questioned the authority of the landowner or furnishing merchant. Many tenants often sank deeper and deeper in debt as the years passed, and they were forbidden by law from leaving farms until they had paid off the landowner or furnishing merchant. Often, landless families became locked into an endless cycle of hard work and debt with few options for getting out.[9]

The crop-lien system helped shape farm life in the upcountry. Tenants usually farmed smaller amounts of land than landowners, even marginal landowners. Tenancy was more common in upstate South Carolina, where fewer than half of all upstate farmers owned their land in 1920, compared to two-thirds in east Tennessee. The average farm size was also smaller in upstate South Carolina, meaning that farmers were less likely to have enough land on which to earn a living and feed their families. For example, in Spartanburg County, South Carolina, the average size of a farm operated by a white farmer was forty-nine acres, considerably less than the average farm size of ninety-eight acres in east Tennessee and far too small to adequately support a family of four or more.[10]

The crop-lien system offered large landowners a fairly steady and easily controlled labor supply and enabled them to make a minimum of cash outlays. But small landowners were often little better off than tenants. Although they were independent from landlords, they often found it hard to earn enough cash to pay their property taxes or to buy the equipment and supplies they needed to farm efficiently and successfully. Small landowners were often deeply in debt and dependent on outside wage labor to remain afloat.[11]

By the time the so-called Golden Age of Agriculture dawned in the first two decades of the twentieth century, the crop-lien system was firmly entrenched in the rural South. During those prosperous years, national farm income more than doubled and demand for farm products soared. World War I intensified the prosperity as the United States sought to feed wartorn Europe. The federal government encouraged banks to ease credit strictures, making more loans available for farmers wanting to modernize or expand. Many farm families sought to update their farming operations, buying new labor-saving equipment. Landowners often borrowed money to buy additional land, believing that the prosperity would last. The federal government also encouraged farmers to adopt more modern (and expensive) agricultural practices by providing them with education through the Agricultural Extension Service (AES). Founded in 1914, the AES provided trained professional advisers who would help farmers become more prosperous and more efficient. Agricultural extension agents had female counterparts known as home demonstration agents whose charge was to help relieve the drudgery of farm women's lives by teaching them better methods of operating their households.

Many upcountry farm families lived so much on the economic margins that they scarcely knew a Golden Age existed. Then after World War I, a downturn in the agricultural economy hit all southern farmers hard. As the Europeans resumed farming and normal international trade was restored, farm prices plunged. Cotton prices dropped from 40 cents a pound in the spring of 1920 to 13.5 cents by December of the same year. Tobacco fell from 31.2 cents a pound to 17.3 cents in the same period. By 1922, prices would recover slightly, but they would never reach prewar levels, and they would plummet again with the onset of the Great Depression in 1929. Farmers who had gone into debt in order to purchase land or equipment found themselves unable to pay their bills. Tenants found themselves becoming more deeply indebted to landlords as the prices for commodities such as cotton and corn fell.[12]

During the 1920s, some struggling farm families found economic opportunities in the small towns and cities that dotted the rural South. As the experiences of several of the women in this collection illustrate, poor farm families often moved to town to seek work in textile mills and heavy industry. Many returned to the land because they found town life unpalatable or because their jobs ended, especially as the Great Depression generated massive industrial unemployment.

In spite of intense lobbying from farm organizations, the federal government took only limited measures to assist farmers in coping with the agricultural depression during the 1920s. Congress attempted to raise farm prices by raising tariffs, a measure designed to make competing foreign agricultural commodities more expensive. President Coolidge vetoed the McNary-Haugen bills designed to raise commodity prices to a fairer level. In 1929, Congress passed the Agricultural Marketing Act that sought to facilitate the formation of marketing cooperatives that would sell farm products in bulk and thus raise prices.[13]

These limited government efforts did little to improve the farm economy. For the most part, rural southerners coped with the economic downturn without outside assistance throughout the 1920s. The onset of the Great Depression only made things worse as farm prices fell again. To make matters worse, many farmers who had been able to supplement farm incomes with jobs at local lumber camps or textile mills during the 1920s lost their jobs. It was not until Franklin Roosevelt took office in 1933 that the federal government sought to address the problems of farmers. The first and most far-reaching agricultural reform implemented by the Roosevelt administration was the Agricultural Adjustment Act, passed by Congress in early 1933. The Agricultural Adjustment Act sought to reduce farm overproduction and thus raise commodity prices. The Agricultural Adjustment Administration (AAA) achieved this goal by paying farmers to reduce their production. Like later programs designed to address the problems in the agricultural economy, the structure of AAA programs favored large landowners to the detriment of tenant farmers and indeed provided landowners with incentives to get rid of their sharecroppers. Often the first land that landowners removed from production was that farmed by their sharecroppers, and they did not always share acreage-reduction payments with tenants as the law required. Instead, landlords used their government checks to buy tractors and other equipment that eliminated the need for sharecroppers. Landowners soon found that modern equipment made economies of scale more efficient. In other words, they could maximize profits by buying up small landholdings around them to develop large commercial farming operations. As a result, small landowners often succumbed to economic and social pressure and sold out to larger landowners. Historian Pete Daniel has called this process the "Southern enclosure," because the way landless farmers and marginal landowners were pushed off the land resembled the effects of the enclosure of pastureland in England in the seventeenth century.[14]

If the New Deal profoundly altered the agricultural economy, World War II accelerated the movement away from the land and the trend toward large-scale commercial farming. World War II created new opportunities for off-farm employment, both within and outside the South. As a result, many tenants and marginal landowners left the land forever. The war also stimulated a revolution in agricultural productivity. Improved varieties of crops and livestock, mechanization, and the use of new insecticides and herbicides revolutionized the way farming was practiced all over the country, but especially in the South. For example, the introduction of mechanical cotton pickers during World War II and the use of DDT to treat insect pests such as the boll weevil eliminated the need to chop and pick cotton by hand, making vast armies of sharecroppers and wage laborers obsolete. Between 1940 and 1960, nearly half a million sharecroppers left the land.[15]

After the war ended, the federal government continued its efforts to reduce the agricultural overproduction that helped cause low commodity prices. A complex system of acreage allotments replaced AAA's acreage-reduction payments. The allotment system assigned each landowner a specified number of acres for overproduced commodities such as cotton, rice, and tobacco. The allotments quickly became assets in their own right, with farmers buying or leasing their allotments to other farmers. The largest landowners held the largest allotments and thus reaped the most benefits from the system, often buying out the allotments and the acreage of smaller landowners who found their allotments too small to be profitable.[16]

Thus in the first half of the twentieth century, upcountry agriculture was transformed from a labor-intensive combination of subsistence and market-oriented production to a capital-intensive "industrial agriculture." This transformation would profoundly alter the lives of upcountry women.

Women's Work on the Farm

Living conditions varied widely on upcountry farms. Some of the women who tell their stories here lived in comfortable, large farmhouses that offered plenty of protection against the weather. A few landowning families enjoyed fashionable furniture and modern household conveniences, but most made do with simple serviceable furnishings. Some women enjoyed water piped into the house from a gravity-fed system supplied by a spring or a well, but most carried water. Poorer families lived in substandard housing, often in meager cabins that were not sealed against the weather, insects, rodents, or dirt. Few families, rich or poor, obtained electricity until World War II or later, but a handful of the most prosperous enjoyed Delco or carbide systems that powered lights and a few appliances.

In spite of diverse patterns of farming and racial and class differences, the patterns of daily life varied little for farm women in the upcountry South, and their counterparts in other parts of the South and in the rest of the country would have easily understood the gendered division of labor on southern farms. Women's lives were dominated by endless hard work, the needs of their families, and the rhythms of the seasons. Upcountry farm women engaged in four types of work: (1) reproductive work such as the cooking, cleaning, and child care that "maintained people on a daily basis and intergenerationally,"[17] (2) producing goods for the household and market, (3) field work, and (4) neighborhood mutual aid.

Caring for households and children occupied countless hours of the farm woman's week, and she spent a large proportion of that time on food production. Although men plowed the gardens, women and children were generally responsible for raising the corn, beans, greens, tomatoes, peas, and other vegetables that provided much of the annual food supply. In addition to tending the gardens and harvesting the fresh vegetables, women spent endless hours preserving food for the long winter months. They dried fruit and beans, and they canned vegetables. In the fall, men and women shared the work of killing hogs and preserving pork for the winter. Women were responsible for grinding, seasoning, and canning sausage, rendering lard, and other tasks. Women also usually tended the cows and the chickens. Not only did they feed these animals, they also milked the cows, separated the cream, made the butter, gathered the eggs, and killed the chickens for meals.

Of course, women cooked for their families. Cooking on most southern farms in this period was an arduous task, usually performed on inefficient wood-burning stoves that kept kitchens toasty in the winter and oppressively hot in the summer. Women cooked everything from scratch, including breads and desserts. During the harvest and other peak labor times when hired hands or neighbors were present to help with the field work, farm women could find themselves cooking for a veritable army of hungry men.

Farm women also manufactured most of the family's clothing. They sewed dresses and blouses, coats, and men's shirts. Some women knitted socks and winter hats. They reused the colorful cotton sacks that packaged chicken feed and flour to make children's sunsuits, dish towels, and even sheets. A few very talented women crafted men's suits. Most enjoyed the assistance of at least a treadle-powered sewing machine, but a few had to do all their stitching by hand, often by the light of weak kerosene lights after long days of working in the fields, cooking, cleaning, and child care.

Child care was not the only nurturing responsibility that fell heavily upon farm women. They were also responsible for caring for sick family members, and they often possessed a vast store of knowledge about effective home remedies. Most ailing elderly relatives were cared for at home, and this burden fell on the farmwife as well.

In addition to their reproductive labors, farm women were producers. They not only raised food for the family's consumption, but they also produced goods for the market. Most farm women sold surplus garden produce, milk, butter, and eggs to the local country store or bartered these items with an itinerant peddler in exchange for salt, coffee, sugar, flour, fabric, or other necessities that could not be produced on the farm. Often they used their earnings to buy shoes and schoolbooks for their children, to pay the real estate taxes on their farms, or to pay doctor bills.

Southern farm people, like all Americans, subscribed to the notion that men and women were suited for different kinds of work, and most southerners believed that fieldwork was men's work. Nonetheless, in reality most farm women labored in the fields at least some of the time, and many worked in cotton fields and tobacco patches regularly. Although women often downplay field labor in their oral narratives, it occupied hours of their time, especially at peak times such as planting and harvest. Wives of the most prosperous landowners were less likely to work in the fields because their husbands could afford to hire extra hands, but the wives of poor landowners and sharecroppers formed a vital pool of surplus labor to meet the demands of peak seasons. Some women of all classes even admitted to preferring to work outdoors. Whatever the reasons women worked in the fields, their labor was often essential the farm's success or the family's survival.

Farm women saw their work as an integral part of a family economy. That is, they saw every economic activity as directed toward the well-being of the family. Every item that a farm woman could produce at home was an item that the family did not have to purchase, thus saving their limited cash for more important needs. "Making do"—that is, stretching scarce resources as far as possible—was an important part of the family economy, as were canning and drying homegrown foods to feed the family through the winter. When women earned extra income from the sale of eggs or butter, they usually used it to benefit the family. Working in the fields contributed to the well-being of the family by helping to produce a crop without the expense of hired help. In short, all of the women's work as reproducers, producers, and fieldworkers proved central to the family economy.

Farm families, however, could rarely survive solely on their own resources; they depended on the help of neighbors and kin to survive financial or health crises and to cope with the excess labor demands of the harvest. Farm women were the backbone of these mutual aid networks. They exchanged garden produce with neighbors, sat up all night with a cousin's sick child, took spare clothes to families who lost their homes in fires, and cooked for families who lost a loved one. They assisted relatives and friends with canning, and in return, the relatives helped them. When the men of one family helped the men of another family with the harvest, their wives usually went along to help with the cooking. Farm women's informal visiting helped build and maintain these networks that were crucial to surviving hard times. The strength of mutual aid networks varied from family to family and from community to community. Some long-established communities had strong networks of neighbors and kin, and landowners were more likely to enjoy the fruits of mutual aid networks than tenants because they had long-standing ties to communities. Nonetheless, most rural women reported that mutual aid networks were an important resource.

Upcountry farm women dealt with the agricultural depression of the 1920s and 1930s by intensifying their traditional coping strategies. Whenever possible, they raised bigger gardens, canned more vegetables, and preserved more sausage. They turned old coats or dresses inside out to revive their appearances and make them last a little longer. They saved more eggs or butter for sale at the crossroads store. A few took jobs off the farm or took in boarders to supplement the family income. They picked blackberries by the side of the road and sold them in town. Nonetheless, for the poorest women, the Great Depression taxed their skills and their ingenuity. As unemployment took its toll in cities, many families who had left the land for industrial jobs years before returned home to the farm where they could live rent-free (even if overcrowded) with extended family members and raise their own food. Such strategies helped many families survive, but they also put additional burdens on farmwives. Moreover, the poorest sharecropping women sometimes found themselves homeless, as landowners evicted tenants from land that was removed from production in order to comply with New Deal crop-reduction regulations. Upcountry farm women's experiences of the Great Depression varied widely. Some described those dark years as "more of the same"—as virtually indistinguishable from the poverty of earlier years. Others noted that living on the land allowed them to sustain themselves adequately. But many found that the economic downturn closed off even the limited options they had once enjoyed.

By the late 1930s, as the southern agricultural economy changed, women found their work transformed. As men focused more and more of their energies on specialized commercial farming, developing peach orchards, dairy farms, or staple-crop operations, most women continued to provide most of the family's subsistence. By providing food, clothing, and other goods, women enabled precious cash to be channeled into buying new equipment, more land, and better seed or livestock. Nonetheless, in spite of the continuing importance of their contributions, farm women found their work was valued less in the larger community. Men's work came to be seen as the "real work" of farming because it produced the cash income. Women's food production simply saved money. Their petty commodity production came to be seen as merely providing "pin money," even though most women continued to use their incomes to provide necessities.

As capital-intensive commercial agriculture took hold in the South, a few women actually took more of a role on the farm. They saw themselves as farm partners and helped make management decisions. Others farmed on their own because they inherited land and a farm operation. Still others withdrew from fieldwork entirely and embraced the role of middle-class homemaker, focusing on developing a welcoming home and caring for the children. Some women took advantage of new economic opportunities to take off-farm jobs. They became schoolteachers and storekeepers and school lunchroom supervisors. Many saw these jobs as a way to provide better lives for their children, using their incomes to pay college tuition. Others saw off-farm jobs as a relief from the drudgery of farm work.

By the 1950s and 1960s, life on the farm had changed in profound ways. Most upcountry women who remained on the land found that their lives were more comfortable and more prosperous. Technology had changed the nature of farming, and it had also eased the housekeeping burden of women. Women whose families left the land for industrial jobs and life in towns and cities missed some aspects of country life but usually relished the fact that their standards of living had improved dramatically.

This book includes the stories of the women who experienced the dramatic changes of the twentieth century. The best way to understand the women's lives is to read their words.

Notes

Epigraph: Alessandro Portelli, *The Battle of Valle Giulia: Oral History and the Art of Dialogue* (Madison: University of Wisconsin Press, 1997), 42.

1. Rhys Isaac, "Stories and Constructions of Identity: Folk Tellings and Diary Inscriptions in Revolutionary Virginia," in *Through a Glass Darkly: Reflections on Personal Identity in Early America,* ed. Ronald Hoffman, Mechal Sobel, and Frederika J. Teute (Chapel Hill: University of North Carolina Press, 1997), 206–37, quotes on 206–7.

2. For more on the way people shape stories to explain and give meaning to the past, see for example, Elizabeth Tonkin, *Narrating Our Pasts: The Social Construction of Oral History* (Cambridge: Cambridge University Press, 1992); Raphael Samuel and Paul Thompson, eds., *The Myths We Live By* (Routledge: London, 1990); Alessandro Portelli, *The Death of Luigi Trastulli and Other Stories: Form and Meaning in Oral History* (Albany: State University of New York Press, 1991); Paul John Eakin, *Making Selves: How Our Lives Become Stories* (Ithaca: Cornell University Press, 1999).

3. Tim O'Brien quoted by Susan Engel in *Context Is Everything: The Nature of Memory* (New York: W.H. Freeman and Company, 1999), 161.

4. The Tennessee interview transcripts are archived at the McClung Historical Collection, Lawson-McGhee Library, Knoxville, Tennessee. The Quinn interview transcript is deposited at the Kennedy Local History and Genealogical Collection, Spartanburg County Public Library, Spartanburg, South Carolina.

5. Donald A. Ritchie, *Doing Oral History* (New York: Twayne Publishers, 1995); Lu Ann Jones, "'Mama Learned Us to Work': An Oral History of Virgie St. John Redmond," *Oral History Review* 17 (fall 1989): 63–90.

6. For my other work on rural African American women, see *All We Knew Was to Farm: Rural Women in the Upcountry South, 1919–1941* (Baltimore: Johns Hopkins University Press, 2000); "Shifting Boundaries: Race Relations in the Rural Jim Crow South," in *African American Life in the Rural South, 1900–1950,* ed. R. Douglas Hurt (Columbia: University of Missouri Press, 2003); and "The Changing Character of Farm Life: Rural Southern Women," in *Southern Women at the Millennium:*

A Historical Perspective, ed. Melissa Walker, Jeanette R. Dunn, and Joe P. Dunn (Columbia: University of Missouri Press, 2003).

7. All analysis and statistics are drawn from the U.S. Bureau of the Census, *Census of Agriculture,* vol. 2, pt. 2 (Washington, D.C., 1930), 870–84, 894–902, 470–75. For more on rural east Tennessee, see William Bruce Wheeler and Michael J. McDonald, "The Communities of East Tennessee, 1850–1940: An Interpretive Overview," *East Tennessee Historical Society Publications,* 58–59 (1986–1987): 3–38; Robert E. Corlew, *Tennessee: A Short History,* 2d ed., (Knoxville: University of Tennessee Press, 1990), 284–303; and Ronald D. Eller, *Miners, Millhands, and Mountaineers: Industrialization of the Appalachian South, 1880–1930* (Knoxville: University of Tennessee Press, 1982). On upstate South Carolina, see David L. Carlton, *Mill and Town in South Carolina, 1880–1920* (Baton Rouge: Louisiana State University Press, 1982), 18–25.

8. For more on the crop-lien system, see Pete Daniel, *Breaking the Land: The Transformation of Cotton, Tobacco, and Rice Cultures Since 1880* (Urbana and Chicago: University of Illinois Press, 1985), 4–5; Rebecca Sharpless, *Fertile Ground, Narrow Choices: Women on Texas Cotton Farms, 1900–1940* (Chapel Hill: University of North Carolina Press, 1999), 5–12.

9. Ibid.

10. U.S. Bureau of the Census, *Census of Agriculture.*

11. See Pete Daniel, *Standing at the Crossroads: Southern Life in the Twentieth Century* (New York: Hill and Wang, 1986), 139–41.

12. Figures compiled from U.S. Bureau of the Census, *Census of Agriculture,* pt. 2, (Washington, D.C., 1925), 736–45.

13. David Danbom, *Born in the Country: A History of Rural America* (Baltimore: Johns Hopkins University Press, 1995), 183–92.

14. Daniel, *Breaking the Land,* 162–68.

15. Gavin Wright, *Old South, New South: Revolutions in the Southern Economy Since the Civil War* (Baton Rouge: Louisiana State University Press, 1996), 248.

16. Pete Daniel, *Lost Revolutions: The South in the 1950s* (Chapel Hill: University of North Carolina Press, 2000), 40–58.

17. For this definition of reproductive labor, I am indebted to Evelyn Nakano Glenn, *Unequal Freedom: How Race and Gender Shaped American Citizenship and Labor* (Cambridge, Mass.: Harvard University Press, 2002), 70.

Country Women
Cope with Hard Times

Elizabeth Fox McMahan

THE FOLLOWING NARRATIVE is the only one in this collection that did not begin as an oral history interview. I met Elizabeth McMahan Adamitis serendipitously. Mrs. Adamitis's mother, Elizabeth Fox McMahan, attended Converse College, where I teach. In 2001, Mrs. Adamitis made a gift to Converse in memory of her mother, marking the hundredth anniversary of her mother's graduation. With the donation, she included a marvelous four-page letter describing her mother's life on a farm in Sevier County, Tennessee.

Bobbie Daniel, the alumnae information director at Converse, read the letter and recalled that I had done research in Sevier County, Tennessee. She pointed this out to Alumnae Director Melissa Daves Jolley, who passed along a copy of Mrs. Adamitis's letter to me. I was fascinated with her mother's story, and I immediately wrote to Mrs. Adamitis to ask if I could come see her the next time I was visiting my parents in east Tennessee. Mrs. Adamitis agreed.

On August 16, 2001, I visited with Mrs. Adamitis. I met her at her apartment, which was located on a secondary road just off the main tourist artery that connects Pigeon Forge and Sevierville. These towns are now booming tourist meccas, rather than the sleepy agricultural villages of Mrs. Adamitis's childhood. At eighty, Mrs. Adamitis was still lively and spry. She had strawberry blonde hair and wore glasses with large attractive frames. Her vitality and energy were striking. She devoted the entire day to driving me around Sevier County, showing me the sites where her mother had lived and worked. Along the way she provided me with details of her mother's hard life on the farm. She also gave me copies of family photos and a copy of her own handwritten memoir of her mother. I frantically took notes and taped the conversation, but I quickly discovered that Mrs. Adamitis's memoir was far more articulate, poignant, and detailed than any transcribed oral history interview could be. With Mrs. Adamitis's permission, I have included her story here. This version comprises several letters that Mrs. Adamitis sent to Converse's Alumnae Office and to me, as well as the handwritten memoir. In places, I have reorganized material in order to put similar

Elizabeth Fox upon her graduation from Converse College
in 1901. *Photograph courtesy of
Elizabeth McMahan Adamitis.*

information together. I have added explanatory information in brackets or in footnotes. I eliminated small amounts of extraneous material. I have added some punctuation for clarity, bracketed some additional explanatory words, and spelled out abbreviations, but otherwise I have left Mrs. Adamitis's language and spelling intact. In June 2002, I asked her to read my edited version and make additions or corrections, which she and her sister, Ernestine McMahan Steele, did.

Elizabeth Fox was born October 1, 1879. Her parents were farmers in rural Sevier County. Elizabeth attended Converse College on scholarship, graduating in 1901. Elizabeth Fox's father was already blind from retinitis pigmentosa and probably glaucoma. During her senior year in college, he died. Fox's mother was left with five small children to raise. Fox returned to Sevier County and began teaching school to help her mother make ends meet. In 1903, she married Ernest McMahan, son of a wealthy Sevier County landowner. The marriage was not a happy one, and Elizabeth Fox McMahan found herself burdened with a husband who was not interested in the day-to-day operation of the farm and with a large debt. She had three children early in the marriage and two more children in middle age.

Elizabeth McMahan Adamitis, her daughter and fourth child, was born in 1921. After graduating from the University of Tennessee, the younger Elizabeth attended graduate training in occupational therapy at the University of Pennsylvania and went to work for the United States Army. She spent her career working as an occupational therapist in army and Veterans' Administration hospitals, retiring in 1988. She was married for thirteen years to a man who turned out to be an alcoholic. After her divorce, she devoted herself to her work and to caring for her aging mother. She also had a lively social life, engaging in regular ballroom dancing. She remains active today, working out at the local gym three days a week and attending the meetings of community organizations.

Sevier County was one of the first areas settled in east Tennessee. The county's geography is marked by rolling hills and fertile river bottoms in its northern third and by steep mountainous terrain on the southeastern side. Sevierville, the county seat, was also the trading center for the county, and it anchored the more fertile farming area. The McMahans lived a couple of miles from Sevierville on rolling farmland along Middle Creek. By the early twentieth century, most Sevier County farmers engaged in general production for home use and also produced some wheat, corn, tobacco, and livestock for the market. In 1920, the average Sevier County farm was eighty acres. Thus, the McMahans were among the largest landowners, farming over one thousand acres at one point.

Here is Elizabeth Adamitis's account of her mother's life:

"A Tribute to My Mother"
Written by Elizabeth McMahan Adamitis

My mother's father, Tilmon Fox, was a farmer in the small community of Middle Creek, near Sevierville, Tennessee. Her ancestors had come to Tennessee before it became a state in 1796. The Fox family came to Sevier County by way of Philadelphia and down through the Shenandoah Valley of Virginia. Her great uncle, Mark Fox, was killed by the Indians. He was the first person buried in Fox Cemetery in the Fox community in Sevier County.

The Fox family had been influenced by Quakers so none of them participated in any of the wars that touched this community until my oldest brother was drafted in World War II and served with the Eightieth Division in Patton's Third Army.

The Fox family were educated farm people with teachers and ministers [in the family]. My mother's grandfather was a circuit rider Methodist minister in three local counties.

My paternal grandfather, Thomas DeArnold Wilson McMahan, came out of the mountains in Richardson Cove and married Melinda Trotter, daughter of Dr. William Trotter on Middle Creek. He was an intelligent, aggressive man who started out teaching school and then bought land in Richardsons [*sic*] Cove. He owned a store, tannery, and mill. So he continued to acquire land after moving in with Dr. Trotter, his father-in-law.

My mother and father were raised one mile apart near Middle Creek Methodist Church. The Tilmon Fox and Dr. William Trotter families were closely related for years since Tilmon Fox first married Dr. Trotter's daughter, Elizabeth. When she died, Tilmon Fox married Martha Lawson, a good friend of Elizabeth Trotter.

The first child of this [second] marriage was my mother, Elizabeth Fox, born October 1, 1879. She was highly intelligent and with the help of her great uncle, Dan Lawson, she received a scholarship to Converse College in 1897. Her family had to take her in a buggy part of the way (twenty-five miles to Newport) to catch the train [for Spartanburg]. They spent the night with relatives and continued next day to put her on the train. For her scholarship, Elizabeth chaperoned the girls when they went shopping, to church, to the dentist, etc. She loved Converse and often said it was the happiest time of her life. She wrote a twenty page letter to her family [describing] the funeral of Dr. Converse her first year there.[1]

During her four years at Converse, her father, Tilmon Fox, died, leaving Martha Fox with five young children to raise. In spite of this, she was able to graduate in 1901. She was the only college graduate in her family or in my father's. After she graduated from Converse, she tried in every way to get a job. She made applications in many counties and other states without success. She had to settle for a three month, one room school at twenty dollars a month, paid by local citizens. That was at Jayell School in Middle Creek. She paid one dollar a week for room and board near the school and walked home on the weekends. The next year she taught at Middle Creek as principal of a two-room school for thirty dollars a month, made up [contributed] by people in the community. She applied for jobs in many states and couldn't get a job anywhere. There were few paying jobs for women in 1901. Women could only teach or work in a store at low wages.

She felt she was a burden to her widowed mother and in desperation married my father, Ernest McMahan. My father lived one mile away. He was the son of a wealthy landowner. His little brother died the year before he was born, and the family spoiled him without any discipline. He only went to fifth grade and put my mother down for going to Converse. My mother had no idea what he was like, only that he came from a prominent family.

They were married December 9, 1903, in a buggy after church at Middle Creek Methodist Church. My mother stepped into a life of physical and mental abuse by my father. They moved into an old dilapidated house with only two good rooms on a 420-acre farm that had once belonged to my grandfather, Thomas DeArnold Wilson McMahan. My parents rented from my grandfather until 1921, when he died. The land was part of a one thousand acre farm that my grandfather owned. Before that, my mother told me it was owned by a widow, Nancy McMahan, who farmed it by herself. This must have been following the Civil War.

My mother told me the bottomland was used as a military mustering ground for the Civil War. It seems logical since the largest skirmish here during the Civil War was on the farm of Dr. Hodson which was only about a mile away. There were estimated 265 casualties.[2] When I was a teenager, people found buttons, etc., there.

Before they were married, my father told my mother he owned a team of mules and a cow and horse and buggy, etc. It turned out he owed for all of them, and she had to pay for all of them out of her hard-earned school teaching money. My mother's life was extremely hard from day one when she had to move into that shack of a house. My father never worked a day in his life on the farm. He was lazy and rode off every day on a horse and later in a car to spend all day around the stove in stores in town, telling jokes, always jovial, slapping men on their backs. People cannot believe he was a different personality at home because that was all they ever saw. My mother wouldn't let us say a word of the dysfunctional behavior at home. He would ride off to town every day and leave my mother to raise the children and run the farm, so she was forced to take two hired hands into the house until about 1910 and cook for them and take care of three babies in seven years. My mother tried to get him to work on the farm, but he would beat the horses till my mother couldn't stand it.

My mother loved flowers and trees and working in the flowers was the therapy that saved her with all those babies and being in debt thousands of dollars all those years. She planted an orchard with apple, pear, and peach trees between the house and barn. My father didn't care what he did to her flowers and drove the herd of cattle through the yard, and they trampled many. He tied a goat to one of her trees, and it butted the bark off with its horns, letting bugs into the tree killing it.

Home of Ernest and Elizabeth McMahan, built in 1912. *Photograph courtesy of Elizabeth McMahan Adamitis.*

Before I was born, my father had a sawmill up in Blalock Woods.[3] I can remember an old house where hired men lived and piles of rotting sawdust. Some fields [there] had been cleared and planted in corn. One field was called the "Ten Acres." Every field had a name so the hired hands knew where to work. My father had a herd of Aberdeen Angus cattle which were pastured at times after the corn was gathered. There was no source of water in the pastures, so a big pond was dug for the cattle. We called that the "Pond Field."

My parents built a big white Victorian farmhouse with fireplaces in 1910. My mother had a plan for a compact, low ceilinged house, but my father insisted on nine-foot ceilings like his childhood home on Middle Creek, and we froze in those big rooms heated by fireplaces until some time in the 1930s they brought circulating heaters on the market. It was wonderful to have heat in the back of the room. We still had kerosene lamps and outhouses until the TVA came in the '40s with rural electrification. All the farms in the county were like this. The TVA was a boon to farmers even though it took away some of the best farms in the county. The river bottoms were the richest soil and lots of them are under Douglas Lake. My father cried when they put the big power lines across our fields.

In 1921, when my grandfather Thomas DeArnold Wilson McMahan died, my father bought out all the heirs of the land. We were paying 6 percent compound interest to all my aunts and uncles. I found letters from my aunt demanding money in the midst of the depression when no one had a cent. All my childhood, every cent that was made went to my father's brothers and sisters, and my mother was feeding and dressing us five children with her chicken and egg money. People in the county thought of us as wealthy, but I was the only one in my high school class (1938) who couldn't afford a class ring. My mother paid twenty-five cents a lesson out of her egg money to pay for piano lessons for us three girls. We had lots of land, but very little money.

They now had three hired hands' houses. These men would come to the back door every morning to know what to do. My mother usually had to tell them what to do because he was never there. The hired men called it petticoat government.

In my earliest memory there were three hired men's houses. There was an old log cabin over at the forks of the road. It was really primitive with only one little window. Later a lean-to with windows for a kitchen was built on to this. They had a cistern for water from the spring. I guess before that they carried water from the spring.

The barn, granary, corn cribs, and sheds for machinery were north of the house. They built a building at the barn to house the scales to weigh the cattle. They also built a large machine shed to house the tractor and farm machinery. At the edge of the woods was another frame house for hired hands. It had three or four rooms. I guess there was a cistern for water.

In the Depression, farmers only paid their field hands fifty cents a day, $2.50 a week, all over the South. They got cow pasture, a garden, and a percent of the tobacco crop. Most of them raised hogs to kill so they were better off than poor people in town. Every day for years in the depression, men would come walking up our driveway to try to hire on or to beg for food. My mother always gave them food from her stove—bread, sweet potato pie, or whatever she had extra of. My mother looked after the hired hands' families. She gave the children our outgrown clothes. She gave them food and went to help when they had their babies. She begged every family to buy land with their tobacco money, but only one in all those people did. Papa sold him ten acres of new ground[4] on what's now Pullen Road. He [the buyer] sold that at a profit and bought a small house, barn, and farm on Denton Road. He sold that and bought one hundred acres on New Era Road which is probably worth a million dollars. His two children have no children. They are both high school graduates and still own the one hundred acres. The boy served three and a half years in the army and went into the D-Day invasion of France. They have been solid tax paying citizens for forty years or more, all because their father was willing to buy his own land and work at back breaking work to make a living and own his own land.

My sister and I were born when the three older siblings were already in high school. This made it very hard on my mother. There she was in middle age with two babies.

My older brothers had walked across to Harrisburg to elementary school near the covered bridge. When my sister started to school, my father went to Grainger County and bought a pair of trotting ponies and a buggy so they could drive to Middle Creek Elementary School three miles away. My brother Glenn, who drove the ponies, said the ponies could really move fast since they were trained to compete. My father bought a stallion and started to raise ponies. We always had a herd of twelve to fifteen Shetland ponies. There were six to eight mares who had colts every year and were sold when they were about a year old. In the depression, my mother sold one pony for forty dollars and took our family of seven to Florida for a week.

My two brothers started working on the farm when they were ten and twelve. My brother Glenn tells me they had steers to plow.[5] He said he could get the wooden yoke on one but it was too heavy to lift the other one. I guess the hired man helped him. Our first tractor was a Fordson. My brother Glenn started driving the tractor when he was twelve years old. My brother Wilbur operated the farm machinery behind the tractor.[6]

When my brothers were in college in the 1920s, one summer they dug a well by hand with shovels and buckets to bring up the dirt. My younger sister and I played everywhere on the farm. We were about ten or twelve then as I remember. The hole was about five or six feet in diameter, wide enough for a man to go down on a ladder to dig and send the dirt up in a bucket. In my childish memory they must have struck water about twelve feet down. They sealed it off with stone and concrete. I guess my brothers could do anything. My younger sister and I followed our brothers everywhere. That was part of the fun of living on a big farm and having loving brothers who let us tag along.

In 1929 when the banks closed and "the Great Depression" started, no one had any money. My mother sold eggs for six cents a dozen. With her chicken and eggs and butter, she traded with Mr. Ward the peddler who drove his team and wagon to trade with farmers' wives in our area. My mother bought blueing for the laundry, coffee, sugar, and spices from Mr. Ward. He threw all the butter in a five gallon lard can. I never knew where he sold it. When we got into high school and college, my mother raised more chickens and got enough hens so she could sell a case (thirty dozen) eggs every week. My father went to stockyards in Knoxville every Wednesday, so my mother took the case of eggs to restaurants in Knoxville that day. It gave her an escape from the farm. She would visit some department stores every week and could watch for bargains. She got to know many clerks and they would alert her to coming sales. She was a keen trader. With five children she had to be. I don't think she ever paid more than fifty cents a yard for beautiful yard goods that would sell for two or three dollars a yard. When she died I still had a trunk full of all kinds of fabrics.

The farmers of this county lived through all the many regimes [*sic*] ordered by President Franklin D. Roosevelt. People had to sign up for a tobacco allotment which still stands today, seventy years later. They could be handed down with the land or traded with other farmers, but never increased. Farmers had to kill pigs and cut back on production to raise the price. I thought this was so wrong when there were so many starving people in the world.

We grew everything we ate on the farm as most farmers in the South did. All summer we canned tomatoes, beans, beets, grape juice, etc. My younger sister and I got one cent a dozen for washing the hundreds of quart and half gallon fruit jars that my mother stored in the cellar. My two brothers dug out and built a basement to store the cans of fruit and vegetables and have a place on the dirt to spread onions, sweet and Irish potatoes for the winter.

My father, brothers, and the hired men killed and dressed two hogs. My father shot the hogs and they were dipped in scalding water to get the hair off and they were hung up on a scaffold of fence rail to be scraped. Then they cut the hog from head to tail down its belly, and the innards fell out into a wash tub. They saved the liver for my mother to make liver hash. My father gave the head and feet to the hired men. The intestines were thrown over the fence into the chicken yard.

Hog killing time was hard work for all of us. That day my mother worked from 5 A.M. till 9 or 10 that night. They had to know the temperature to kill the hogs. If it was too cold, the meat in the smokehouse on tables would freeze before the inside had cooled out and would spoil when it melted. If the temperature was too warm, it would spoil. The hams and shoulders were packed in salt on big heavy tables in the smoke house. They were safe to eat until summer. Every night my mother would cut slices of ham and bacon for breakfast the next day. She cut off the rinds and threw them out to the many cats that were kept to catch the mice and rats in the granary and barn. The fat was cut up in small pieces and boiled in the wash kettle to make lard. My brother Glenn built a lard press. It was a square box on legs with a groove cut so the lard could run down into the five gallon lard can.

I don't know what part of the hog was used for sausage, but the men worked far into the night grinding the meat with a grinder attached to a plank laid over a wash tub. At the same time, my mother was frying balls of sausage and canning it in half-gallon jars. She would turn them upside down so the grease would seal the lid. Without refrigeration, it was important to get this done as soon as possible to save the meat. My mother grew red pepper and sage to put in the sausage. It [the red pepper and sage] hung behind the stove. Next morning she would fry the tenderloin, the strip of meat along the spine. This is cut as pork chops in modern times. My mother also fried and canned this to keep it safe until later in the week. Also that week, she would cook the ribs with sauerkraut as soon as possible.

I loved all of this food. The tenderloin she fried for breakfast. I was in hog heaven! The people who got the heads made souse meat with the jowls. When it cooled, after being boiled, it formed a clear gelatin over the meat and could be sliced. I never liked that. Also they ate the brains and ears, I guess.

Behind our kitchen was a pantry where my mother kept a can of that lard [that we had made during hog killing]. She had a flour chest my great uncle Isaac Trotter had built of poplar. The lid lifted up and it held one hundred pounds of flour on one side and one hundred pounds of corn meal on the other side. The corn and wheat was taken in tow sacks to the mill owned by Mr. Reed Wade in Sevierville. Back then, the miller took a toll of the wheat and corn to pay for grinding.

In the 1930s we also got fifty pound blocks of ice from the same mill on Saturday. We made ice cream from pure cream from our Jersey milk cow. It was made in a crank freezer which had a dasher to stir the milk. One of the treats of childhood was the chance to lick the dasher after it was removed.

Our only way to preserve milk and butter was to keep it in a trough of cold water to keep it cool. We had to change the water every two hours in the summer. The water from the well house went into a tile under the driveway into the chicken yard to water the chickens. I envied people on farms around us who had spring houses and cool water to keep their milk cold. The milk would sour or clabber in a few hours so we had to churn often or make cottage cheese with the milk. The cream was skimmed off to churn and the thickened clabbered milk was put in a dish pan on top of our big wood burning cook stove and slowly heated until the curds and whey separated. We put that in cheese cloth and squeezed out the whey which we put in a trough for the chickens. The cottage cheese was dry and firm, so we usually added some cream to it and put it in a dish where we sliced it out. My sister Dorothy would take the leftover biscuits from breakfast and put canned tomatoes on them and a slice of cottage cheese and baked it in the oven. It was delicious. With seven in our family, my mother made a huge pan of biscuits every morning so we kids could take them to school for lunch. We used the sausage, ham or bacon or whatever was left over from breakfast. We loved to take brown sugar from a one hundred pound bag in the pantry and mix with butter and put between saltines. We usually had apples and pears from the orchard which was between the house and the barn. My mother spread them out on newspapers in a storage room upstairs we called the "long room."

We put our lunch in a newspaper and folded it over until it became a square. All the country kids stored these on the shelf in the cloak room which was behind each class room in the old high school. We called them duck nests. I would trade my apples and pears with the town kids for their bananas. The town kids always looked down on us country kids, especially in high school. I think of all the fun things on the farm. I sure am glad I had a sister sort of my age. We knew every inch of that farm.

When I first remember, we had a T Model Ford and a small garage at the bottom of the hill. The T-Model had Eisenglass curtains that snapped in during the winter. Then when my father bought a big Essex sedan so that seven of our family could ride together, they built a two-car garage to accommodate the length of that car. This was in 1928 when I was five years old. My mother told me she had not been off the farm in twenty-five years [at that point]. She told us we were not going to grow up on that farm as "red necks" or something to that effect. So with the new big car that would hold seven people, she started planning trips. Our first trip was to Charleston to see the ocean.

There were no paved roads in 1926. The road to our farm was mud with deep ruts up the hill to the Nelson Fox House. At the forks of the road, there was a quarry that my brothers and hired men worked at to crush rock for the road. At that time, there was a law requiring men to work seven days a year on the public roads or pay a poll tax. So my brothers dynamited the limestone rock and crushed it with the powers of a gasoline engine. They hauled it in a specially-built rock bed on the wagon. It was heavy timbers—like two inches by four inches. The side boards were only about a foot high because the rock was so heavy. The bed was made of many of these timbers. They were not attached so one plank at a time was pulled out so the rock could fall out on the road. Then through the years, they [my brothers] rocked the public road all around our farm and up the driveway to the house.

Anyway, when we went to Charleston, there were no paved roads—all "wash board" gravel roads. When we got to Folly Beach there were no hotels or tourist cabins. We rented a tent on the beach with a wooden platform and army cots. I can still hear the palmettos and tent flapping.

In the 1920s, there were very few public bathrooms, so out on the public roads that trip we had to stop at a wooded area and go in the bushes. It's a miracle we didn't get bitten by a snake. I cut my bare foot there.

Our second long trip was about 1931 when we went to Florida [on that forty dollars my mother made selling a pony.] In the depression, there were many people who left Sevier County to get jobs packing oranges. Some of my father's cousins lived in Winter Haven and Lake Wales, so we stayed with them. With seven in our family, they had to spread us around at different homes. For years we went to Florida every year at Christmas when the schools closed. It was the Depression. My mother saved enough from her eggs to take us. Gas was about fifteen cents a gallon. For lunch we would buy a loaf of bread for five or ten cents. She would buy bologna for a few cents and a half gallon of milk. We took eggs, ham, bacon, and potatoes from the farm to cook for supper. There were a few tourist camps with separate little houses. In Georgia and Florida they were heated with little stoves burning pine wood. They used the heart pine for kindling. They called it fat wood. I loved the smell.

My mother was determined that we would know the history of this country by touring it. We were actually there sometimes when it [history] happened. I can remember going with my family to Bristol to hear Herbert Hoover when he was running for president in the 1920s. In 1932, we went to Washington. That year the veterans from World War I marched on Washington demanding the bonus that Congress promised them in 1918. It was the third year of the Great Depression and times were *bad*. The bonusers had built a huge encampment of cardboard boxes to live in. They had effigies of President Herbert Hoover hung in trees and sitting on toilet bowls. The men had ridden trains in like hoboes. When we were downtown, President Hoover called out the army under General McArthur to force the bonusers out, and they threw tear gas to quell the riot. We were in the middle of it and eyes stung. The tanks rolled through the streets. A black man standing next to us was calling the tanks "catpullers" for the caterpillar-type tracks on the tanks. That night the army or police burned the veterans' boxes. We were in a cabin on the edge of town and we could see the flames. We saw history in the making. I never knew if the veterans got their bonuses at that time.[7]

In 1936, my mother bought a tent from Sears Roebuck. It was completely sealed against moisture and bugs. There were two windows with mosquito netting. My brother fastened the front over the car and staked the back. We had a new car without a trunk, so my brother built a big black box and attached it to the back of the car to carry the oil stove, our clothes, tent blankets to sleep on, and the food my mother brought from home. We could rent a place to set up the tent for fifty cents. They always had a building with showers, bathroom, and laundry shared by the whole camp. We spent three

Elizabeth Fox McMahan with her daughters Ernestine and Dorothy in the family buggy around 1940. This pony and buggy carried the children to school each day for years. *Photograph courtesy of Elizabeth McMahan Adamitis.*

weeks in all the western states except Washington and Oregon. When we were in California, we bought fruit on the side of the road. Glenn would turn the motor off on the hills, and we would coast to save gas. We crossed the bay in San Francisco on a ferry long before the Golden Gate Bridge was built. Very few people in Sevier County went on trips then. By the time I was fifteen, I had seen forty states. My mother scraped and saved and got us there.

My brother Wilbur drove us to Philadelphia and New York. Another time I drove my parents and Dorothy through all the New England states and Quebec and back by upper New York State. I also drove my parents all over Oklahoma and all the way to the Mexican border. We drove all over Texas visiting people who left Sevier County fifty years before that. They could start talking like they left yesterday. It was amazing. I am so glad my mother got to take all those trips. It gave her the strength to tolerate life on the farm.

When I was five years old, my sister Dorothy drove me to school in a pony buggy with one pony named Betsy. My mother would go over to the barn every day and hitch up the pony and bring it out for us rain or shine, and she would be waiting for us to take the pony to the barn. We had a heavy lap robe to put over our laps and legs and often the snow would be piled up on that robe when we got home. We boarded our pony with the Ballards who had a small barn across from the old Sevier County High School. This building had all grades from primer to senior high school. In 1930 Dorothy graduated from high school and went on to college so that year we had to depend on my father to pick us up [from school]. My father spent his day sitting around the stores in Sevierville or at his mother's house on Middle Creek, so many nights Ernestine and I were standing outside the school in the dark waiting for him to pick us up.

I was always hungry when we got home [from school]. My mother always had big pans of peanuts baked in the shell or roasting ears of corn or some tasty thing waiting for us.

The year my sister [Dorothy] was fifteen years old and in high school, the schools in Sevierville, Knoxville, Newport, and Maryville collected pennies to buy land for the start of the Great Smoky Mountains National Park. There is a book in the library of the Sugarlands Visitors Center that lists the names of all the children and teachers who gave money. The teachers gave one dollar and kids gave from ten to twenty-five [cents]. There are names of people still living in this area. The total amount was over one thousand dollars. Wilma Dykeman, genealogist for the state, said that would be worth twenty times that in today's money.[8]

At that time my father, Ernest McMahan, and about ten other lumbermen in Sevier County were hired by Champion Lumber to cruise timber and estimate value for purchase by the park. They were provided with mules and they slept in deserted log houses, and my father brought bed bugs home. We ruined every mattress in the house using kerosene to kill them. There were no insecticides then.[9]

My mother was an excellent farmer. She was forced to be since my father was never there. She took *Progressive Farmer* and all the farm magazines to keep up on the latest and best methods. She knew as much about farming as any man in the county. She knew about rotation of crops which must have been a new idea in the thirties since so much of the farm land in the South was worn out with planting cotton every year. She knew to plant lespedeza for hay and red clover; then it was plowed under to enrich the soil.[10] Before 1920, she encouraged my brothers to grow the first Red Burley tobacco in our county. They were teenagers [at the time].

After breakfast my mother would go to feed the chickens and milk the cow after all us girls were off at college. Her work was *never* done, but after lunch she could lie down for about an hour. The mail came by rural carrier about one o'clock, so she could read the newspapers. She read the farm news and the financial news. She took *Saturday Evening Post* at five cents a copy during the Depression and *Collier's*. Both of these magazines came every week. She subscribed to *McCall's* and to *The Knoxville Journal* which came through the mail the next day.

Our farm was a totally working farm with herds of cattle, ponies, sheep, and hogs. If the market was good for hogs, the corn was fed to the hogs. If the market was best for corn, it was sold. We always had at least thirty acres of wheat. Before combines[11] came on the market, my brothers used a wheat binder to cut the wheat and tie it into sheaves and throw the sheaves off. My brother Glenn drove the tractor and Wilbur operated the binder. Then the hired men would stack the sheaves into shocks. (I see in the dictionary that this word came from Middle English in the fourteenth century.) A pile of sheaves of grain set up in the field with the butt ends down. Then this was covered with a sheave spread out to protect the wheat from the rain. They started threshing July 1. My father would drive to the neighboring farms and ask them to bring a wagon and an extra man. It took about twenty-five men to haul the wheat to the thresher and then haul the wheat to the granary where the wheat was dumped out in bins about three feet high.

The year I was fifteen years old, when the threshers came, my mother had taken my two sisters to Nashville for surgery, so I had to cook dinner for those twenty-five men. I sent for the hired man's wife to help me. She wanted to fry chicken and make biscuits, which was our usual Sunday dinner. The men ate it, but they were asking where the ham and cornbread was! We cooked beans, corn, sliced tomatoes, and blackberry and apple cobbler pies. The men out on the back porch waiting to eat would laugh and joke and weigh each other to see how much they ate. We seated eight men at a time. When they finished eating, eight more sat down after we washed the dishes and set the table again.

There was no plumbing in the house. There was a rail on the porch where we kept wash pans. The men pumped water from the well and washed their hands and faces and tossed the water in the yards as was the fashion until after World War II when farm electrification came in. We had a water table with a two-gallon bucket of water with a long-handled dipper which every-one drank out of and put the dipper back in, never knowing or thinking about germs. People who had springs always had one dipper and everyone drank out of it.

Back to threshing day—when I was a child it was exciting to see Mr. McKelder and his tractor and threshing machine arrive just at night. We rarely had overnight guests. They [the threshers] would travel from farm to farm and stay overnight.

Farming is a treacherous way to earn a living whether it is four hundred acres or forty. Every year the lightning would strike and kill animals. The animals would get under trees or near a wire fence where lightning strikes. We lost ponies, hogs, and cattle to lightning. We lost fields of new corn, wheat, and tobacco stripped and blown down by hail and wind. When there was drought we could lose the whole crop of corn. Years ago there were no drugs to save the animals. In 1938, when I was to start the University of Tennessee, the hogs got cholera and all died. That was our cash crop for the year. The germs stayed five years, so we couldn't have hogs again. It could be walked in on feet. The money to pay U.T. was lost, but somehow they managed.

My brothers had to get up in the night when the hogs were having pigs. The sows would roll over and kill their pigs or sometimes they would eat them. Often a heifer would die when having a calf. We had a flock of sheep with bells on, and we didn't hear them. The next morning they were all dead, scattered all over the field with their throats cut and ears chewed off by a blood-thirsty pack of dogs. That was a loss of two crops. The sheep were sheared and wool was sent off to market and every year there was a truck-ful of lambs to sell.

I was always there when they sheared the sheep. They took them to the barn and caught one at a time, and the wool had to be sheared and folded and tied just right for the market. Then men would seat the sheep on its rear end and hold its back against their legs and then start shearing from their neck down their belly and the wool would roll back on each side. Years ago they used old-fashioned hand clippers with long blades that had to be pressed together to cut and the sheep came out with bloody cuts all over them. Then my brother got a shearing machine on a stand with a wheel to turn to power the clippers similar to those used in barber shops. They sheared the sheep real clean, no more bloody cuts all over the sheep.

Back then before veterinarians, the farmers cut the tails off the lambs and castrated the pigs, calves, ponies, etc., with the pocket knives—nothing for the pain or germs. My father would use his knife to castrate a shoat and then come to the house and peel an apple or turnip for him to eat with that same knife! Imagine!

All the animals had to be watched all the time. My favorite pony got out of the barnlot and came over to my mother's garden and foundered on corn.[12] Horses and ponies will do this, but mules are smarter and will never over eat. Back then there were no veterinarians, no shots. Every farmer had to treat his animals as best he could. My brother did everything he could think of. He got the pony off her feet and supported her on straps hung to the rafters and gave her enemas. I wonder what a modern veterinarian would do? He kept copper sulfate in the gear room to pack sores made by harness on the miles. My mother used that in the water for the chickens. It prevented some disease.

My mother bought our clothing and paid for our piano lessons with her egg money, and it was precious. In 1934, I wanted to take painting lessons, so my mother let me raise frying chickens to pay for them. In three months, chickens would weigh the three pounds needed to sell as fryers. There were many enemies to deal with when raising chickens. The foxes, skunks, cats, hawks, and snakes ate her little chickens and eggs. In the night, we would hear chickens squawking with thieves stealing her chickens. My father would shoot the shot gun in the air to scare them off. Finally the hired men hauled in a covered pig pen with a floor and a door where she could lock them in at night.

Now for the fun things about living on a farm. After our chores were finished in the house at lunch, I was free to work with ponies and horses. I enjoyed training the colts to ride, to pull the buggy in double and single harness. I begged and begged and my father bought me a real five-gaited riding mare I saw at the horse show in Sevierville. My sister and I would saddle up Patsy Pat and Old Pearl, an old mare that had survived pulling logs in the time of the sawmills. My younger cousins would come, and we would bridle up five or six of the ponies, and we would ride the logging roads [on our farm].

When my sister and I were eight to ten years old, we had play houses everywhere, under the rose bushes in the front yard and under the lilac bushes in the back yard and in the basement when we were older. We played restaurant and served our cousins tomato and biscuit sandwiches from food left over at breakfast. We had an unfinished room upstairs where my mother's books from Converse, unused furniture, and clothes were stored. There was an old cylinder record player and an old telephone we pretended to call our boyfriend on—we were about ten years old!

My sister and I rode all over the farm in wagons with our brothers or on horseback, so we knew every inch of it. We knew where the dog tooth violet grew up in the "Ten Acres." Where the wild raspberries and wild strawberries grew near the road in the woods across from the house. Where the muscadines grew in the woods at the "Hill House" and the chestnuts and chinquapins (which all died out years ago) and the persimmon tree.

Families in Sevier County did lots of visiting kinfolks on Sunday afternoons in the 1930s. We would take turns going to different homes with cousins. I really enjoyed this. In turn, they came to visit us. When company came, we sat in the parlor. My mother served the canned grape juice and cake to our guests. At our house, I took all the children out to the barn to ride the ponies and down to the basement to play house.

When we went to my mother's old home on Middle Creek, we played softball down in the pasture field and dammed Middle Creek so we could swim. We walked over to my uncle's house on Ridge Road to get the Sunday paper. At one uncle's house, we played in the storm cellar. It was fun.

When I was living at home on the farm, we were the only family on what is now Ernest McMahan Road. In summer the whole family sat out on the porch till about nine o'clock at night waiting for the house to cool off. There weren't many cars in the neighborhood going up the hill to Middle Creek. At night we could identify all the neighbors by the sound of the cars. Some cars came from Sevierville to pick up the bootleg liquor hidden in a big stump back along the road at Blalock Woods. My mother always warned us not to tell anyone or the bootleggers would burn our barn.

Then there were the lovers who got stuck in the mud back there. They would knock on our door and ask my father to pull them out, and he actually went to the barn and got the tractor and pulled them out. He would never have done that for us.

The road was mud all the way until about 1931 when my father was elected road superintendent. He rocked the road and put in a culvert at the bottom of the hill at Judge Holt's. He put bridges and culverts all over this county. When I came back to Sevier County to live in 1988, many of the men who worked on his road crews in 1931 were still living in nursing homes, and they told me how grateful they were to have those jobs when there were no jobs. Later those men got jobs at the Aluminum Company and earned enough money to retire well-to-do financially.[13]

Sitting on the porch at night, we could hear Shannon Sims playing his guitar on the porch of John Sims' house. We could hear the fox hunters' hounds up in the Blalock Woods. They would build campfires and sit around and talk and listen to the hounds. We could hear Laura Snapp who was a widow who lived alone and farmed the Snapp farm. She would wait until dark to call her cows up to the barn. I never understood that.

My mother loved the mountains so every chance we could go on Sunday after church, she fixed a picnic lunch—fried chicken, pimento cheese sandwiches, ice tea, stuffed eggs. We would go as far as the road went up Newfound Gap. I remember giving Easter eggs to the workmen on Easter when they were building that road. Sometimes we went to Elkmont to watch the swimmers in the river. I remember a man made a pond that people swam in on the road to Newport on Sundays.[14]

When I was little, we had an old radio with a big speaker that we could get WLW in Cincinnati, Ohio, a station in Pittsburgh, KDKA, and one in Chicago. When my brother started teaching agriculture at Sevier County High School, he bought a big battery radio and kept it in his room. Every night we would go upstairs to listen to the news. We listened to "Amos and Andy," a mystery about Sing Sing prision, Mormon Tabernacle Choir on Sunday, and the Farm and Home Hour from Chicago on Saturday. They would start with "It's a beautiful day in Chicago," whether it was raining or snowing. We listened to other programs that I can't remember.

Before we had the radio, my mother read to us at night. All seven of us would be sitting around the fireplace and later around the stove after supper. Early, we only had very dim oil lamps. Sometime in the thirties, Rawlings store [in Sevierville] got Aladdin Lamps which burned kerosene, had a net-like mantle, and made bright light. We had one in the living room for Wilbur to grade his students' high school papers.

At night my mother would read to the whole family. She read *The Life of Lincoln* and *The Life of George Washington*. My mother would read the newspaper to all of us and discuss current events. She was a strong Republican and couldn't stand Mrs. Roosevelt because she served liquor in the White House. She had no use for Pearl Buck because she and Mr. Buck swapped marriage partners while in China.[15]

My whole family enjoyed this [reading]. My father was a sullen man who never contributed to the conversation, so she talked about current events and news in the community. My brother Glenn had a happy personality, and he kept us laughing at meals. He was a joy to be around.

We went to bed at 8:00 because my parents got up at 5:00 every morning. My father built a wood fire in the kitchen stove and in the fireplace in the living room. In the winter, he shoveled ashes over the back log to keep fire till morning.

It seems all my treats as a child were food. My aunt on Middle Creek came to Sevier County as a missionary teacher from South Dakota. She could bake wonderful yeast bread which no one in my family could do, and it was a treat to open her door and smell those beautiful cinnamon yeast rolls.

At our church on Middle Creek, there was a nice man who owned a little country store near the church. Every Sunday he gave us a thick pink mint about the diameter of a quarter, and I remember that as a treat for seventy-five years. I wonder if adults ever know how little it takes to please a child.

I think of the food treats my mother made. We kept home made sorghum molasses in the pantry to eat on hot biscuits. My mother made wonderful molasses cake in a stem pan. At Christmas, she made boiled custard with real whipped cream from our Jersey cow. When I was real little and believed in

Santa Claus, my sister and I got an orange in our stocking. It was the only time of year we had one. My mother would cut a hole in the orange, and we could suck the juice out through a stick of peppermint. Then we started going to Florida at Christmas, and we could have all the oranges we wanted.

And when we went to Key West to visit my father's cousin and her husband, I thought the turtle steaks and Key lime pie was the most wonderful thing I had ever tasted.

And I loved the Keys—the blue green water and the Spanish-speaking people were so nice. That was the first time I ever heard Spanish (age fifteen), and I loved it. In 1935 when we went to the Keys, a hurricane had destroyed a lot of the highway between the keys so we had to drive our car on steamboats brought over from the Mississippi to run between the Keys. There was a Civilian Conservation Corps camp in the Keys and they were warned to get out before the hurricane, and they didn't so they all were killed.

Another treat came once a year. Every Christmas when we went to Florida, my younger sister and I would beg to be at Melbourne, Florida, for Christmas Eve. There was a huge tourist camp with cabins, and they had a big recreation room where they had a band and music and dancing. They gave all the children a paper bag of treats. I loved being there. They played a song called "The Missouri Waltz," and I loved it. When Mr. Truman was president, he used to play that on the piano, but I learned to love it as a child.

The circus came to Knoxville every year, and one year when I was little my father and mother took my younger sister and me to see it. It was the first time I had ever been on a street car. My father bought a coke for my sister and me. It made me sick, and I threw up. I never drank another coke till I was at U.T.

One year my parents took my younger sister and me to the East Tennessee State Fair at Knoxville. I loved the animals and exhibits. We stayed for the fireworks, and I was terrified. Coming from Knoxville, my mother would buy a small loaf of bread for five cents, large for ten cents, no slices. My sister and I loved that. We could eat a whole small loaf before we got to Sevierville. To me it was like angel food cake. Back then we called it light bread.

Things we didn't like to do: milk two cows before we went to school, especially if it was rainy and the cow's tail was full of mud. We didn't like to churn. We took turns cranking the Daisy churn.

My mother believed that education was the only answer for a better life financially and socially, so she worked like a slave on that farm from 1903 to 1963 when she fell and broke her hip and needed assistance until her death in 1971. My mother knew the only way to prevent her five children from

Elizabeth Fox
McMahan around 1940.
Photograph courtesy of
Elizabeth McMahan
Adamitis.

being hired hands on my father's farm was to get college educations for us all. With her prayers and hard work, she finally got us all through University of Tennessee [U.T.]. My brothers, Wilbur McMahan and Glenn Fox McMahan, both earned B.S. degrees in agriculture in 1931. My brothers lived on one good meal a day in a cheap boarding house to make it. My mother did their laundry and mailed it to them in a laundry bag that resembled a twenty-two-inch suitcase, but it was covered with a water proof material that looked like tent material. My brother Glenn worked at odd jobs to help and of course they came home on summer vacation and raised crops like hay, wheat, corn, hogs and calves to sell in the fall.

My sister Dorothy only lacked three months finishing at U.T. in 1938. Ernestine McMahan Steele earned her B.A. and Bachelor of Music at U.T. Chattanooga in 1944. I earned my B.S. in home economics at U.T. in 1942 and then I studied at University of Pennsylvania for two years. My mother got me into a cooperative dormitory at U.T. where twenty-four girls did all the work. This was fall 1938. We had five committees, cooking, dishwashing, cleaning, hostess, and guest, and alternated these every week. The cost for one year—tuition, room, board, and books—was three hundred dollars.

When I graduated in 1942 and went to University of Pennsylvania, it cost eight hundred dollars a year.

My mother was very religious but not overbearing with it. From her I learned the stories of the Bible. She never had us say grace at meals or prayers at night. Some people have a powerful experience to know they are saved, but I always knew from her that I was. When I got to U.T. most of the girls in the dormitory went to church, and my senior roommates would get on their knees and pray every night, so I learned to do that because of them.

Because of my mother's awful experience with marriage, she wouldn't let us date till we went off to college, so I was green as grass as far as self esteem and social graces. My mother was told by Dean Greve, dean of women, that I improved more than any freshman she had ever seen. I had never been in a cafeteria, and my roommate had to show me how to go through the line; I was that inexperienced.

After he graduated from U.T., my wonderful brother Glenn Fox McMahan came home and worked for five dollars a week [on the farm].[16] He and my mother influenced my father to sell the Emert Place on Middle Creek Road. It connected up on top of the hill to my father's home farm. They sold the "big holler" across Middle Creek Road from the Dollywood parking lot. My father had a sawmill and sawed out that holler for years. There was a shack where very poor people lived until about 1938. They sold the Lawson field which connected on back of Judge Holt's farm and extended to the Trotter McMahan farm. By selling these strips of land that didn't produce farm produce, we were able to get out of debt for the first time since 1921, thanks to my mother and brother, Glenn.

My other brother Wilbur taught agriculture at Sevier County High School from 1932 to 1942. He lived at home but never worked on the farm any more. He was drafted into the army and served three and a half years, much of it in Europe with Patton's Third Army. He was in the Eightieth Division.

My mother was a beautiful caring woman. A prominent local business-man who owned a large furniture store and funeral home told me she was the prettiest girl in the county in 1901, and she certainly was the most educated. She was one of the first woman college graduates in the county.

With her intelligence and creative thinking, I believe she would have been in charge of some big company if she had been born in modern times. With her perseverance, enthusiasm, and love of education, she would have thrived in modern times that give women independence and freedom to use their skills.

Everything good in my life I owe to my mother. She gave me faith in God from the time when I can first remember. She gave me the education to have an enjoyable productive professional life and the chance hopefully to have made the world a little better with my forty-four years as a registered occupational therapist in army and Veterans Administration hospitals. I worked with veterans from five wars: Spanish-American, World War I, World War II, Korean War, and Vietnam. In 1988 when I retired I was still working with one hundred veterans a day, four groups of twenty-five in all stages of disability using group activities in reality orientation, sensory awareness, and activities of daily living.

NOTES

1. Dexter Edgar Converse, a textile mill owner who was one of the founders of Converse College, a liberal arts women's college in Spartanburg, South Carolina.

2. This was the battle of Fair Garden, Tennessee, January 27, 1864. A small Confederate cavalry force seeking to curtail the activities of Union troops south of the French Broad River engaged Union cavalry near what became the McMahan farm. The Union troops won the battle but withdrew due to the fatigue, heavy casualties, and lack of supplies. See "Fair Garden Tennessee," *American Civil War,* available on-line, www.americancivilwar.com/civil.html.

3. The name the family gave to a small forest adjacent to their farm.

4. "New ground" is newly cleared land.

5. They used cattle as draft animals instead of mules or horses.

6. Early tractor-drawn farm machinery usually required at least two people to operate. One person drove the tractor while the second sat on a seat on the equipment and operated it. For example, an operator was required to turn the hay rake in various directions to catch the mown hay and thrust it into orderly windrows. As equipment became more sophisticated and the power takeoff was developed to power the equipment with power from the tractor, the process became more mechanized and a second operator was no longer required.

7. It was actually 1924 when Congress promised to pay World War I veterans a "bonus" in 1945. The Bonus Army included unemployed World War I veterans and their families who marched on Washington to demand early payment of the "bonus." About twenty thousand camped on the grounds of the United States Capitol and across the Anacostia River in a swampy area. Hoover indeed ordered the army, under the command of Gen. Douglas MacArthur, to remove the marchers from Washington, but historians generally believe that Gen. George Patton exceeded his orders by attacking marchers and their families with tank and mounted cavalry.

8. Schoolchildren collected $1,391.72. Wilma Dykeman is actually a Tennessee writer and historian. For more on the purchase of land for the national park and its impact on Sevier County, Tennessee, see Melissa Walker, "The Land of Do Without: The Changing Face of Sevier County, Tennessee, 1908–1940," in *All We Knew Was to Farm: Rural Women in the Upcountry South, 1919–1941* (Baltimore: Johns Hopkins University Press, 2000).

9. Champion Fibre was the largest single landowner within the boundaries of the park. The company hired veteran timbermen to survey the standing timber and

estimate its value. The company then used this information in its lawsuit against the federal government, seeking additional money for the land the government had condemned. In the end, Champion received $2.35 million for their land, a figure within a few dollars of their asking price.

10. Farmers had actually known about the value of crop rotation for centuries, but the practice was rarely used in the South before the 1930s. Lespedeza is a nitrogen-fixating plant. Nitrogen was an important crop nutrient for such plants as corn. During the growing season, nitrogen attaches itself to nodules in the roots of nitrogen-fixating plants. When the roots of nitrogen-fixating plants are plowed into the soil at the end of the growing season, the soil is naturally fertilized for the next crop.

11. A piece of equipment that combined the functions of mowing and threshing grain.

12. Horses and ponies that overeat can develop laminitis, a potentially crippling inflammation in their hooves.

13. The Aluminum Company of America (ALCOA) opened an aluminum smelting and fabrication plant in nearby Blount County in 1913. The plant operated with a reduced workforce and schedule throughout the Depression, but with the onset of World War II, many farmers and farm laborers from outlying counties were able to obtain relatively high-paying industrial jobs at ALCOA.

14. Newfound Gap was the pass over the crest of the Great Smoky Mountains on the Tennessee–North Carolina border. The road over Newfound Gap was completed. Elkmont began life as a lumber camp built by the Little River Lumber Company. The camp could be reached by rail, and the lumber company operated a scenic excursion train to Elkmont on Sundays. The excursion train brought middle-class visitors from Knoxville and Maryville to enjoy mountain vistas. The Wonderland Hotel at Elkmont housed and fed visitors who wished to stay more than a few hours. Eventually tourists began buying small parcels of land and building their own cabins at Elkmont. By the time Elizabeth McMahan Adamitis was born in 1921, Elkmont was a small rustic resort community.

15. After Prohibition was repealed, Eleanor and Franklin Roosevelt did indeed serve alcohol in the White House. Pearl Buck was an American novelist and essayist.

16. Glenn also taught school.

Hettie Lawson

HETTIE LAWSON AND her husband, John Oliver Lawson, lived "across the mountain" from Elizabeth Fox McMahan's home. Although they lived less than twenty miles from the McMahans' Sevierville home, a visit would have required a half day of traveling by horse and buggy and well over an hour by car. The Lawsons lived in isolated Wear's Valley in Blount County. Here they engaged in farming, emphasizing livestock and subsistence crops.

During the Great Depression, Oliver Lawson worked for the federal public works program, the Works Progress Administration, at times. He also found work as a supervisor at a local Civilian Conservation Corps camp. The Civilian Conservation Corps employed single, unemployed men between the ages of eighteen and twenty-five to construct roads, campgrounds, trails, and other facilities in national and state parks. While Oliver Lawson was away at work during the day, Mrs. Lawson and her children did the farm work.

World War II generated an enormous demand for manufactured goods, creating new jobs in factories all over the region. As a result, in the early 1940s, Oliver Lawson obtained a job at an Aluminum Company of America (ALCOA) plant near Maryville. Although it was a thirty-mile commute to the ALCOA plant, the company transported employees from neighboring counties with an extensive network of "work buses," giving ALCOA access to a large pool of rural employees who did not own cars. After the war ended, the Lawsons moved to a small community near the plant, and Mr. Lawson worked at ALCOA until his retirement.

Mrs. Lawson was in her nineties when we spoke, and she was in poor health. She and her husband lived with one of their daughters, and we spoke in their home on August 16, 1993. Her memory was failing, and she did not have a great deal of energy, so our talk was short. Nonetheless, she provides an interesting picture of life on a mountain farm. At the end of the interview, Mrs. Lawson's daughter, Betty Lawson Coulter, told a colorful story about a mischievous cow that brings home the hardships that Mrs. Lawson often endured while her husband worked off the farm. Mrs. Coulter's words are indicated in italics. In the fall of 1994, Mrs. Coulter completed the family history questionnaire for her parents and made a few corrections to the transcript.

I grew up on a farm in Wear's Valley. I was born July 31, 1901. We had, they called her the home demonstration agent. I guess I joined the 4–H. One year we planted beans. I guess we were supposed to can then. I got a few rows of beans.

I went to Knoxville several times. They used to have, Ringling Brothers and Barnum and Bailey used to have a parade. And me and my neighbor and another girl, we'd go down there to see the parade.

We [she and Oliver] went to school together.

It [the Depression] was hard. I had four children.

We had cows for our own use. And raised corn, and we raised tobacco. We had apples. I don't know now hardly how we did it. Just by hard work, I reckon. I put up a lot, canned and put up a lot of stuff. Through the summer, we always had a garden, and I canned all the vegetables. We depended on those through the winter. Of course, we raised a little corn. But we managed some way to buy flour. We never did raise much wheat. We had hogs. Salt and brown sugar and pepper, I believe, was what we put on our hams.

And Oliver, my husband, worked for the WPA some. And he was in the CCs [sic] a while. They had civilian employees. They went under the same rules, but they wasn't actually members of the CCs.

The neighbors pitched in and helped each other quite a bit. At that time, we lived close to Oliver's parents and mine, too. And, of course, they helped out with things. They gave us food and helped us out a little bit.

When people were having hard times, the neighbors would help them. Sometimes the churches did [provide aid], sometimes they didn't. At that time, I don't think, now I may not be telling you right, but I think it was mostly neighbors. Maybe they had some quilts that they didn't really need or something.

For fun, we played ball. Just with family, a lot of the times. Sometimes we'd have some of the neighbors or somebody up there to play with us. We didn't have much time to do things. Most things we done for fun was on Sundays. We worked about six days a week.

We went to church. And we'd visit people around in the community. But we didn't do much visiting; I mean, any distance away from home. Only where we could walk. I didn't [visit with other women] very often. Most of 'em was like me; they had to work.

We had little grocery stores. We could get groceries there. For clothing, we could go to Sevierville. Back then, we usually made our clothes. They kept some cloth. They didn't have a big variety, but they had some. Sometimes we'd get something there. Most of it you had to go somewhere else to get it. To get to Sevierville then, with a wagon or buggy, you started early of a morning and come home late at night with your traveling time and the time spent in the stores.

We had, there was a spring up on the mountain, way up above the house. And we had water piped down to the back porch. We had plenty of water. Just get it out on the back porch. No, we didn't have any electricity for several years.

Well, I believe the oldest one, Hugh, was a child [when we got our first car]. I remember what the first we had was a secondhand Ford. Wish I had one of them.

I worked in the garden and the field, too. I milked. We had a mule, but I didn't have much to do with him, only just feeding him and, and after he started to work down here, Hugh [her son] took care of that. I was about halfway afraid of these mules.

DAUGHTER, BETTY LAWSON COULTER: *We lived up next to the mountain. And Daddy bought a cow. This was in the late '40s, wasn't it, when he bought old Lucy. And they had a bell around her neck so we could find her. She'd get somewhere and hide, and she'd stand so still that that bell wouldn't tinkle, and we couldn't find her. And mama would climb those hills till she was just give out.*

We had to have the milk.

Yeah, we needed the milk.

That was the coldest house we lived in up there [in the mountains] *I've ever seen. And I made myself a promise then that when I get out, and I ever get a home, I'm gonna stay warm. And I have. And of course after we moved down here* [near Maryville], *the house we lived in wasn't as bad. It wasn't as cold as it was up there* [in the mountains].

I had a brother in the First World War. And then our sons were in the second war. The oldest one went first, of course. He was in Belgium and France. The younger one, he went to Japan.

We moved to Blount County, I guess it was in the early '50s. I can't remember. It was after the war. He [John Oliver] worked for the Aluminum Company. He worked there a while before we moved here [near Maryville].

I encouraged them [her children] to get educations and get a job [rather than farm]. I had enough of it.

Wilma Cope Williamson

WILMA COPE WILLIAMSON was born in Sevier County, Tennessee, on April 27, 1915, the oldest of ten children. Her father worked for the Little River Lumber Company, and the family spent much of Mrs. Williamson's childhood living in various lumber camps in Sevier and Blount counties. The lumber industry was a fickle one, with frequent layoffs because of an oversupply on the world market, fires in the forest, or the logging out of an area. Mrs. Williamson's father, Frederick Cope, was often out of work. During these periods of unemployment, the family sometimes moved in with Mrs. Cope's parents, Robert and Delilah Woodruff, at their farm on Sevier County's Middle Creek. The Woodruffs proved to be the strongest influences on Wilma Williamson's life.

First settled in the 1780s, Sevier County is situated in the Great Smoky Mountains in east Tennessee. Until the end of the nineteenth century, Sevier County's economy was agricultural. In the rich river bottoms and valleys of the northern part of the county, large farms that balanced commercial and subsistence enterprises developed. Sevier County's commercial farmers sold fruit and livestock in nearby Knoxville. Most Sevier Countians like the Woodruffs lived on more marginal farms located on the upland slopes. The coming of the lumber industry in the late nineteenth century provided these struggling farmers with an opportunity to supplement their meager farm incomes with wage labor for the timber companies. Mrs. Williamson's grandfather Robert Woodruff worked for Little River Lumber Company off and on for most of his adult life and used his wages to pay for his small farm. He worked on the crew that built Little River Lumber Company's railroad line up the middle prong of the Little Pigeon River into a mountain valley known as Elkmont. Here the lumber company built a hotel and housing for workers.

In the early years of the twentieth century, Sevier County was gradually transformed by the lumber industry, but the 1920s and 1930s brought other sources of change. Pi Beta Phi, a service organization for college women and alumnae, established a settlement house in the county in 1912. The settlement workers opened a school near the village of Gatlinburg, and they soon established a program to revive traditional mountain handicrafts as a way of providing mountain people with additional income. They hired elderly local residents who remembered the old crafts to train many county residents, including some of Wilma Williamson's relatives, in weaving, wood carving, and other traditional handicrafts. Pi Beta Phi products were sold in northern cities and to local tourists.

Tourism in Sevier County predated the arrival of the national park. Once the lumber company's railroad provided easy access to the mountains from nearby Knoxville, city residents began to frequent the Elkmont Hotel for day trips. Men from the city came to Gatlinburg for hunting trips. These tourists fueled the growth of the handicraft industry and a fledgling tourist industry including small motels and restaurants. The establishment of the Great Smoky Mountains National Park in 1925 simply accelerated the process of developing tourism in the county. Today Sevier County's economy is almost totally dependent on tourism.

The economic changes in Sevier County shaped a very different life for Wilma Cope than for her grandmother. Wilma married Tommy Williamson, a Civilian Conservation Camp worker, in 1934. Although Tommy worked as a logger for a time, much of the land logged by Little River Lumber Company was purchased for the Great Smoky Mountains National Park in the early 1930s, curtailing logging activities. When Little River Lumber Company shut down its operations in 1937, Tommy Williamson took a job with the Aluminum Company of America (ALCOA) in Blount County and moved the young family to the Sevier County town of Pigeon Forge. Like Hettie Lawson's husband, Tommy Williamson commuted the forty miles to his job on ALCOA's series of "work buses." After World War II, the couple moved to Blount County, Tennessee. Mr. Williamson worked for ALCOA until his retirement. He also worked as a vocational (non-seminary trained) minister for a number of Southern Baptist Churches in Blount and Sevier Counties. In Pigeon Forge and later in Blount County, Wilma Williamson continued her subsistence patterns, raising a large garden and keeping a few cows to supply milk for her family and to sell for extra income.

In the process of trying to identify potential oral history subjects for the dissertation that gave rise to this project, I sent a standard author's query to newspapers in a number of East Tenenssee counties. The *Maryville-Alcoa Daily Times* published my query in March 1994, prompting a letter from Mrs. Williamson. I responded with some questions, which she promptly answered. At that point, I requested an interview, and she graciously agreed to talk with me. I have included all of Mrs. Wiliamson's letters here because they are full of details about rural life before World War II.

This interview was conducted July 18, 1994, on the front porch of Mrs. Williamson's neat frame house near Maryville, Tennessee. In the fall of 1994, Mrs. Williamson reviewed the transcript and corrected some minor mistakes. She concluded her corrections with this personal note: "I told my grandson [the transcript] showed me up for what I was—a dyed-in-the-wool Smoky Mountain woman."

Mrs. Williamson's younger sister, Florence Cope Bush, published an account of their mother's life. *Dorie: Woman of the Mountains* (University of Tennessee Press, 1992) focuses more on the lives of the younger Cope children. It provides interesting companion reading to Mrs. Williamson's account.

MARYVILLE, TENN.
MARCH 8, 1994

Dear Melissa Walker

I read your letter in today's *Daily Times,* and decided to share what I remembered with you.

I don't have any diaries or letters, only first hand experience. My mother and father lived with my grandparents on a farm on Middle Creek in Sevier County. One of my earliest remembrances is of hog-killing time, I always crawled under a bed in the back room. My grandmother could use everything about a hog except his squeal. She made sausage, and seasoned it with her own special spices and then pack in corn shucks, tie the end and hang it up to dry.

Strangely enough it never spoiled.

She can[ned] the ribs, backbones, and tenderloin, and cured and smoke[d] the hams, shoulders, and middling. She cooked the head, feet, ears, tongue, and liver and made souse meat from it. Some times she would pickle the feet, they were my favorites. She would then take fat and make lard from it which left cracklings. If you've never eaten crackling bread you don't know what you have missed. She would then clean the intestines and make lye soap from them. That is the only kind of soap she ever used, even to wash her face and hands with.

They kept a few sheep, too, and she would shear them, wash the wool and card and spin it into yarn, she had her own loom that she wove cloth on. It was called "linsey." She would dye part of [the] yarn and use it with the white to make her cloth. She always grew her own cotton to make quilts with. I well remember setting by the fire and helping pick the seed from the cotton.

When I was growing up, cow feed was bought in a cloth bag in 100 lbs. size. She washed those bags in lye soap to bleach the letters out, and then she would dye part of them and use white to go with the dyed material to make quilts. I still have one she made from feed sacks. She made sheets, pillowcases, towels and underwear from them. That was the only underwear I had until after I was grown.

She always kept the string she raveled out of the bags,[1] and used it to crochet with. She made bedspreads, doilies, door panels and just anything she decided she wanted.

She always put up all kinds of fruit and vegetables. Put up was the term they used for canning. She could take a bushel of apples and end up with apple sauce, jelly, apple butter, dried fruit and sulphured fruit. She made kraut from cabbage she grew then would bury some of the good ones [cabbages] along with the potatoes, and they would keep all winter. She canned beans, dried beans and made pickled beans with big ears of corn on the cob in them, makes me hungry to think of them. I still make them. She had a big iron wash kettle that she used to make hominy in, then would can it.

She made her brooms from broom corn she grew, and her mops by using hickory limbs that she would shave back so far and then tie to hold it in place.

She could take small willow limbs and weave them into some of the most beautiful baskets you ever looked at.

I remember how she used hickory bark, onion skins, black walnut hulls to color easter eggs with. The hickory bark made yellow, the onion skins orange, and the walnut hull made brown, and for red, she used Putnam dye.

At that time school was only for three months of the year so the children could help on the farm. Needless to say, very few ever went beyond the eighth grade. If you went that far you could get a job teaching.

There was no government help available at that time.

My grandparents came from the Cherokee Reservation.[2] They both grew up over there. Grandmother was ¼ Indian. She told me about the first jars she ever had to can in, they always dried everything, even berries. She also told me about growing tomatoes in her yard for flowers. They were called Love-apples and people thought they were poison.

Maybe this will give you a glimpse of one very resourceful lady. She has been a wonderful influence to me.

Wilma K. Williamson

P.S. Her name was Delilah Woodruff.

MARYVILLE, TENN.
MARCH 29, 1994

Dear Melissa,

I am happy to have been a little bit of help to you.

I think many people should be interested in finding out about our heritage, or the young people growing up will have no knowledge of it. So, I'm always ready to help when I can.

My sister, Florence Cope Bush, said she was going to get some material together to send you. She wrote a book about our mother, *Dorie: A Woman of the Mountains,*[3] that tells about how things were then. She won the Tennessee Literary Award for it, and U.T. bought the rights to it and use it [as] a textbook. She can be of more help to you than I can because she has done so much research.

My grandparents didn't live in the part of Sevier County that [was] affected by the [Great Smoky Mountains National] Park.

All the men of the family worked for Little River Lumber Company when the park took over. Grandad and his one son moved back to the farm, and my Dad went to work for KUB [Knoxville Utilities Board] in Knoxville, building power lines from Waterville, N.C. It wasn't too steady a job, so that is where WPA came in. My oldest brother worked for them to help out at home.

Of course, by that time, I was grown and married, which is another story altogether since it starts with the CCC's [Civilian Conservation Corps].

Very few people that we knew had any chance for an education. There just wasn't that many schools and if you were lucky enough to get to go to high school you had to leave home and stay in a dorm.

I never remember the churches being involved much, of course in a community if some one got sick the neighbors all worked to help out. They were never too busy to help in that case. I think churches play a bigger role now because people are too busy to help now.

If there is anything else I can answer for you, just let me know. I know this is [not] very much, but in our case, it pretty well covers it.

Sincerely,
Wilma Williamson

INTERVIEW:

I have some things in there I'd like to show you that my grandmother did. You know, I wrote you about them. I have a quilt, and I have some crocheted things that she crocheted out of bran sack twine. She looked at the picture; she never had a pattern. Can you remember when people used to have half of their door glass? Well, she would crochet door panels, she called them. And she had some of the most beautiful ones she had crocheted deer in, and she didn't even have a pattern. My granny was a smart lady, and I've got a book in there that's got her picture in it that I want to show you.

And until I got to writing a few of my earliest memories, I had never realized what an impact she had had on my life. It was always Granny and never Mom.

Granny and Grandpa moved over here from North Carolina when Mama was six years old. And it took them two days to cross the mountain in a wagon. They spent the night on top of the mountain, camped out that night and then came on to Sevier County the next day. And they left over there because Granny was afraid that some of the Indians were going to steal her boy. He was blond-headed, blue eyes and [had] fair skin. And they had never seen children like that. She said she could just catch them peeping around the door facing or in the window at him. And she got afraid they was just gonna steal him. And I guess he was just about two years old when they moved over here. Loaded all their worldly goods in the wagon, and they had to walk most of the way. Well, Mama said they got to ride a little bit when they'd get tired—they'd set them up on the wagon and let them ride. The wagon they moved over here in belonged to Granny's brother-in-law. He went over there to move them over here. He was married to Granny's sister who already lived over here. And they moved Grandpa and Granny to a little house on the farm where they all lived. Way up next to what they call the Glades. Up next to Gatlinburg. There's where they lived when they first come to Sevier County.

Oconoluftee Church is where my grandparents were married and where they went to church until they came to Sevier County. And Granny always said, how did she say it, anyway? Their church letters [memberships] are still in the trunk. They never joined anywhere over here. They went to church at Boogertown. Ogle's Creek was the official name of it, but it's always been Boogertown. And that was the church there where they went, but they never did join.[4]

I was born in 1915, April 27, 1915. I'm the oldest of ten children. Daddy was working for the lumber company—Fish Camp first, up in above Elkmont. Up in there is where I was born. Me and my oldest brother were both born up there. Granny practically raised me because Mama was busy having babies. And I was busy helping Mama. Up until I married and started having mine. [laughter]

But so many times they [Grandpa and Granny] came to our rescue. When Dad would get out of work they'd take us in. I don't know what would have become of us had it not been for them. And the last time they took us in they was six children. And they lived in three of them little railroad cars at Tremont.[5] Dad had been working for KUB [Knoxville Utilities Board], and they got the power line built from Waterville, North Carolina to Knoxville; they laid him off. And he had to go back to Little River [Lumber Company] to try to get work again. But after they closed down the logging job up there, he finally went back to KUB. And he worked for them until he died.

Granny sold butter. She took it to a peddler that came and [also sold] eggs. That was how she got her sugar, salt, and coffee. They call that the barter system. Well, the peddler came by once a week in his wagon. She made all the clothes. She made grandpa's clothes. She made practically everything they used. About the only thing they bought was shoes and Grandpa's overalls. Other than that, they were all made. Well, even after my boys was born, she made shirts for them. And she wanted everybody to wear these big old high wool socks that she knit out of the wool. They itched. My oldest brother had somewhat of a temper, and he had on a pair of these high wool socks, and he got mad, and Mama just had what they call a little old step stove, you know, just the flat part, no warmer on the top. And he threw something, I don't remember what it was, but the coals fell off on his leg. And when he died he still had those [scars in] the pattern of the sock on his leg.

Granny taught me to cook. Who else? Who taught me to do everything? Who taught me to crochet? Who taught me to make a quilt? [laughter] Mama did teach me to use the sewing machine. She put me at it early. Said she didn't aim for me to grow up like she did, couldn't sew anything. No and after I come along, Granny made me a dress one day, and it didn't suit Mama, and she said something to Granny about it, and it made Granny mad. She throwed it down, and she said, "You make the next one." And that's the last one she done for her. [laughter] Mama had to learn how. And, oh, she was good at it. She could look at a picture in the catalog and cut out any pattern of a dress. And crochet some of the most beautiful afghans. I guess she made about sixty of them in all, and all the same pattern. And after she made them, she embroidered roses up and down them. They said she sold a lot of them at Gatlinburg. And she made [them for] all the family. She made them and sold them after Dad died. She sold her place in Knoxville and moved to Lakemont[6] where Paul, my oldest brother, lives. She bought her a trailer and put it in behind his house over there. And then's when she got started at it [making afghans in large numbers]. Of course, she'd crocheted and made things all of her life about it, but she didn't go into it like that until after he died. He died in 1961.

But I was sitting here talking to somebody the other day, and we were talking about that [how Granny was thrifty and talented]. Granny used to, when she made her sausage, she would take a dry corn shuck, and she'd roll a piece of sausage about that long [about six inches], and she'd stick it down in that corn shuck and tie the top and hang it up and it never spoiled. She used her own recipe, of what she had in it. She raised her herbs and spices. Everything except black pepper. And she would smoke the middlings of the meat, and the shoulder and the ham.[7] But she's told me many a time about raising tomatoes in the yard for a flower. People thought they were poison. Love apples.[8] [laughter] You know, I've wondered since then who was brave enough to take the first bite.

My grandmother canned with jars after they moved over to Sevier County. Well, Mama said that she could remember the first jars they got.[9] They had never heard of it before. And they dried everything from cut corn off the cob and dry it, blackberries, apples, whatever. And I've seen Grandpa dig a hole in the ground, oh, about so big around [indicates about three feet], and four or five feet deep, and fill it, line it with straw. And he'd bury his potatoes when he dug them out of the ground; he'd bury them in that and cabbage heads and cover it up, and you had good potatoes and cabbage all winter. That's how they kept them. The hole would be four or five feet deep. And we lived up on Middle Creek, she had what you called the flume house, a pretty good-sized little house built over the spring. And she had, well like the walls were lined with shelves. And that is where she kept her cans. And you know, they never froze? I just can't even remember when we did first get ice. But it came from the icehouse over in Alcoa. And they would deliver once a week.

My grandmother raised chickens and sold eggs. And she raised ducks. I can still hear the old ducks saying "quack" when she pulled the feathers out when she picked them. She made her own pillows. And for years I used the featherbed that she made that she gave me. If you needed it, she either raised it or made it. She bought coffee, sugar, and salt. That was it. And a lot of the time, she used molasses instead of using sugar. And they made their own molasses. And they ground, had their own corn ground for meal. Now I believe she did buy flour because where we lived back there on Middle Creek, you couldn't raise wheat; it was too steep and hilly. She was a very resourceful lady.

And she was beautiful. Her grandmother was full-blooded Indian; her mother half. And she was a fourth. But she had Irish blood in her. And she was fair-skinned, very fair-skinned. Blue-eyed. And the blackest hair you ever seen on anybody. Come to think of it, I guess she was pretty young when I was born, because she was only seventy-four when she died. And I had four boys when she died.

She was pretty. She's got those high cheekbones. That was where the Indian showed up in her. And I have been told since then that my family had enough Indian heritage till they could have gone through college free.[10] But I didn't know it at the time.

There's never in my estimation been a better man lived than Grandpa. He was my idol. He built railroads. And you know, the first thing I can remember about Grandpa, he had a handlebar moustache. And it was black as it could be. Ted[11] makes me think of him a lot. Grandpa was tall and big old hands and long arms.

To pay his taxes, my granddaddy had to work a certain number of days on the country road. They called it poll taxes. That was how [he paid his taxes] when he lived on the farm. You know, taxes wasn't very much then. And when he worked for Little River, he made enough till he could handle the taxes on his land then. And he always raised a beef to kill in the fall of the year. I can remember canning beef many years. He'd have it killed and dressed out and then he divided it among the family so we all had meat. And they always raised hogs. [They] always managed to have at least one to kill. And they say now pork'll kill you.

Grandpa raised bees. And it was the oddest thing about that. He could go and take the honey out, and he never had to put anything over his face. They didn't sting him. [He] didn't wear gloves. And he's the only person I've ever seen that did that. And he took part of his white pine lumber he had bought to build the house out of to make our table out of. And I'm not sure but what that table's in the basement today.

You know when the banks failed, Grandpa and Granny lost every cent they had in the bank. Every penny. I can't remember how much they lost, but it was a tidy little sum. They never had anything to do with banks anymore. I've seen them stuff their money in a quart jar. And they didn't have mattresses; [they] had straw ticks. And [they would] stuff it in under the straw ticks, between the straw tick and the springs. And when Granny died, she had eleven hundred dollars pinned to her gown. They never trusted the bank anymore. Every penny they could scrape, they'd save. Granny kept boarders—four or five at a time—and cooked for them, washed for them. And she saved her money, too. They had an extra room, and they had bunk beds in it where they could sleep. These were people who worked at the lumber company and lived too far back in the mountains for the hotel at Elkmont to be able to handle them.

And I can remember many a mornings, me and Grandpa would shovel snow out from in front of the little stable where they kept the cow to get in and milk her, the way it would snow up there. About like our blizzard we had last year.[12] People talks about they'd never seen anything like that. I was used to it when I was growing up. [laughter] In fact in March before Max [her son] was born in May, it came one [snow storm] like that up there, and we had to carry water. Every bit of, [every] drop of water we used, had to carry from the community spring. And Tommy [her husband] fell in between some crossties on the railroad [after the storm], and the snow was so deep, he like to not got out.

When we were home, we never celebrated Thanksgiving and Christmas. Mama was a person that it never seemed to mean anything to her. Of course, Grandpa and Granny always seen to it that we got a little gift. But I never had a Christmas tree until after I had family of my own. Never celebrated Thanksgiving till after I had family of my own. My husband's family hadn't either. They was so busy trying to make a living.

There was some lady at Newport,[13] I can't remember what her name was now. But anyway, every Christmas she seen that they [rural Cocke County children] had something for Christmas. She would send a huge barrel of stuff, all kinds of stuff in it, clothing, candy, and things they didn't have on the farm. But I cannot remember her name.

The company was good for looking out for the children up there [at the lumber camp]. They always made sure there was school available and church. And before we lived there at Tremont, a couple of the superintendents said that [school] building was dedicated to education, salvation, hellfire, and then damnation because they showed movies in it. There's where I went to see *Uncle Tom's Cabin*. And they always had a western serial going [at the lumber camp], you know. And there's where I got hooked on reading because they had a little library there in the school. Grades one to eight, just one teacher. Flo [her younger sister] said when she was researching to do that book that she went to the library over here and checked back.[14] And she found that all of the family that went to school there but me had made the honor roll. And my name wasn't on the list. [laughter]

At Tremont, it was a little Methodist Church, and they [the lumber company] always seen there was a pastor there, and they paid him. And they paid the teachers. And they always came from around Maryville. Well, one, the one I had when I was in eighth grade, lived at Townsend. Miss Melinda

King. She was an old maid schoolteacher. Then where they had the CCC camp[15]—they called it Lynn Camp—I went to school there. They had the school there. And the teacher I had when I went to Lynn Camp was Hansell Proffitt from Sevierville. And his wife went with him to school every day. They lived in the hotel at Tremont; they didn't have any family. I think he finally, when he left up there, went to Sevierville and went to law school. [He] ended up a lawyer.

They'd have church service and different people would come preach. And I remember, too, one of them was the Olivers from Cades Cove, Kerry Oliver. And the other one was a man from Sevier County, Alan Sizemore. Anyway, that morning Kerry Oliver preached a little sermon, and then he made the announcement, "Brother Alan Sizemore will preach for you tonight if he gets back from bee hunting in time." [laughter] They'd go to the woods and hunt bee trees, they called them, where the bees had found a hole in the tree and moved in. And they would cut that tree and catch the bees and put them in the beehive. That's how they got started. That's how Grandpa got his [bees].

I remember when we first moved back to the logging job [after a layoff and time living on her grandparents' farm], we went to Jake's Creek up above Elkmont, and we lived there till they closed out that prong of the logging and moved to the Middle Prong up toward Tremont. I can well remember it because the first time I ever came down the Little River Gorge, I rode the train.[16] We moved to what they called Wildcat Flats in between Walker's Valley and Tremont.

I remember the little houses we lived in were built on railroad cars. You didn't have to pack anything but your dishes. And they was a little hole right in the center of the room where it was built on the, well you wouldn't call it a joist, I don't guess. A joist is overhead. But anyway, there was a pretty good-sized little timber that run across and under the floor. And it had a big old metal eye of a thing that was screwed down in there. And they used to lower the tongs down through the top of the house—there was a little hole in the top of the house—and lift that thing up and set it on a flatcar and haul it where ever they wanted it. And they used logs to build what they called a house seat out of. That's what they called the foundation. Where they would set these little rooms on them. And the middle room, it didn't have any walls on the end; it was open. That's where the other two fit against it on the end. It was like three railroad cars long. And you didn't have to go to the store; you just write out your grocery list and send it in there. They would fill it, and they shipped out the groceries on these cars once a week.

My mother only kept one boarder. And that was when I was about twelve years old. And that was the only one she ever kept except when a couple of Dad's brothers would come and stay a while and work up there.

You couldn't buy ice cream then like you can now. They kept it in a big gallon container in a freezer-like thing, and you'd have to take your own vessel to the store to get your ice cream. And I guess that's why I took to cherry ice cream, because they had it more than any of the other. Go and buy a half a gallon and take it to the house and dish it out and eat it. Didn't have ice cream cones. [We] ate it out of a dish or a saucer. Had to eat it quick. [laughter] And they only had it in the summertime.

Everybody had what they called their own milk box. They'd take a plank and build them a little box and set it down in where the water flowed out from the spring. And you kept your milk and your butter in that. And you'd be surprised at how cold it kept it. It'd keep a couple of days like that. If it got the chance.[17] [laughter]

I only got to go to high school one year. I went to Townsend. From Tremont to Walker's Valley, I walked. That was about three miles. And from Walker's Valley to Townsend, I rode the bus. But that was in 1931–32. Dad couldn't buy books, and they didn't furnish them then, so I didn't get to go back to high school after the first year. And the year I did go, I had one dress that I wore to school. And I'd wash it and wear it again the next day. I still— well I don't even have to shut my eyes to see it. It was white background with little black print in it with red binding on it. Bought it ready-made at the company store. That was the first bought dress I ever remember having. And I can't remember how I came by it. We wore tennis shoes in the summertime.[18] And old brogans in the wintertime with long cotton stockings. And if it was real cold, we wore overalls to school. You know, though, we all grew up together like that; one person didn't have more than the other. You didn't feel better than somebody else. And, in fact, everybody was in the same boat.

Dr. Montgomery was the [lumber] company doctor until he retired, and then Dr. Griffitts at Townsend took over. And as long as the logging job lasted then, he was the company doctor. Oh, lands, I don't know how many years Dr. Montgomery was the company doctor. He had just one of them little rooms up at Tremont, set off to itself. That was his office. And I don't guess you've heard about calomel. That was supposed to cure everything from pneumonia to a stumped toe. Little tiny pink tablet. And you couldn't eat anything when you's taking it. And the next day after you'd took all of that, you had to take a good dose of castor oil. And that was what he doctored with.

I got married September 9, 1934. Married in the middle of the Depression. I married a CCC boy.[19] We [her family] lived up in the mountains above Townsend at Tremont. But one Sunday morning after they [the CCC workers] first came up there, he [her husband-to-be] came to church. In the Sunday School class I was taking up offering. And he winked at me, and I made a face at him. [laughter] That's how we met. And he told his friend that was with him, "I'm going to marry her." Well, we had our usual ups and downs, of course. But all in all, well, we'd been married almost fifty-two years when he died.

[My husband] grew up in Cocke County, up on [Interstate] 40 as you go toward Asheville. Now he grew up the hard way like I did. They farmed those hillsides up there, and they just barely made a living. And when he was in the CCC camp, he got thirty dollars a month, and twenty-five dollars of that was sent to the family. He got five [dollars for his own use]. And he helped his daddy pay off what he owed on the little piece of land he owned over there [in Cocke County].

I was talking to a friend of mine the other day—we [both] lived there up in the mountains—and we were just wondering, how would young people react now if they had to start out like we did. Tommy sold his guitar to buy our marriage license. Marriage licenses cost five dollars. We lived in one room. And it would have fit in here [a one-car carport] with room to spare. We had the cookstove. We had a bed. And we had a very small table my grandad made. And he [her grandfather] built a cabinet on the wall to put what few dishes we had in. And Granny gave me a big old trunk to put our clothes in. And that's what we had in that one room. And we lived in it for over two years.

Now he [her husband Tommy] worked for Little River [Lumber Company] till 1937. We lived at Tremont. In 1937, Tommy went to ALCOA [the Aluminum Company of America] and worked for ALCOA thirty-seven years. We moved to Pigeon Forge. Now when we moved to Pigeon Forge, oh, we was modern then. We even had electricity. And we had a well over there. We used the round buckets that you rolled the, let the bucket down in the well with the rope that had the pulley on it. Then you'd pull it back up with that. Yeah, we got modern then. Even had a radio. We moved up in the world.

We gave five hundred dollars for our place. A house and about a half-acre of land. It was a lot of money. In fact, he got laid off at ALCOA, and had it not been for Grandpa, we'd have lost it for a hundred and twenty-five dollars. I don't know how Grandpa found it out, but a lawyer in Sevierville had the note. And we got a notice. But Tommy couldn't pay it. He was working whatever he could get for ten cents an hour to put food on the table. That was 1936 and '37. And Grandpa come over there one morning, and he said, "Son, I want you to take me to Sevierville." Well, Tommy walked back and got the car and come back and picked up Grandpa.[20] And they got to Sevierville, and Tommy said he said, "I want you to take me to Lawyer Ogle's office." He didn't tell him what he was wanting to go for. Then he got down there and told Tommy where he wanted to go. Tommy said they went in. He said to that man, "I hear you're about to take this boy's place." And he paid it off. And Tommy didn't have a car at the time; he always drove Grandpa's, took them places. And then when Tommy went back to ALCOA, he was gonna pay Grandpa back the a hundred and twenty-five dollars plus interest. Grandpa wouldn't let him. He said, "You buy a car instead." So he bought him a car, but he paid Grandpa back.

After I was married, I sold milk. When we first moved to this community [in Blount County] in 1946, we lived down at the bottom of the hill out there where the first big house is when you come off Blockhouse Road. There was a big two-story farmhouse there. We owned it. We owned a sixty-four-acre farm there. I milked three cows and sold the milk. And we raised pigs and sold them. But I never did like chickens.

And meantime [while working for ALCOA] Tommy was a vocational pastor. He pastored Niles Ferry and Greenback Memorial. And West Miller's Cove. And then he went to Sevier County. And then he went to Oak City in Sevier County up on Boyd's Creek, and he pastored there thirteen years. And that was his last church. He had his first heart attack in 1978 on a Saturday, after he had preached his last sermon at Oak City.

[Her children were] Ray and Max and Kit and Ted, I've got four boys and a girl, Sue.[21] They all graduated at Everett [High School in Blount County]. And Max is director at Overlook [Mental Health Center]. And Kit's playing ranger up at Cape Cod.[22] He's been up there since Memorial Day and will be through Labor Day.

Ted's in a wheelchair now; he was injured in a wreck. And he plays wheelbilly basketball.[23] But he's more like Grandpa than any of my other boys. And Ray, the youngest one, has been a mechanic ever since he could walk. I said he was born with motor oil in his veins instead of blood. But you know, though, all in all I'm very proud of my family. Sue's been a nurse at Blount Memorial for twenty-six years.

When Max was born it cost five dollars to have the doctor. Even on up till Ted was born; it was only five dollars. He's my third son. And then Ray was next, and Dr. Broady that used to be at Sevierville—he's dead now—he delivered Ray, and I think it was thirty dollars. Ray was born in 1940. And Sue was born during the war. She was born in 1947.[24]

We lived in Blount County when Sue was born. But Ted and Ray was both born at Pigeon Forge. And Max and Kit were both born at Tremont. We went up there one day—Ted likes to get out and ride around—so we rode up there. And there's a man got out of the car that's wanting to know about hiking up there. And Ted told him, "Can you believe that I was almost born here?" and pointed to the place. [laughter]

Granny took care of Max when Kit was born; she just took him over. And somewhere I guess have a picture. And she dressed him; she called the wool cloth she wove linsey.[25] And she made him petticoats out of that, and she took Grandpa's old shirts and made him some dresses, and she had him in those wool stockings [laughter], and Kit was born in November. And by that time Max was used to wearing those things, and I had to let him wear them all winter. [laughter] He was just a little over two years old.

I have eleven grandchildren. And four great-grandchildren. Three, four, five of the grandchildren are in Florida. Wait a minute, now. No, I've got four here. Let's see, let me name them. Jeff and Jake and Eric and Cindy and David, that's five here. And I've got one dead. And then the five in Florida.

I never did learn to drive. Tommy tried to teach me, but my mind went blank when I'd try to drive. And after we moved here, for my sixty-fifth birthday, he bought me a lawnmower, a riding lawnmower. And he put me on it. And the first thing I done was knock a dent in the fender of his car. [laughter] He never said a word! [He said,] "Anybody that can ride that thing around these trees can drive a car!" [laughter] I thought that was some birthday present though, a riding lawnmower. But I used it right on up till I had to have back surgery.

I've always been a person that had to be doing something with my hands. The first quilts we had when we went to housekeeping, Granny gave us the tops. We quilted our first quilts ourselves. And then after Tommy retired, we quilted in the wintertime and gardened in the summer. One winter here, counting two weeks out to go to Florida where two of the boys live, we quilted forty quilts between Christmas and time to make a garden. We quilted for people. I wish I had been smart enough to have kept down how many we had quilted. But he could quilt better than most women. In fact, the last book my sister put out has got a little story in it about him and his quilting, "The Boy Who Liked to Quilt." And they put his picture in the paper quilting. And Ted's wife had one of them enlarged and framed for me. And a whole group used to get together up here in the community and quilt for charity. And one day we were down at Lee Garland's [home] quilting. And Tommy sat there looking at the quilt. He said, "Wilma, did you do that?" I looked to see where he was pointing, and I said, "No." Merle

Davis, one of my friends, spoke up and said, "Tommy, I did." He said, "Well, I didn't think she did." And ever time we've quilted since then, Merle said that, "I feel like he's looking over my shoulder." [laughter]

I told them, though, that after we moved out of the mountains, it took me years to get used to seeing the lightning. I was afraid. Back there [in the mountains] you could hear thunder and hear the railroad rails crack when lightning run on them, but you never could see the lightning. And ever time they'd hit a jump where those rails would come together, it'd pop. That's all I knew about lightning. I knew it made a lot of noise.

Flo's working on another book.[26] U.T.'s[27] pushing her to get it down because they're wanted to publish, have it out by October. And it's going to be on the customs and ideas of death among the mountain people. And she's got pictures of what they call an angel crown. Have you ever heard of that? It's a little halo-like thing of feathers; they're interwoven. And you can't hardly tear them apart. And Merle Davis I mentioned a while ago? She's got one. She found it in her husband's pillow after he died. And that where you find them. They form in pillows. They form on their own. And that was one of their beliefs was that was indication they [the deceased] were all right, you know, and they had gone on to heaven, when they found that angel crown. Flo said about all she lacked was coming and talking to Merle and taking a picture of the one she's got.

Grandpa died in 1947. And Granny died in '56. She still lived in the old home place by herself after he died. Of course, Uncle Luke lived just across the road from her. But she lived there by herself just right on, well in fact, she died there. She made garden and kept a cow. But right on up until she got real bad sick, she had a garden. And Mama and Aunt Lola would fuss about it. And I said, "Leave her alone. If she dies out there, she'll die happy." And not try to make a monument out of her, you know. Just set her down and not let her do anything? They're not gonna do me that way. [laughter]

In July 1995, I wrote Mrs. Williamson to ask her about the advent of tourism in Sevier County. Here is her reply:

Undated, July 1995

Dear Melissa,

I am happy to tell you what I remember about how tourism helped the people in Sevier County. It was the opinion of most people that it was one of the best things to happen to the county. Of course, there were the usual hard-nosed people that resented the D-Yankees.

The business of arts and crafts started before the Park[28] was established. When Phi Beta Pi[29] came to Gatlinburg, they began to teach many things. They opened Arrowmont Crafts and hired people to work for them. I have a cousin who wove placemats for them for fifty years. She worked for them until they closed about a year ago. She also wove dish towels and scarves for them. I happen to own some she gave me.

Aunt Lola, mom's sister, made scatter rugs for the Shop. They weren't woven, they were hooked rugs.

My oldest brother Paul was quite a talented wood carver, so he worked for them also. In fact, for a time what he made was the money the family had for living. One of the clocks he carved is in the Governor's home in Nashville. It was an owl with every feather in place, and he did it with a pocket knife. I have a pair of book-ends he made when he first started, squirrels sitting on an acorn.

The school also taught a class for mid-wives. My grandmother's sister took the training and was a qualified mid-wife. I don't know very much about the school, except my second oldest brother, Charles Cope, graduated there. They recently had their forty-ninth class reunion. He thinks highly of the school.

Lots of my relatives worked at the motels. Some of my nieces drove from Newport to work, and in some areas buses ran to transport the workers. One of the distant cousins did so well that he owns Brookside Motel in Gatlinburg and has recently built a huge one near the Apple Barn on the Parkway.

Personally I think tourism has been a blessing to all of East Tennessee. . . .

I was sitting here wishing I had a tape recorder. You could probably make more sense of it.

Good luck!!
Wilma

NOTES

1. String used to sew the bags shut.

2. The Qualla Reservation in Cherokee, North Carolina, is home to the Eastern Band of the Cherokee Indians. Mrs. Williamson's grandparents lived on or near the reservation as children and young adults. Delilah Woodruff was descended from Cherokees and whites.

3. University of Tennessee Press, 1992.

4. She means that the Woodruffs attended a church in the Ogle's Creek (or Boogertown) community of Sevier County, but they remained members at Oconoluftee Church.

5. Little River Lumber Company housed workers at its more remote camps in an early form of mobile home. They outfitted railroad boxcars as housing and moved them from camp to camp. Usually two or three of these boxcars were joined together to form temporary housing for a family. Tremont was one of Little River Lumber Company's main camps with a company store and a school/church building provided by the company. Nonetheless, some of the housing at Tremont, particularly the family housing, was in the railroad cars. Single men lived in dormitory-style housing.

6. A community on the Knox County-Blount County, Tennessee line.

7. "Middlings" referred to cuts of meat from the middle of the hog.

8. Until well into the twentieth century, many Americans believed that the fruit of a tomato plant was poisonous. Apparently some people grew them as ornamental plants.

9. For more on the use of canning jars, see the LaVerne Farmer interview.

10. Mrs. Williamson is referring to various scholarship programs that exist today for college students of Native American ancestry.

11. One of Mrs. Williamson's sons.

12. In March 1994, Blount County was hit by a blizzard that dumped fifteen inches of snow on the county.

13. The county seat of Cocke County, Tennessee, where Mrs. Williamson's husband grew up.

14. Florence Cope Bush, Mrs. Williamson's younger sister, was researching documentary records of the family's past for her book *Dorie: Woman of the Mountains.*

15. Civilian Conservation Corps, a New Deal program which employed young, single men to do work in state and national parks. The workers lived in dormitory-style accommodations, and they built roads, picnic areas, campgrounds, hiking trails, and other facilities. They received a monthly wage, and they were required to send most of it home to their families.

16. The railroad followed the course of the Little River.

17. She means if the milk lasted that long before being consumed by family members.

18. Canvas shoes.

19. Civilian Conservation Camp worker.

20. Mrs. Williamson's grandfather owned a car, but he never learned to drive it. Various family members drove him wherever he wanted to go. On this particular day, Tommy Williamson walked to Robert Woodruff's (Grandpa's) farm to pick up the car and then picked up Mr. Woodruff and drove him into town.

21. The Williamsons lost a son who was born in 1956; he lived two days.

22. Kit, a retired policeman, worked for the National Park Service as a seasonal ranger during the summers.

23. Wheelchair basketball.

24. Mrs. Williamson was confused about the dates of the war but not about the birth of her daughter. Clearly, the birth of her daughter is more important to her than a world war.

25. A sturdy wool or wool/linen, wool/cotton blend.

26. Mrs. Williamson's sister, Florence Cope Bush, the author of *Dorie: Woman of the Mountains*.

27. University of Tennessee Press, also the publisher of Mrs. Bush's first book about her family.

28. Great Smoky Mountains National Park.

29. Actually Pi Beta Phi. This Ohio-based women's sorority established a settlement house and a school near Gatlinburg in 1912. They also established a handicraft cooperative, a clinic, and a school for midwives. For many years, Pi Beta Phi's high school provided the only opportunity for secondary education in the county. Students left their local communities and lived in dormitories in order to complete their educations.

LaVerne Farmer

LAVERNE FARMER PERSONIFIES many of the changes in rural southern
women's lives over the course of the twentieth century. Born at the height
of the Great Depression on July 12, 1931, she grew up the only child of a
prosperous farm family. She attended college at the University of Tennessee,
eventually earning a master's degree, and she enjoyed a career as a home
demonstration agent and later as an administrator with the Tennessee Cooperative Extension Service.

Farmer was born in Townsend, Tennessee, an old community nestled in
Tuckaleechee Cove of the Great Smoky Mountains in eastern Blount County.
First settled in the 1790s, generations of Tuckaleechee Cove residents made
their livings as subsistence farmers. Then in 1890, Knoxville lawyer and
businessman John English began to acquire tracts of timber in Tuckaleechee
Cove and the surrounding mountains. The Cove became the center of his
fledgling lumbering enterprise, which he sold to Pennsylvania-born businessman W. B. Townsend in 1901. Townsend called his timber operation
Little River Lumber Company, and he established a sawmill in Tuckaleechee
Cove. By 1902, a post office was established at the site, and the community
became known as Townsend. Little River Lumber Company gradually expanded, constructing a railroad into the Great Smoky Mountains, and provided hundreds of mountain men with new job opportunities off the farm.
In the early years of the twentieth century, many Townsend families combined subsistence farming with lumbering jobs in order to make ends meet.

As Little River Lumber Company grew, other Townsend residents seized
on new economic opportunities, Farmer's grandparents among them. They
turned their subsistence farm into a thriving dairy farm and creamery operation, bottling milk from their small herd to sell to residents of the nearby
lumber camps and later to workers at New Deal public works projects in
the area. By the time LaVerne Farmer was born, the farm and creamery
employed her grandparents, both her parents, and several hired hands.

Government intervention would ultimately transform the lives of the
Farmers and of most Townsend residents. Little River Lumber Company
weathered a series of economic ups and downs but went out of business in

1938 after the federal government purchased most of its timber holdings for the formation of the Great Smoky Mountains National Park. Farmer's family ceased their dairy farming and milk bottling in the late 1940s when the federal government enacted new regulations designed to guarantee the safety of bottled milk. Complying with the new rules would have been prohibitively expensive for the family. In addition, Farmer's grandparents were quite elderly by this point. Farmer's father continued to do some part-time farming, but he made his living as a school bus driver and a rural mail carrier after the demise of the dairy.

On August 9, 1993, I interviewed Miss Farmer at the Blount County Farm Bureau Building where she had just attended a meeting. Now retired, she lives with her mother on the farm where she was raised. Miss Farmer's interview reflects her education and her broad perspective on the changes in southern rural life. At first, she talks in very general terms about the conditions of rural life early in the century, but as the interview progresses, she speaks in more personal terms. I sent the transcript to Miss Farmer in the fall of 1994. She corrected a few errors in the transcript and completed the family history questionnaire, but she offered no further comments on the interview.

I was born in 1931, but of course, I've heard the family talk about the Depression. I was an only child, but my parents lived with my dad's parents when they were first married, so it was a three-generation family for a while.

Mother was from a family with six children. Families back in the teens and World War I and the twenties were pretty much self-sufficient as far as the farm families. They produced most of their own goods, maybe purchasing a few staples like sugar and things like that. The families did most of their own work. Sometimes they would share with neighbors to get jobs done. But if they were large families, the children and the parents did most of the work themselves.

Now, as far as food production, they raised most of their vegetables. Pork was the main meat source. Occasionally if they had sheep, they would have mutton—they called it mutton. Occasionally I think some families would kill a beef, but pork was the main meat source. Plus, the men did a lot of fishing and hunting, depending on that for a food source.

There was no means of preservation except pickling, drying, [and] curing of meat. There was very little canning. Now, as a very small child, I can remember we started putting food in tin cans. There were no glass jars at that

time, but they did have tin cans beginning along about the thirties.¹ There
was a little sealer. It had the lid to fit on it, and there was a little device that
sealed the can.

[To cool food,] they had crocks, and they would set that down in the
creek. The woman did most of the milking, too. Some men would milk, but
most of the time, the milking was left up to the woman. And then the milk
would be put into these crock jars. And usually . . . if there wasn't a lid for
it, they'd put a plate on it and a rock on it, to help weight it down. And it
would be cooled in the spring. If there was a big rain or something, and
water got up, they'd have to go to the spring and get the milk out so it
wouldn't wash away. [laughter]

They had dried fruit. They had their own apple trees. Some peach trees,
but it was a little cold for peaches. Most families had apple trees or access to
apple trees. And they also had an attic or somewhere close to the chimney
where the heat would come up, and they'd put [dried] apples up there, and
they'd last till after Christmas. And then most of them had cellars that they
used to store potatoes, sweet potatoes, turnips, and things like that.

The wood cookstove and the fireplace was usually the heating source for
the family. And the men on the most part got the wood, but sometimes if the
men were real busy, the woman would have to chop the wood for the cookstove, especially in the summertime because they [the men] were busy in the
fields.

Laundry, of course, was done on the old washboard, and the water heated
in a big black pot out in the yard. Most of them had spring water close by.
There was some wells, but when people settled in that area, they looked for
a spring. So they used spring water as a water source, most of them. And, of
course, a lot of them lived very close to the river, and they would use river
water for washing and things like that. But they had to carry water in buckets. It wasn't an easy life.

For their clothing in the thirties, if they could afford it, they began to buy
some of their fabrics. Well, even before then, they would buy fabric. But
ready-made clothes were just almost a thing . . . unheard of. [laughter] The
mother did sewing for the children. Knitting was another thing they did
quite a bit of. They would knit socks. They did a lot of weaving, especially
household fabrics, you know bedspreads, coverlets as they called them.² And
they would shear the sheep. There was some cotton grown in this area. Of
course, this has never been a big cotton area. But they did grow some cotton, but fabrics were available, I guess, at that time.³

That was another thing they made, their bed linens. I'm amazed at the
fancy underclothing that they made and how they had time to do all that. So

much of it had to be done by hand back then. Of course, sewing machines did come along, but in earlier years, it was hand sewing. Mother had an electric sewing machine, but my grandmother had the treadle. I used to think that was great fun to just play with the sewing machine. It was an interesting toy.

And the rolling stores would come around. Are you familiar with the rolling stores? Well in the rural areas, they didn't go to the store too much, but the little rolling stores was kind of like a big U-Haul-it, one of the big colored things. And they had staples, and they would buy eggs in exchange for groceries. This, too, was a source of income. The mother would take care of the chickens and gather the eggs and take the eggs to the store and exchange those for staples.

Church was the social center. The ladies in church, the ladies sat on one side of the house and the men on the other. They generally wore their bonnets to church. They had sewing circles, mission circles, and quilting bees.

There was no transportation much. Roads were very poor. Of course, in our community, we had the lumber company, which came in around 1900, and there was train service to Maryville after that.[4] But up until that time, your transportation was just horse and wagon or horse and buggy. People did a lot of walking then.

Now, my mother walked to school. And it's about six miles, one way. Now for grade school it wasn't that far, but when they went to high school [it was about six miles]. And they didn't have a high school when Mother first got through grade school, so she and her sister had to wait two or three years for them to complete the building of the high school. They walked to high school.

My mother taught school a year before she was married. My mother got one year of college. Her sister got two years and started teaching, but she eventually finished college going in the summertime. And their youngest brother was a college graduate. Several of the local people went on to school and are teachers now, the women especially. A lot of them came back to Townsend.

A lot of the older teenagers that were high-school age had no transportation out of Cades Cove.[5] See the families didn't move out of there until the late '30s. So those that went on to high school would come out and board somewhere during the week, and they would go home with him on Friday afternoons and come out on Sunday afternoons. It was the only opportunity they had. It was either do that or not get an education.

By the time I came along, there were a lot of little two-room schools in the community. I can remember three; there were others before my time.

There were three little two-room schools when I first started to school. But the one I attended had all the grades and the high school. And then, I guess I was ten years old, it was about '41, the '41 school year I guess, they combined all the little two-room schools and sent them all to Townsend.

I can't recall exactly when the school buses started running, but there were buses when I started school. They didn't pick up a lot of the students close by, but they did bring students in from [further away]. . . . Well, let's see, I guess there was just one bus, and it ran, now there were a lot of the families that worked for the lumber company that were living up in the mountains, up in Tremont area and that section, and they did run a bus to pick up those children.[6] But most of the other sections of the community, they still had the little two-room schools. So they were just mostly running the bus to pick up the high school students. I guess they did travel the main roads to pick up high school students.

But when Mother and Dad were married, we were in the dairy business. We had to keep people—we called them hired people—and they boarded in the home because there were no places for them to stay. So Mother did most of the cooking and the housework. And my grandmother helped process the milk. Labor was very cheap at that time, but of course dollars were very scarce. But we did hire people to come in and help with the dairy farm operation. There would usually be a lady and a couple of men.

At the beginning, they [Farmer's family] grew a lot of corn and ground feed to feed our cattle in addition to the hay. Then after we really got into the dairy production, he [her grandfather] would make a trip or two every week to get feed, the ground feed, in Maryville. It was close to an hour's drive one way on the old Highway 73. If we needed to come into Maryville to get supplies for the farm, for a lot of people who needed to go into Maryville, Granddad was the taxi service.

Dad had helped with the dairy operation. He delivered some milk and took milk to the CCC camps. And that was his income. And then Mother was paid a little; of course it would have been a lot to them for doing the cooking and the housekeeping. So they had their own income. And then my grandparents had the main operation. Then when I was six years old, Mother and Dad built a house, and they moved out from my grandparents' house. Mother still helped some. She would go and help do the cooking and all, but they lived in a separate house.

And it was interesting then: in building their homes, they usually cut their own lumber. When my parents built their house, Mother's dad gave them most of the lumber, and they cut it. They took it to the lumber company and had it sawed. And most of the labor had to be done by hand because they didn't have electricity so they had to use hand tools. Mother is still living, and we live there [in the house her parents built].

We were the producer, processor, and distributor all. And we sold milk in that area [Townsend and its environs] and even here in the Maryville area some. But we supplied . . . the CCC camps.[7] There were two in our area in the thirties, and we supplied milk to those.

To cool our milk, we used ice. The Little River Lumber Company had an ice plant, and we would go, usually every other day, to the plant and get one-hundred-pound blocks of ice. And I've been cleaning up an old building that still has the old icebox that was used. And the ice was put in the center and then the milk on the side. We did some cooling with the spring water. And we had just a big, long trough about the size of this table [six feet long] I guess, and the water ran into that trough and then out in a continuous flow, and we used that for cooling the milk down before we put it in the ice box.

We didn't have hot running water. But we were a little bit modern; we had the spring water piped to the house. We got electricity in '38. There was a little plant, privately owned plant put in at Townsend. It was mostly for the lumber company. But because we had to furnish milk for so many people, they did supply us with electricity at that time. Then we modernized: we built a big walk-in cooler that had a compressor that cooled the milk. Then we started pasteurizing the milk shortly after that. Up to that time, it was just the raw milk.

I helped on the farm and in the house as far back as I can remember. Mother was always real good at helping me learn to cook. She took time and patience. And I always liked to make desserts more than anything. So I learned to do cakes before I started school. I had just a basic one-egg cake that I did. And when I was very small, the churning was done with an old dash churn. I wasn't big enough to do it, but I thought I was. I have a picture of me with the churn, you know.

And then just as soon as I got big enough to carry bottles of milk, I started going with my grandfather to deliver milk. We also went from house to house. And then as soon as I started school, I was able to make change. Some people in the summertime—especially up around Kinzel Springs— people from Knoxville would come, and they would just be summer customers, and maybe just weekend or something. And they would buy and just pay cash, so I had to handle quite a bit of money.

I would go to the hayfield, especially, I can remember, as soon as I was big enough that they would trust me out by myself, I would have to go help drive the cows in for milking. Then when we got the tractor, I was the tractor driver. Especially during World War II, it was difficult to get help because a lot of the men were gone. So I was just a regular hand in the fields at that time, in the summertime, especially hauling hay and working up ground and sowing seeds.

We had a truck, and my dad had an A model car. There was also a tractor. Now, the first one that I recall, and they had it before I was born, it was an old International with steel wheels. Now I don't know if you've seen one of those or not. And it was a great day when we bought the little Ford tractor, you know, with rubber wheels. [laughter] The hay was cut with horses and a two-horse mower, you know. And it was raked into rows and then hauled as loose hay on the wagon and put in the barn loft. You had forks [to throw the hay into the wagon]. And there was a track in the top of the barn, and you had a fork that would come down and pick up hay, and then you had a rope outside on a pulley, and you would take a horse, or as I said when the tractor came along it was a great day, you could hitch the tractor to this rope, and you could pull the fork through the barn, and then you would trip it, and the hay would drop off.[8]

I was in 4–H Club. I wasn't very active, but I did belong to the 4–H Club when I was in my upper grades. I don't recall anything about it before maybe sixth grade or something like that. Now Mother was a home demonstration [club] member.[9] Mother did a lot of sewing. They had dress contests back then, and as I recall, Mother won second place or something in the dress contest. They did a lot of handwork. They did a lot of stenciling at one time; that was a fad. And then food preparation was a major part of it and [food] preservation. They taught people to can in the glass jars and that kind of thing.

We had a country doctor who delivered about all the babies and took care of their runny noses. There was a country doctor around; I've heard my great uncle was one for a long time. They had very little medical training.

Like I said, we had the country doctor, but if there was serious sickness or deaths or needs in the community, the neighbors would just—my grandparents would just go, no matter how much work they had to do. If somebody was real sick and needed somebody to stay, they'd go and stay. You know, all night or whatever. They'd go sit up. Back then, of course, [when] you died, they'd bring the body back to the house for one night before the funeral. And neighbors would come in and sit up with them [the family of the deceased] and talk. And if they needed food during garden season, they'd take surplus food to the neighbors. You know, it was just kindly an extended family.[10] If people around needed things, why, they'd help each other out. But back then I don't recall anybody being much poorer than anybody else. They just shared what they had.

The lumber company of course was the source of income for a lot of people at that time, plus their farming. After the CCC camps were disbanded, people started working [on WPA projects]. I recall one lady started working in the lunchroom at the school.[11]

A lot of the people that lived up in the mountains and worked for the lumber company—they would just set box cars off to the side of the railroad tracks, and people would live in those boxcars.[12] There was one area up there they called Boxtown. And there really wasn't room for, oh, they might have a little garden in the back, but they really didn't have room for a garden. Those people really just survived on what he made at the lumber company. There was a company store at Tremont. And there was one at Townsend.

The elderly worked as long as they could and then their families took care of them. Neighbors would help out. Of course, back then, they didn't live to be real elderly, most of them.

Divorce or separation or anything just really didn't happen all that much when I was growing up. In that community, it was kind of looked on as kind of a disgrace. You know, you just didn't do your family that way. There was always drinking. I don't know if there was a whole lot of what you'd just call alcoholics or not. But they always had their moonshine around, and a lot [of people] made it. That was the source of income for a lot of them. But, you know, I've always heard the saying that the moonshiners don't drink their own brew. I guess they know too much about it. [laughter] But they would make it. They would have their little nips. Of course, alcohol was a big source of their medication, too. They believed in those hot toddies and things like that for colds and things. Oh, I can remember a few alcoholics. They called them sots. That was the word. But there wasn't that many. The families [of alcoholics] struggled. They really did. The mother had the main responsibility to see that the family was cared for. You didn't hear of women drinking much then. The women smoked back then, but they had their little corncob pipes in the chimney corner, and they didn't let anybody see them with their pipes. [laughter] Snuff was still was kind of a little secretive thing. Now, my grandma had to have her little snuff after her meal, but she'd slip off someplace. You just didn't see her using her snuff.

We went out of the dairy operation about '48. My grandfather had a cerebral hemorrhage, and he wasn't able to help anymore. It was just too much for him. And about that time was when rural electricity was going out everywhere, and they were changing the requirements about handling the milk, and you had to have coolers. We had four little milkers,[13] but it still had to be handled by people a lot, and so then they began to require the tank where the milk was run directly into the cooler.[14] So it was going to require a lot of remodeling and expensive equipment. So we just sold out the dairy herd and stopped the operation. But it was also becoming difficult to compete with the larger milk producers, too.

Oh, and another thing. In spite of all that they had to do, the neighbors had to walk to the store or wherever they were going, and especially in hot weather, they would walk and as they was passing by, they stop on the porch and visit and get them a drink of water. People were never too busy to sit down and visit and talk for a while. We had some people who lived up from me near Dry Valley. There was a footpath—it was kind of a gap in the mountain and a hollow that went up by our house and you could go into Dry Valley [on the footpath]. And that was the shortest way out for people who lived in the upper end of the valley. And they walked out to the store. There was a little grocery store down near Bethel Church on the old Highway 73. And that was in addition to the company store. And those people would walk out to the store by our house. And lots of time they would stop by and just visit a while on the way to the store. And they'd walk through there to church.

Then evenings late after everybody would get their work done up, they'd just go sit on the porch and visit with each other. They didn't have TV to watch, and they did a lot more playing of games like checkers and things like that. Children played marbles and hide and go seek, and that was big entertainment. They had battery-operated radios; a few people had those. And neighbors would go visit the neighbors that had radios and hear the radio occasionally. Some had the old crank-up Victrola and records. They had family reunions a lot more back then, too. That was a source of entertainment, too, I guess you'd say. The families would get together. We had the Sears and Roebuck catalog to entertain us. And most everybody had a path instead of a bath [an outhouse]. But it certainly was a different time.

Notes

1. Actually there were glass jars available in the United States at this time. In 1810, Frenchman Francois Appert developed the principles for preserving food in hermetically sealed jars, which were then heated in a water bath. Over the years, a number of inventers in Europe and in the United States developed various types of glass food-preservation containers, but the seals on these jars were never very effective. The real breakthrough in home food preservation came in 1958 when John Landis Mason patented a jar with a tightly sealing zinc cap. Late in the nineteenth century, the cap with a rubber seal was developed, a device that has changed but little down to today. Nonetheless, glass canning jars were not widely used in the rural South until the 1920s and 1930s when home extension agents taught farm women to use the jars and the canners needed to seal the jars. Canning jars were also prohibitively expensive for many poor farm families.

2. Although women in most parts of the country had completely given up home weaving, a few women in the Appalachian Mountains continued to weave into the early twentieth century. This weaving caught the attention of social workers and others interested in the colonial crafts revival. See the Wilma Williamson interview.

3. Some rural east Tennessee families grew a few rows of cotton, which they de-seeded by hand in order to use the fiber as quilt batting.

4. Little River Lumber Company.

5. Cades Cove was another farming community nestled in the Great Smoky Mountains, about twenty miles from Townsend by road. The community was part of the Great Smoky Mountains National Park, and the National Park Service purchased the land and removed families living in Cades Cove in the late 1930s. Until that time, it was quite isolated.

6. Tremont was a lumber camp between Townsend and Cades Cove.

7. Civilian Conservation Corps, a New Deal program designed to give employment to young, single men between the ages of eighteen and twenty-five. They worked in state and national parks, building trails, roads, and picnic grounds, and they lived in military-style barracks.

8. The fork grabbed a chunk of hay from the wagon. Using pulleys, ropes lifted the fork up and into the barn loft. Once inside, the fork traveled the full length of the barn loft to distribute the hay evenly.

9. The Cooperative Extension Service established local 4–H clubs for farm youth and home demonstration clubs for farm women. Through these organizations, professional agriculturalists and home economists trained youth and women in new skills designed to improve the standard of living and quality of life on the nation's farms.

10. "Kindly" is mountain dialect for "kind of."

11. The Works Progress Administration, another New Deal public works program. The WPA hired unemployed workers to build roads, bridges, and schools and to run recreation programs in cities and school lunch programs in the country.

12. Lumber companies used a form of mobile housing that resembles the modern mobile home. Two or three boxcars would be moved into a remote location, placed on a temporary foundation, and bolted together. These would become temporary housing for lumber workers and their families. When logging moved to another area, the boxcars were simply loaded onto trains again and moved on. See Wilma Williamson interview.

13. The portion of the milking machine that attached to the cow's udder.

14. New federal regulations required that Grade A dairies install pipelines that carried milk directly from the cow to an electrically cooled bulk tank. Grade A milk, the milk designed for drinking (rather than use in ice cream, cheese, or butter) was the most profitable to produce.

French Carpenter Clark

FRENCH CARPENTER CLARK was born January 21, 1905, in Blount County, Tennessee. She was the fourth of thirteen children. Her parents were farmers. Mrs. Clark had little to say about her childhood, perhaps because I did not ask her specific questions about those years. I asked her to tell me about rural life, especially during the Great Depression, and as a result, she focused on the early years of her marriage.

French Carpenter married Ole (pronounced Ol-ee) Clark on November 1, 1924. Like many Blount Countians, Ole took advantage of the new industrial opportunities at Blount County's Aluminum Company of America (ALCOA) to try to earn a more secure living than the farm provided. ALCOA constructed its first Blount County aluminum-smelting operation near the county seat town of Maryville in 1914. Although the company constructed some housing for its workers, many local farm folk commuted to jobs at "the plant," as the locals called it. Some men drove their own cars to work or carpooled with neighbors, and at some points in its history, the company operated a "work bus" system that provided transportation for workers who lived in the countryside. In response to the booming demand for aluminum created by World War I, in 1920 the company added a rolling mill, which rolled aluminum ingots into sheet metal. By 1920, ALCOA employed 3,672 men, including Ole Clark and eventually six of French Clark's brothers.

Ole and French Clark never owned a farm. In the early years of their marriage, they lived in ALCOA's company town, also known as Alcoa. After one of ALCOA's periodic layoffs in 1926, the couple went to Detroit, Michigan, in search of work, a common strategy among many southern Appalachian people. Their first son was born in Detroit. Ole Clark worked for a time in Detroit. The couple returned to Blount County three and one-half years later, renting a house in the country. Ole returned to a job at ALCOA, commuting daily for his shift. In the countryside, they kept a garden that provided much of the family's diet. For several years, the couple ran a crossroads store. Mrs. Clark tended the store during the week with help from Ole in between his shifts and during the periodic layoffs that were common for ALCOA employees. The couple raised four children.

I have known Mrs. Clark all my life. I grew up in the same community. She and her husband were friends of my grandparents. (In fact, Ole made kitchen cabinets for both of my grandmothers when they remodeled in the early 1970s.) One of her granddaughters was formerly married to my mother's brother, and another granddaughter is one of my closest friends. Nonetheless, I knew little about her life until I conducted this interview.

On July 22, 1994, I interviewed Mrs. Clark at her home, a small ranch house in the community where she and Ole spent most of their adult lives. Ole had died in 1986, and by this time, Mrs. Clark's health was failing. Her mind was sharp, but she found it difficult to move safely around the house unassisted, and her hearing was impaired. A home health care worker was present for the interview, and Mrs. Clark's daughter, Irma Tulloch (pronounced Tull-ock), arrived at the end of the interview. After I sent the transcribed interview to Mrs. Clark, she completed the family history questionnaire, but she made no corrections to the transcript. Mrs. Clark died in 1997.

Ole and I got married in 1924. November 1, 1924. We set up housekeeping in Maryville. We had an apartment on Lord Street. Then we moved to a house in Alcoa. He was working at ALCOA.[1] Irma was borned out there. We lived up there three years and a half. Kenneth was borned up there, but I didn't want to raise them [the children] up there, so we moved out here.[2]

Ole worked there at ALCOA, and at that time, they was bad to get laid off up there. That's what made it so hard. We ran the store there at Big Springs for five or six years. Sometimes people [customers] would bring eggs [to trade for supplies]. We took them to the market I guess. Your grandpa and grandma traded with us. They'd get in that car and come down and get the groceries, your grandmother and all of them [her children].

But it was pretty hard. The Depression started in '29 and seemed like it lasted a long time, harder at different times than others.

When we moved to Binfield, we rented a house, and we paid five dollars a month for the house.[3] We lived out there at the railroad [not far from the tracks]. They had a big apple orchard there, and I said I never eat as many fried apples and biscuits for breakfast in my life. [laughter] Or fed as many hoboes. The train stopped out there, you know. And they'd get off them trains and come out to the house to get something to eat. I grabbed what I had. If it wasn't nothing but bread, I'd grab it and give it to them. I know one day one come out there and wanted something to eat, and I put something in a poke[4] and give it to him and looked out, and they was five in a boxcar with their heads a sticking out, you know. He took it out there and divided it with them.

But one time they was one [hobo] come of a night. And I was laying on the bed in the bedroom. And there was a door coming in off the porch onto the bedroom, and something hit the porch, and I looked up and I saw him; he was standing up over my bed. Ole was in the living room. He was standing up over the bed there and just looking at me. But Ole was in there by that time, you know. And he asked him what he wanted. And he wrote on a piece of paper: he was deaf and dumb, and he wanted water. He didn't want anything to eat, just water.

One time, one [hobo] came at five o'clock in the morning and knocked on the back door, and Ole had done gone to work, and I went to the door, and he was standing there. Ole had done gone to town. I said, "What do you want?" And he said, "Something to eat." And I said, "All right, you stand right there and I'll get you something." So I give the children's breakfast to him, and when he left and headed back toward the railroad, I got Kenneth up and—he was about seven years old—and I said, "Go up there and tell John [a neighbor] to come down here." And he [John] come, and by that time it was getting light, and John went out to the railroad, and he [the hobo] had gone way down the railroad and built him a fire.

We picked blackberries and sold them ten cents a gallon to buy books for the kids for school. Ole was working for the plant, and he was making fifteen dollars a week. Can you imagine that? So he worked on the farm for a neighbor up there [on days he was not working at the plant], and he got a dollar a day. That was the wages.

But still, things wasn't so expensive then. You paid five cents a pound for coffee, and five cents for a loaf of bread, and I think nineteen cents for five pounds of sugar, yeah about nineteen or twenty cents then. We could take that dollar and buy groceries. And our shoes, Ole would give me five dollars, and I'd buy our shoes, and I could buy me and the children a pair of shoes. And his, I think, were two dollars. They were cheap shoes, but everybody wore them. They were about all you could get.

I had four children in all. Two boys and two girls. That was a pretty big family. A lot of kids to keep in school. We bought their books, and a lot of times before school started we could swap [books] with other people.[5]

I made all our clothes; I even made the boys' shirts. You could get material for ten cents a yard. Irma never had a bought dress till she graduated. I got her two dresses. I guess Inez never did [have a store-bought dress] because I made their clothes.

I raised a big garden and canned. We had our chickens, and we always raised a hog. About the hardest thing was when they rationed things [during World War II]. That was the hardest time for us.

Things picked up at the plant when the war hit. [M]oney wasn't so scarce, but there was nothing to buy. No gas. It was so hard for us to get gas, and we always went to church, took them [the children] to church. We carried that little old Bob to church up here at Binfield.[6] We didn't have no gas, you know.

We just had to make our own entertainment, because we didn't have a television or a telephone or a radio; we finally did have battery radio. And made our own. And I used to try to, well I did try to take the children every time Shirley Temple was on, and I think we saw all her shows [at the cinema in Maryville]. And people visited then, and we'd make ice cream. [At Christmas] we always had our Christmas tree, and the children hung their stockings, and we always visited with my family and his family. It was a family tradition, and [we] still do with my children. We didn't make a big deal of buying presents and things like that. We strung popcorn together for the [Christmas] trees. We always went out and cut our trees. I still like to do that.

People would help [each other] if they needed it. But they had to live, too. Everybody lived like that; we weren't the only ones. And I raised my four [children] that way. Churches helped, but they didn't help people like churches do now. They'd give the preacher something. We always took so much wheat to the mill and had it made into our flour, and we gave some to the preacher. They didn't ask a salary, you know.[7]

The doctors would come out here. They'd come out for five dollars. I know Dr. Brickey Lequire would come out. Sometimes they'd have medicine with them. There was a time when Ole had surgery, he had appendicitis, and uh, I had a tumor in my breast then, and the doctor told me I needed surgery then. And I know I went to the doctor one day, and a friend of mine was a nurse, and she said, "You've got to see about that," and I did. And he looked at it and said I needed surgery, and I said, "When we get Ole's surgery paid off I will." And he said, "You'd just as well have it done now. You'd just as well owe me for two as one." And he only charged me thirty-five dollars and sent it [the tumor] to Nashville to be checked [biopsied]. He did it [the surgery] in his office.

I had the kids at home. Irma and Inez were ten dollars. They was ten-dollar kids. Kenneth was twenty-five dollars; he was worth a little more.[8] [laughter] And Bobby—he wasn't but five dollars. He was cheaper because he was so little. And then old Dr. Brickell, Dr. Brickell at Friendsville delivered him. Dr. Crowder delivered the two girls. I don't know what that doctor's name was that delivered Ken [in Detroit], he was a little bitty doctor is all I remember. I don't remember his name. We didn't have no phone. Ole had to go to Maryville to get him [the doctor].[9]

Bobby was about six years old before we lived over there close to electricity. That was in the forties. We had had it when we lived in town. That was an adjustment [to move to the country and live without electricity]. When we got our electricity, then we got our stove and refrigerator, and the children were so thrilled with the refrigerator because we had just had an ice-box, and they were thrilled to death with making ice. And they made ice and then took it and threw it in the yard. [laughter] And somebody said, "Well, did you let them throw it out?" And I said, "Yes, I just let them throw it out because," I said, "they was so thrilled with it." It wasn't going to hurt anything. They'd fill up the tray and throw it in the yard. It was pretty rough old times, but we was happy.

I'll tell you another story. We was living up on the hill over there [near her present home]. Ole had one denim shirt. And I'd wash that, and I'd iron it to get ready for him to wear it to work that evening. Well, back then they had these patches that you could iron on. Kenneth had a red one, and one day Kenneth put it on that shirt, and you couldn't get it out. I know he [Ole] was embarrassed to death—he had to wear that shirt with that red fox on it every day to work. You know I told that story to somebody the other day, and she didn't have no kids, and she couldn't believe it. She said, "You know he had more than one shirt." And I said, "Well, that was all he had. He did have a Sunday shirt, but he did not have more than one shirt to work in."

It was hard times, but still I think people expect a little bit too much now when they start out. Yeah, they do. And all down through life they expect too much.

Notes

1. The Aluminum Company of America. The couple moved from a Maryville apartment to a company-owned house in the company town, Alcoa.

2. They moved to the country. Apparently Mrs. Clark was referring to the family's move to Detroit here, but that was not clear to me at the time. I learned of the family's time in Detroit much later from other family members. In the family history questionnaire Mrs. Clark completed later, probably with the assistance of daughter Irma Tulloch, she indicated that Kenneth was born in Detroit.

3. Binfield was a rural community in southwestern Blount County. It was about eight miles from town.

4. In east Tennessee, the term "poke" was used to refer to a paper bag. In other parts of the South, it referred to burlap bags.

5. At this time, most public schools in the South did not provide free textbooks to students. Families had to try to provide textbooks, an obstacle that sometimes prevented children from attending school.

6. Bob was Mrs. Clark's youngest son, born in 1933.

7. Most rural churches were staffed by ministers who served several churches or by part-time lay ministers who made their living in other ways. During the Great Depression, it was common for parishioners to "pay" their ministers with gifts of foodstuffs.

8. Kenneth's delivery was probably more expensive because it took place in Detroit.

9. Dr. Crowder.

Korola Neville Lee

KOROLA NEVILLE LEE was born December 10, 1911, in Blount County, Tennessee. Blount County, situated between the Tennessee River and the Great Smoky Mountains south of Knoxville, was settled in the 1780s. By the early twentieth century, the county's economy was a mix of agriculture and industry. The Aluminum Company of America established a large manufacturing facility near the county seat, Maryville, and several other small industries provided wage work for many town dwellers and rural people who continued to farm part-time after they took factory jobs. The majority of Blount Countians continued to farm full-time until the Second World War, however. Large farms lined the county's rich river and creek bottoms while smaller farms dotted the upland slopes.

Korola Lee's father, Ephraim Perry Lee, was a prosperous landowning farmer born just after the Civil War, and Miss Lee shared the Civil War stories she had heard from her grandmother. Miss Lee had a half brother and half sister from her father's first marriage. She was the middle child of five from her father's second marriage to Mary Ann Eliza Josephine McCammon, a local schoolteacher.

The Lees were devout Quakers and well respected in their home community of Big Springs, south of Maryville. Two of Miss Lee's ancestors had founded the Quaker boarding school, Friendsville Institute (later known as Friendsville Academy), in 1854. Another ancestor had drawn up the plans for the town of Friendsville.

The Lee children attended public schools in the county. When Korola Lee and her younger sister Thelma finished high school, they were still too young to obtain teaching certificates, so they attended Maryville College for a year. Miss Lee began her teaching career at Mount Vernon Elementary School in southern Blount County. She and sister Thelma finished their college degrees by attending summer sessions at East Tennessee Teacher's College (now East Tennessee State University), alternating summers so that one sister would always be home to help out on the farm. Korola Lee served a series of one- and two-room schools for a number of years before the consolidation of community schools into Friendsville Elementary. She taught three generations of Blount County children, including my father and his siblings, before retiring in the late 1960s. She and sister Thelma cared for their parents in old age and maintained a large garden. A number of years after their parents' deaths, Thelma Lee moved in with a single nephew who had lost both his parents, leaving Korola Lee alone in the family home. Miss Lee remained active in the Friendsville Friends Church and the local home demonstration club.

This interview took place on the front porch of Miss Lee's rambling, white frame farmhouse, the home where she was born and where her parents lived until their deaths. We talked on August 10, 1994, and she corrected the transcript in October 1994. Her spoken dialect was typical of east Tennessee and contained syntactical and grammatical errors, but Miss Lee had not forgotten her schoolteacher's training in standard English: she corrected her grammar in much of the transcript. I have made corrections as she indicated but left mistakes intact in portions of the transcript she did not correct. Although she was eighty-three when we talked, her memory and her wit were sharp. In her narrative, Miss Lee was meticulous about local geography, constantly placing people and events on the land. She shared a couple of her mother's recipes, which are found at the end of the narrative.

I had two brothers older than me and two sisters younger than me. Then I had a half brother and a half sister, Macy Hartsell Lee and Myrtle Mae Lee. My half sister is ninety-five years old, and she lives in California. Macy's daughters, Elizabeth and Margaret Nell, flew out for her birthday last year. And Macy lived to be ninety-two. Their mother [Korola's father's first wife] died when Macy was about eighteen months old.

Macy went down and worked in the gristmill. [It was a] flour mill, flour and corn meal. Then he got to working at night at the marble quarry,[1] and he was a perfectionist [about cutting marble]. He sawed the marble at night for the post office at Knoxville [built in the late 1930s] and also the Smithsonian Institute Museum in Washington, DC. [He sawed at night] because nobody was around to bother him. He said, "If you are off, one-thousandth of an inch, then the rest of it's off."

[After his first wife died], my father married my mother, Mary McCammon Lee. She taught at McConnell's Schoolhouse. And she and Papa were married the twenty-eighth of December, 1905. Chester Perry Lee was born April 7, 1907, Oliver Verne [pronounced Vern-ie] Lee was born April 4, 1909, I was born in December 10, 1911, and Thelma Bernice was born December

20, 1913, ten days different. Mary Frances was born in November 3, 1920. My father was a birthright Quaker, and my mother was a Presbyterian. And the reason we went to Big Springs [Presbyterian Church] was because it was right here close to us. The way they'd pay the preacher was to give him things that they raised on the farm.

Verne was a farmer. Verne sold watermelons in his yard for twenty-three years. And people come from everywhere to get them, even Knoxville. Labor Day is about the last day you can sell them. There was one year when the National Guard was down in Hawaii, and someone was coming back, and they asked them, "What do you want us to bring you back?" They said, "Well, bring us some of Verne Lee's watermelons." And they, I believe they got six. And they had to pack them in ice.[2]

My older brother Chester graduated when he was seventeen from Friendsville Academy [a Quaker school]. He went to Knoxville and took business courses. He stayed with Mama's brother, he was a well-known doctor, a children's doctor. Chester was seventeen. And when he got through business college, he went to work for the telephone company. [He] stayed there forty-three years. [He] worked on up in the office. Then later on, in '36 or '37, they sent him to Athens [Tennessee] to be a supervisor. From the time he left home in 1926, he came home once a month until my mother died. He'd bring people with him. They'd bring their friends, mother-in-laws, father-in-laws. He died sitting in the golf cart. Died happy.

And my baby sister was a registered nurse. And she started at Fontana.[3] Her husband got on up there as the safety supervisor. And he was the last person out when they turned the dam on. They opened the gate and they was trying to keep ahead of that water. They had to check to see that they was nobody in there. He said, "I was the last person out."

We were not hard up back during the Depression. We didn't have very much cash, but where Papa would make his money—when he'd sell a calf, he would put that [money] in bank. And we sold baled hay, and that's where I learned my arithmetic. People would come here from miles and miles around and buy hay. And he [her father] had one of those old-fashioned scales. Did you ever see any of them? It had a hook on it. And we'd go down there [to weigh the hay], and I added it. He'd take that money. We'd raise the chickens, and [we had] the cream money; that's what bought the groceries and the food and clothes. And my mother, how she made our clothes I don't know. How my mother did all those things. I learned to sew when I was nine years old.

And we got up at four o'clock. And one song I remember my father sung going to the barn, [sings] "Get up in the morning, have a little chow, Hal-le,

Hal-le-lu. In the morning, have a little chow, Hal-le, Hal-le-lu. Get up in the morning, have a little chow, Hal-le, Hal-le-lu. In the morning have a little chow, Hal-le, Hal-le-lu." They laughed an awful lot. They were happy people. And we went to bed by eight o'clock.

I remember one time a big steer fell in the creek up here and backed the water up. And they found it on Sunday morning. And they did skin that because he said, "It's an emergency." But otherwise we didn't. And from sundown on Saturday night to Sunday night, it was the Sabbath, and we did not work. We sat out on the porch. We played ball. We visited neighbors on Sunday afternoon. We'd look out and say, "Oh, there's so and so a'coming." Old people would come back here and visit. That's where I got a lot of my history. Elderly people would come to visit.

People would come in and quilt. And we killed hogs. And my uncle was building a barn and putting a roof on it. And people would come in [to help build the barn], and the women would cook.

Back then, did anyone tell you about the apple orchard and drying their apples? Well, they used to make peach brandy and locust wine. Did you ever hear of locust wine? Well now, I've made it. Did you ever see these locust trees? See they had thorns on them. And the brown seeds hanging in them have a pus on the inside of them that's good to eat. They'd gather those [seed pods] up and put them in a big jar and put water [on them] and let them sit for two or three weeks and ferment. And that was locust wine. They made peach brandy. And they made their own vinegar. I remember Mama making her own vinegar. Aunt Elizabeth had an apple press. They raised a lot of apples. Now we had an apple orchard right out across the road, a big one, when I was growing up. We also had an apple orchard down here, and we had a persimmon orchard. We had about eighteen or twenty trees, persimmon trees. Nobody told you about persimmon trees? Boy, I wish I had written that recipe. My mother would make persimmon bread. Grandmother made it, and my mother made it. You'd take persimmons and squeeze the pulp out of them and use that with your flour and your egg and your sugar and make it just like a loaf of bread. I thought everybody had heard of that. Did you ever hear of Green Tomato Pie? Well, we made it. She'd make elderberry jam. We'd go pick elderberries, and we'd make pies out of them. People make blackberry wine. You could take blackberry juice and let it sour, and it would make wine. Do you have a recipe for egg butter? I wrote that off yesterday and also how to make lye soap.

We raised peas. Well now, we raised whippoorwill peas. They growed about this high [indicates knee high], and Papa would bring them in and let them dry. I remember we'd bring them out on the porch out here, and we'd take an old quilt or something, and we'd take a stick or something when they was dry, and that was the way you'd break the hulls. And we'd save some for seed. Did you ever hear of hominy? We made that. And they had black-eyed peas and hog jowl meat for the first day of the year. We had a big garden, and we raised our beans. And we holed up our turnips and cabbage and sweet potatoes.[4] We kept watermelons upstairs under the beds till after Christmas. They finally got mushy up towards Christmas. We kept them in those rooms upstairs. It was kind of cool upstairs in the fall and the winter. We sold watermelons in the wagon. And we had a cotton patch.

Up in Kentucky or Virginia somewhere, Sam Lambert[5] had a rock quarry. And this old Negro, Jimmy, didn't have anywhere to live. He was too old to work [in the rock quarry anymore]. So, Sam Lambert didn't have any room because he took in so many, so he asked Papa about it.[6] And we had a dairy house where we used to keep our [chickens]; it had layers in it, and we'd keep our milk [there].[7] And he [Jimmy] slept there. He helped milk, with the cream separator and the chickens. Once in a while, he helped in the truck patch. He was too old [to do much]. I don't know how old. But anyway, he was kindly crippled. Not too bad crippled. But he helped around about hauling watermelons, just the odd jobs around the house. And Thelma and I were teaching school, so he helped Mama an awful lot. He was just a handyman. And he ate with us. We had an old-fashioned bench at the table. And he sat at the end. And he'd sit by the fire in here by the fireplace and get warm. So every Sunday morning, we always got up to eat breakfast to-gether, and we always said Bible verses. And Jimmy's Bible verse was, "Jesus sayeth unto Peter, feed my sheep." And I thought, why did he say that one? I got to studying: Jesus sayeth unto the preachers in the pulpit, give them a sermon they can use.

And he [Jimmy] lived here for fifteen years. When he left here, he went to Will Endsley's and slept in the outhouse down there. I don't know whether he went to Bonny Curtis's or Will Endsley's first,[8] but he stayed with both of them. When he lived here, my father took out burial insurance on him, and my father said, "Always pay it up." So when Jimmy passed away, we still had the insurance. So Hazel Curtis [Bonny's wife] and I went and picked out his casket. A one-hundred-dollar casket. And they brought him up here [to the Lee home] and laid him out.[9] And an old Negro lady brought in a very big bouquet of zinnias in old tin can and set them down in front of him. The Curtis family sitting here and our family sitting here as family. And an old lady, a big old fat lady, Negro lady, preached his funeral.

We had an iron kettle with legs on it we used to use on the stove. I looked out one day, and there was a lady carrying it off. Took it right out of the house.[10] We still have a wooden stool that's one hundred years old. Years and years ago, we had one of those cedar churns, those old-fashioned churns. We'd sit on it when we churned. And a preacher's wife was here; she collected antiques. And she wanted the cedar churn. It was in behind the pantry door. And Mama went to find the churn one day, but it was gone. Thelma says, "Don't you dare show anything to anybody." Somebody said, "You have a lot of antiques in your house?" I said, "Yes, I'm one of them."

My brothers, Chester and Verne, were born in the old house, a big old, two-story house down behind Verne's house down here that my uncle had lived in. They were building this house here in 1911. And Mr. Morton and his son, Rupert, walked from Clover Hill over here every day to build on the house, and they didn't have a new well out here. They had a cistern. And they was digging this well, and when he [Mr. Morton] went home and told his mother that they had a new baby girl here, she went in there and told him, says, "Tell them to name it Korola." And he forgot it and told her to write it down. So the man digging the well's mother is the one that named me. So we had water right here in our door all the time. But in the summertime, before we built the well house there, we carried our milk [to the spring]. We've got a spring down here right at the foot of the hill. And also down behind Verne's house there was another big spring. So we would carry our milk for dinnertime and our cream to the spring. We didn't even have a springhouse. Then it would come up a storm, and we'd have to go down there [and remove the milk and cream so it wouldn't wash away].[11]

I don't remember when we got electricity. But we had the Aladdin lamp, and we had the other kind of lamp that we used.[12] Before we had electricity, we had carbide lights. Did anybody tell you about carbide light? Well, it's c-a-r-b-i-d-e, carbide.[13] And they had a carbide plant over at Knoxville, and it was in a drum that you would buy, and it was little pellets. You bought it in fifty-gallon drums. And we had to go to Friendsville to get it off the train. And we put it down there [in the basement in a tank]. And little by little, we had to fill it up with water down in the big tank. And little by little that dropped down and come out, and we had a pipeline into the house. And we had carbide lights, and that gas would come through those lights. And we even had a carbide iron. We kept the iron for a long time, and I think one of the grandchildren had broke that cord; it was old. But we would iron. And the gas came in, and in the iron there was a little place that had a fire in it. So we had carbide lights before anybody else. I think Carsons up here had it. So I guess we was modern.

We used to have an old-time telephone. Then back in 1923, Southern Bell come through. And the people from down in there would come up here to use our telephone after we got a telephone. I don't know when we got our Southern Bell telephone, but anyway people from Marble Hill[14] would come down here to use it. I know one time a lady who worked at Oak Ridge died suddenly sitting on her bed. They phoned here to have her mother and brother to come and make arrangements with them and claim the body. Another time a lady working at Oak Ridge had to have a major operation— an appendicitis operation. They called here to get her family word that night. They [the family] lived near Marble Hill, three and a half miles from us, so we had to go at night after them.[15]

Well, [once we got a car] Papa wouldn't let us drive very much. We'd go around in the fields out here. And we had this garage over here, and he'd let us back it out and bring it around. So I learned how to back first.

Back during the Depression the peddler came here. Aunt Sarah Jones lived in an old house back off the road there. And she would gather up her eggs in a basket over here and give it to him [the peddler] off the rolling store. That's what she called it.[16] And Aunt Sallie Dunlap lived down here, and they'd walk up here sometimes from way down here in Dunlap Hollow to meet the peddler. He come at the same time every week. It was right around dinnertime [lunch]. And he didn't have many things out there, but if they wanted butter or something like that. They would feed the horses out here right in front of the house. And one day they gave him oats in those crates. Did you ever see an old-fashioned crate? They'd take those out and feed their horses out there. And one day the chickens were roaming around the yard, and one old hen got in that crate and flew up and scared the horses. Well, they took out up that road around there and around the corner . . . by a big spring up there. And as they turned that corner, the corner of our field, everything in there [the wagon] went over into that ditch. They had butter . . . in a big lard can, homemade butter, and it [the buggy turned] over in there [the ditch]. And eggs were broken. And they had chickens in it, too, and they went out. And we went up there—I remember going up there, I was real small—and we went up there with lard cans. And the neighbors came and we picked up butter; it was still in butter paper. And [we picked up] the eggs that were only just cracked. And they, I don't remember who stopped them [the horses], but I remember when they turned around up there.

They [her family] gathered sixty dozen eggs a week. Now we didn't have ours [chickens] fenced in. We had them in a big chicken house; we raised our own chickens.[17] And we have gathered as many as sixty dozen. We sold eggs to the peddler.

That was the old road to Friendsville. [She pointed to the road in front of her house.] And there was a quarry down here right this side of Friendsville where they got the gravel for this road. And the rock for it came from the quarry was this side of the creek at Big Springs.[18] That's where a quarry was. That's where they got a lot of gravel. And one day, it was Frenchie's mother-in-law [French Clark's mother-in-law] lived in that house [across the road from the old quarry site]. And they were blasting over there, and Aunt Sarah Clark was cooking dinner, and for some reason or other, she moved away from the stove. And they blasted out a stump, I remember seeing the stump. And it went up over, [it] blew the stump that far, and went down and like to have hit Aunt Sarah [in her kitchen]. And I saw the hole in the house. That's when they were building this road. Now this road was built in 1923, so it had to be before that.

That road was where Maude [the editor's grandmother] was courting Rex Clendenen. Her father didn't like him. [laughter] She would take cream to Friendsville [to the train]. Now Sam [Lambert, Maude's father] sold cream and took it to Friendsville. And then she met Charles, and he started dating her. And that's how she met Charles Walker [Charles Walker, Sr., the editor's grandfather]. He was a nice man.

Maude raised four fine children. I had Charles, Guy, and Spence [in her class]. And I whipped Charlie one time. It was the first year I came to Friendsville [teaching] in the sixth grade. I transferred here to the school in Friendsville. And I was reading the Bible [to the class], and Charlie looked out the window and saw somebody passing by on the road, and he got up and walked over to the window. I popped [paddled] him for it. Well, that night, Maude called me on the telephone. And I laid the telephone down [off the hook] and walked across the room [letting Maude Walker talk without listening to her]. Well, she let me have it. "Well, what was wrong with a little boy looking out the window?" [laughter] I loved that. But she got over it. No, I've laughed about that. She's not the only person I've laid the telephone off on. [laughter] She didn't know it, but see if all the children got up and went over to the window, I couldn't have class.[19]

I graduated from East Tennessee State. I wasn't old enough to teach when I graduated from high school. Thelma was younger. And she graduated— she was fifteen in December [of the year she graduated from high school]. She was the youngest girl, and Roe Best was the youngest boy in the class. I was not old enough [to get a teaching certificate yet], so Thelma and I went to Maryville College one year. And she still wasn't old enough to teach; I was just barely old enough to teach.

So I taught at Mount Vernon [School] for two years. Mary Evelyn Lane was raised up with Granny Russell [Mary Evelyn's grandmother], and I lived with Granny Russell the first year I taught school.[20] It was eight miles from home. I don't remember, but I believe I made eight dollars a month. I don't remember if it was eight dollars a month, or eight dollars a week. But I had to eat breakfast at home and fix my lunches at home. And I ate my supper there [at Granny Russell's house]. And Friday morning, I ate breakfast and then took my lunch. I had to come home [to her parents' house] on Friday afternoon and come back on Monday. And I used a water pitcher and a big bowl—that was my bath. And she [Granny Russell] told me [that] after she died that I could have that [the pitcher and bowl]. But I said, "Oh, wait a while." Somebody else got it. I wish I had taken it.

I didn't go to summer school in '33 because I didn't have the money. It just cost one hundred dollars a year to go [to college]. So I taught in the fall, went to school in the summer, taught in the fall, went to school in the summer, taught in the fall, went to school in the summer, taught in the fall, went to school in the summer.

I taught four winters and went [to college] three summers and stayed out another summer to recuperate. Then I taught four winters, four to five months at a time, and then stayed home. And then the next time, I finished, and I graduated. Three different times, I'd go four or five months straight to school and graduated. But I learned so much from other people [other teachers], what they did. I learned more than I would have if I'd gone straight to school. And I did my practice teaching in the sixth grade. But I learned so much [from other teachers].

Oprah Winfrey had on a show not too long ago; she said if you have a favorite teacher, be sure and write and tell her about it. So I got a letter from a girl who lives down near Nashville, and she wrote, and I've seen her a few times since then. And I taught her in 1930, and I was eighteen years old. I was teaching at Mount Vernon [then]. I taught at Mount Vernon the first year.

Then I taught at Foggville one year till I set the schoolhouse accidentally on fire. [laughter] People laugh about it. We had a pot-bellied stove right in the middle. We burned our papers [school papers] in the stove. And I burned those papers in the stove, and one day a child came to the window and said, "Miss Lee, the schoolhouse is on fire." So I jumped up and went out to see, and I said, "Children get your books out real quick." And one little boy went in and grabbed his books and stuck them under the schoolhouse. It wasn't burning too fast. And one of them put a table and a chair on top of that, and he had to jump to get up there. And we took the school bell rope and got a rope from Mrs. Russell. And she had a duck pond. So we had a bucket brigade with the children passing water up there, and whoever got on the top poured water on that [flaming stovepipe]. And they had come down and put tin over the top of it. And we put out that fire. And that boy tried to jump up there [on the chair] after that, and he never could. He said, "I don't know how come me to jump up like that." So right before school was out, the windows had been broken by the fire; we had planks in some of the windows.

And the first year I had to carry my kindling in a bag because they'd burn it up over the weekend [for church services].[21] And I had to carry my kindling in a black bag to start the fire. And I had to pick up the pulpit and put it over to the side, and they'd put it back on Sunday. By the way, they had eight revivals that year in that Sunday school.

Down here at Marble Hill [School] the first year, we'd have big benches, put them out, and we'd sit around in a circle. Now I had all seven grades, maybe one or two in one grade, four or five in another. I had twenty-eight or thirty that year. But later on, I had enough [students] for two teachers. And I gave my children treat at Christmas. And I'd get on the bus to go to Maryville. I'd go to Maryville to Mr. Nicely's store and get different candies, and an apple and an orange. And I'd sit down and put paper bags down and do treat for all the children.[22] And I would go to Maryville, and I would carry home books from the library and bring down here. Verne [her brother] or somebody would take me down; I didn't have a car then.

After I burned the schoolhouse, I changed the name of the school from Foggville to Marble Hill. And the community changed it. [laughter]

I had to carry my switch from home because it would have been gone. I had a board that didn't have holes in it, and I'd pop [paddle] them.[23] But I didn't whip hard, and I knew I didn't.

I enjoyed teaching. So the next year, they tore down the two-room Simmons schoolhouse and brought it down to Marble Hill [and reassembled it]. I taught with a missionary Baptist preacher, and he came from Walland down here driving an old T-model Ford with the floorboard out in the front, so I sat in the back. And he stayed [boarded] down there with Mr. Franklin. And the next year I taught with Frank Cox. He was fresh out of college, never taught before, and he lived up at Louisville, and I rode with him to work. So he stayed there, and I walked to school.

So the next year, in that two-room school, they had another teacher with me. She had never married; she was sixty years old. She caught the sheet mill bus at Walland, came to Maryville, caught the work bus, got off down here across the road, carried her suitcase up there and went and taught school.[24] Then after Christmas, they called me in and told me I had to, they didn't have enough students for two rooms, so I had to jump from the fourth grade to all-age grades. Lena Patty and Glenna Weese, two of my eighth-grade students, helped me that last year. I had to call every class. This was in 1933, '34, and '35.

I had a fundraiser or pie supper at my school in '33—Foggville School. We sold pies and cakes. Now we had a "cakewalk." And we had set the cake up on the windowsill, and when the couple who won the cakewalk turned around, the cake was gone. So we had a pie and we gave them a pie. Somebody had reached in through that window [and stolen the cake].

I think I got sixty some odd dollars the first year. And went back down to fifty dollars the next year and then went back up to sixty dollars. In 1933, I got fifty dollars for teaching all seven grades in that old building. But I was told they offered it to him [an unnamed male teacher] down here at Marble Hill for sixty-five dollars, and he went down and seen it, and he went back and told him he wouldn't take it. And I said, "I wished I had known it, that they offered it to him for sixty-five dollars and gave it to me for fifty dollars." I might not have taken it if I did.

Thelma didn't start teaching till '40, and I started in 1932. She taught two different places. I taught at Mount Vernon first. And I taught at Foggville/Marble Hill, Union Grove. Then came to Friendsville. And I moved to eleven different rooms at Friendsville. And I taught the sixth grade to get into the school down there. And the next year, I taught a split grade, third and fourth, over in the boys' dressing room in the old gym. We didn't have desks. We had tables. We did have a desk [compartment to hold books] under our chairs. But otherwise, we'd just leave them [our books] sitting on the table. And every time they had a ballgame, we had to take all our books. I had my third grade on one side and my fourth grade on the other. And we were not allowed to go over to the high school to the toilet; we had to go to the outhouse that was across, it was about as far as from here to the barn [about thirty yards]. Rain or shine, that's where we had to go. And then for the lunchroom, we had to walk over there. And when they were playing ball, those boys would hit that wall, and we had to stop up our ears [because the ball bouncing against the wall of the classroom was so loud].

And that was the year I had my accident and killed a child. You know where Spears Road is? But they [some schoolchildren] had to meet the bus on out where Olivers lived. And the bus came by that morning late. And this little girl, six years old, came across—she thought I was the bus. She had on her snowsuit. She ran across, realized I wasn't the bus and started back, and I hit her right then. And I stopped on a dime because I knew there was children there, and I wasn't driving too fast. And I stopped. Her shoe dropped off. But there was a dent just about like that [about two inches] in the headlight. And I picked her up and started down to that green house. And I said,

"Let's take her down there." So I carried that child, six years old, bleeding in her mouth, carried her down there with her snowsuit on. Thelma took the wheel, and we took her down to the green house. And she [the woman who lived in the house] hollered, "Oh there's the Lee sisters." She knew who I was. So she called the Maryville Hospital, old Baptist hospital, and called her [the child's] parents. And I held that child on my lap, and as we went under the underpass up there, I thought she was dying. And I says, "Lord, don't let her die in my arms."

So I went on to the hospital and called Earl Blazer, my insurance agent. So he came over, and her father did not sue. He was going to, but somebody told him, said, "Go and talk to her." So he stopped me as I came in from school. And he said, "I was going to [sue], but she [Miss Lee] wouldn't have done it for anything.'"[25] And the police came down, and he said one of her shoes had gone over the top of the car. And I said, "I picked up her shoe myself." But I was never charged with manslaughter. Earl Blazer said, "It's already settled." I don't know how much they got, and to this day, I don't know how much they got out. But for weeks and weeks and weeks, I could see that blood coming out. And Mr. Henry [George B. Henry, one of Miss Lee's fellow teachers at Friendsville]—one day his daughter was playing down there and got hurt. And I screamed. To this day, if I hear [a child hurt], you'll hear me scream. And she [the little Henry girl] said, "What did she scream for? It wasn't her that got hurt." [laughter]

Thelma and I used our legs and arms to help out at home [after they were grown], not our salaries. Now Papa did not make a slave out of us. And my baby sister, Frances, when she was at home, after she got big enough, she packed all the hay during the summer because we was, me and Thelma, was at school. Thelma didn't go to summer school at the same time I did. I went during the summers she stayed home. We shelled corn. And we'd walk miles, sometimes we'd know where a big blackberry was, and we'd walk a mile to pick blackberries. We worked in the fields, and my mother worked in the fields hoeing until she was on up in years. She enjoyed working outside. She was a hard worker.

She [Miss Lee's mother] was a beautiful lady. But when she went out, she wore her gloves, she wore her hat. And my father, he was slender when I was born, but he was fat [in later life]. He was the only one out of seven children who was fat. He weighed 237 pounds. He died in February 1953, and Mama died in October 1964. And when she got down [sick], she was six years in bed, and her mind was good. And when she passed away, she was ninety years old. And she had on a blue dress with a white collar and beautiful white hair. And I had helped them set her hair. And they came and when Evelyn

[Mitchell Prater] lifted LeeAnn [Evelyn's daughter] up, she said, "Mommy, she's beautiful."

We had a lady come in and stayed five years and a half [to take care of her mother]. She was so good to Mama. And we let her bring her ironing. She could do her sewing here. She didn't touch one thing; she didn't carry off a thing. And John Crawford, the lawyer, old John Crawford, asked her to come up and houseclean for them, so he called and asked if we'd let her. Well, as long as she can come back here during the winter. But she went up and cleaned house for John Crawford in the summer. So they must have thought she was pretty good.

A Civil War battle was fought right over there in that field across the road. My grandmother said she witnessed it. Right across there [across the road in what is now a pasture]. The old road from Union Grove to Big Springs and Friendsville met right out there at that corner [next to the Lee house]. And right out here by the side of our yard fence was the Union Grove Road. The Rebels had their camp down in Dunlap's Hollow. I don't know how many soldiers there were. The Union had camped at Big Springs, one mile east of us. Somewhere I've got a cannonball. That was years, maybe seventy-five years later. We found it up there in the field. It was about that big. But you don't show anything to anybody because it might walk off. These soldiers, I don't know, I reckon they must have met out here.

A Union soldier was wounded by the Confederates. They brought him here to Grandmother's house and had guards around the house. One morning she woke up, and he was grumbling, and she says, "Now, you can just quit your grumbling. My brother was killed in ambush last night." He said, "How do you know?" She said, "I had a vision there was blood on his cap. On his head." And the way they found out where he was, some of these people went there, and they wanted Uncle Jim and these other two men to show them where somebody was. They wanted him (my grandmother's brother, Jim McBride) as a guide, and so his wife told them where he was. So they shot him and these other two men. My grandmother had a vision and knew it before they told her. She saw blood on his hat. Just had a vision.[26] He [the brother who was killed] was an uncle of Edwin Best's. And Edwin Best told me they used to go over to his great-aunt's home, and she had the vest, and he'd put his fingers in the hole where he [the uncle] was shot by two Rebel bushwhackers.[27]

[On another occasion during the Civil War] Grandfather had his horses a-plowing in the field, I don't know where, but some of these rebels came and was going to take the horses. So Grandfather said, "No. You can't take the horses till they have something to eat." So he brought them down here, and they had to hide their food in the ground. And they brought the horses down to the barn, and when Grandfather put those horses up, he put his horses at the back side and put their horses at the front. And told them to come to the house, and Grandmother would fix them some food to eat. When they got ready to leave they took their horses and left Grandfather's.[28] And the Confederates was up here at Big Springs.

Grandfather had give Aunt Elizabeth a mare. And they [some Civil War soldiers] came down here one day and got her mare. I don't know where Aunt Elizabeth was. They got her mare and took up there and tied it to a tree. Aunt Elizabeth[29] was about eighteen years old. And Aunt Elizabeth [laughter], spunky as she was, she walked up there, she got that mare, she got on it, and rode home. [laughter] They weren't getting her horse.

The Women's Missionary Society [of the Friends Church] last year came down from Ohio and had a meeting down here [at the Friendsville Meeting]. And forty women and ten men came down here, and Joan Sloan talked about the education in Blount County, and she said something about the Quakers building that old stone house next door to me. I wasn't on the program, but I popped up and said something about it, I says, "I live next door to it." And told them what my father told me. And they said, "Come up and talk. Come up front." [laughter] I said, "Now, listen, I'm not on the program." But I told about the Civil War battle and different things that happened that my father had told me. And afterwards, one lady says, "How old are you?" [laughter] And I told her. And she said, "We did not know the Civil War was fought right here."

Did you ever read about the cave in Friendsville? There was a cave, and they'd take the people who did not believe in fighting [Quakers], and they'd go down there and put them in there. And when they'd get so many in there, at night they would take them up to the river at Louisville and send them across to, there across the River so they could go to Ohio.[30]

I saw my first really drunk person in Johnson City[31] at a drugstore. And he was so drunk he didn't know where he was. That's the first really drunk person I ever saw. I was in college. You could go to Maryville and find pure whiskey [in those days].[32]

After I quit teaching, I joined the home demonstration club. It's what I did to get out of the house.

DEPRESSION DAYS RECIPES[33]

Egg Butter
¾ cup sorghum molasses
6 eggs

1 1/2 cups sugar
1/2 cup milk
Pinch of salt
1 tsp. allspice

Heat molasses in saucepan until it melts. Beat eggs well. Ad sugar, milk, salt, and allspice; stir well. Add to molasses. Cook until thickened.

Serve on hot biscuits.

Lye Soap

Mix one can lye with two to three pints of cold water. Place on stove. Solution will get hot. Let stand one hour.

Cool and pour slowly into 5 1/2 pounds of wax grease. Stir till the consistency of honey. Add one cup ammonia and a handful of borax.

Pour into pans and cover. Let stand twenty-four hours. Cut into squares.

NOTES

1. John J. Craig and Co. quarry near the town of Friendsville in southern Blount County.

2. A local unit of the Air National Guard, based at McGhee Tyson Airbase between Maryville and Knoxville, was training in Hawaii.

3. A Tennessee Valley Authority dam in the mountains of North Carolina near the Tennessee border. Miss Lee's younger sister Frances's first job was working as an occupational nurse at the Fontana Dam construction project.

4. "Holing up" root vegetables referred to storing them in a hole dug into a barn, a cellar, or in the side of a bank and covering them with straw to prevent freezing. This cool storage place prevented spoilage.

5. The editor's great-grandfather, who owned rock quarries in several locations around the South as well as a road construction contracting business.

6. In addition to their twelve children, Sam Lambert and his wife, Laura, raised several orphans. As a result, they did not have room to house Jimmy.

7. Layers are laying hens.

8. Two other men in the community who housed Jimmy. When Miss Lee refers to an outhouse, she is referring to an outbuilding. Outdoor toilets were not large enough to sleep in.

9. Until at the least the middle of the twentieth century (and longer in some families), bodies were brought to a family home overnight before the funeral. Friends and relatives of the deceased visited the family home to pay last respects.

10. This incident happened in her adulthood. Miss Lee related several stories of people stealing antiques.

11. Rural families used several strategies to cool perishable food. Many built a springhouse over a spring. A springhouse was a small shelter lined with shelves to hold the food. It usually had no floor but was open to the spring below. Some families simply placed crocks of food into the spring, as Miss Lee is describing. Still others

built a well house around their well pump. Usually constructed of masonry and damp because of the well, a well house provided cool storage closer to the house than a spring. The Lees eventually constructed a well house.

12. An Aladdin lamp was a brand of kerosene lamp that used a special type of mantle to create a clear white light.

13. A compound made of carbon and one or more other elements. When water was added under pressure, carbide could be converted to a gas and used to power lights and other appliances. Many rural families used portable carbide "light plants" to power their homes before electricity arrived in the countryside. Unlike oil lamps that had to be filled individually, a carbide system was fueled by a system of pipes installed in the house, just as natural gas appliances are supplied in today's homes.

14. A small community tucked in the knobs—or steep hills—near Friendsville.

15. These incidents probably occurred in the 1940s. During World War II, the federal government built a uranium-enrichment facility at Oak Ridge, an area near Clinton, Tennessee. The top secret Oak Ridge installation, part of the Manhattan Project that developed the first atomic bomb, employed thousands of east Tennesseeans, who lived in barracks at the project. The women Korola Lee mentions were probably local women who moved to Oak Ridge for government jobs, leaving family behind in Marble Hill. Today, Oak Ridge has grown into a prosperous town and is home to a national laboratory.

16. In general, rural people called itinerant merchants who drove horse-drawn wagons peddlers. Merchants who carried stock in an enclosed truck were usually referred to as rolling stores. Apparently Miss Lee is referring to a peddler who drove a horse-drawn wagon. For more on itinerant rural merchants of all types, see Lu Ann Jones, chap. 1 in *Mama Learned Us to Work* (Chapel Hill: University of North Carolina Press, 2002).

17. She means that they allowed some of their eggs to mature and hatch so that they constantly replenished their supply of chickens with chicks they raised themselves. Some farm families bought their chicks, because raising them could be labor-intensive.

18. Within a half-mile of Miss Lee's home.

19. Miss Lee laid the phone off the hook and allowed my grandmother to continue ranting to open air. My grandmother was famous for calling people to "give them a piece of her mind." Korola Lee found this episode delightfully amusing, and so did I.

20. Korola Lee boarded with Mary Evelyn Russell Lane's grandmother the first year she taught school. See Mary Evelyn Lane interview.

21. Most rural school buildings were used for church services on the weekends.

22. "Treat" was a common Christmas gift given to school and Sunday school children. It was usually a paper bag filled with an apple, an orange, some nuts, and some peppermint or horehound stick candy.

23. Rural schoolteachers routinely used corporal punishment as a form of discipline. Although they sometimes used switches cut from trees, usually they spanked children on the behind with wooden paddles. Some teachers drilled holes in their paddles; they believed that paddles with holes in them inflicted more pain.

24. The Aluminum Company of America ran a series of "work" buses through-out the county. These buses were intended to carry commuting workers to their jobs at ALCOA, but county residents could also use the bus when space was available. Rural residents flagged down the buses from the side of the road and traveled to Maryville to shop or do business. School children sometimes traveled to school on the work bus.

25. Apparently the father meant that his first impulse had been to sue Miss Lee, but after further thought, he realized that she would never have hit the child on purpose.

26. I was unable to confirm any of the details of this story. Guerilla warfare was common in east Tennessee during the Civil War, with roaming bands of militia on both sides hunting each other down and settling personal vendettas as well as war-related ones.

27. Another Blount Countian, Edwin Best became a local historian upon retirement.

28. Apparently they left the family's horses alone because Mr. Lee fed them.

29. Miss Lee's father's elder sister.

30. According to one local historian, over two thousand Quaker conscientious objectors came through Friendsville, Tennessee, on their way north during the Civil War. The Confederate Army might have conscripted them if they had remained in the South. Local lore also says that the cave in Friendsville was used to shelter run-away slaves who were aided in their escape by the town's Quakers.

31. The location of East Tennessee State University.

32. Moonshine whiskey.

33. These recipes have not been tested for accuracy or safety. They appear exactly as Miss Lee wrote them out for me.

Mary Evelyn Russell Lane

MARY EVELYN RUSSELL was born December 14, 1912, in Louisville, Tennessee, a small community south of Maryville near the Tennessee River. Her father combined general and dairy farming with running a small crossroads store. Mary Evelyn was the oldest of five children. She attended local schools and then went on to earn a college degree. As a child, she lost one arm in a cream separator accident.

Mary Evelyn Russell taught in local elementary schools for a year before her marriage in 1935 to Henry Lane, son of a local farmer. The couple moved in with Henry's parents, where they lived for the next twelve years. Henry farmed, and Mary Evelyn gave birth to two children and helped her mother-in-law with household and farm work until she returned to teaching during World War II. She taught until the early 1970s.

Henry Lane died in 1969, and Mrs. Lane eventually sold their farm. The land became one of the first industrial parks in Blount County. At first, Mary Evelyn Lane held on to the family's house in the country, but eventually she bought a condominium in Maryville and moved to town. She served two terms on the Blount County School Board. She remained active in church, club, and volunteer work. Mrs. Lane died in 2003.

I interviewed Mrs. Lane at her condominium on August 8, 1994. As we talked, her phone rang constantly as friends called to update her on volunteer activities or on the health of friends and relatives. She displayed a lively intelligence and a great interest in my project, in my family's current activities, and in Blount County politics. I transcribed the interview in the fall of 1994 and sent the transcript to Mrs. Lane. She responded by making numerous corrections and clarifications. She also completed the family history form. In the summer of 1995, I wrote to her with additional questions, which she answered promptly. I have incorporated her corrections into this edited interview.

I guess some of the first things I remember about it [farm life]: In 1925 we had a drought, and it was dry. I remember Dad made twenty-five bushel of corn to the acre. We did not make enough corn and wheat on the farm to make our bread. We always furnished the bread for the [hired] people who lived on the farm [and] worked on the farm. And [that year] Dad had to buy wheat and corn both to make the bread for the people on the place. You always gave the renters—you didn't pay him a lot of money—but you gave him a house rent, and you paid him, gave him a home, and gave him a cow to milk. You gave him a garden plot. And that was considered part of the pay. Daily wages weren't much; a dollar a day was high.[1]

We just had one renter. We had two renters' houses, but the one up above the railroad we rented to people.[2] He worked at the quarry. And they had to carry their water from down home. And they had two boys. I saw one of them not too awful long ago. Dad was always teasing them [the boys]. They had a new baby up there. So Dad would say, "I'm going up there and get that baby and gonna bring it home with me." "No, you're not." And he'd just get them in the awfulest racket. So he'd been up above the railroad and fixed fence, and he always carried him a tow sack on his back. He'd go up to the railroad and put the milk on the train to town and then he'd go on up and work up [in the fields near the railroad tracks] there a little bit. Coming back down, he had this over his shoulder, this tow sack with an axe and hammer and whatever he'd taken with them up there, so he met these little boys coming back with a bucket of water. He said, "OK, boys, you've been gone, I knew. While you's gone, I went and got that baby." Dad said they didn't say a word, and he thought, well that's funny. And about that time, one of them hit him in the head with a rock. He said, "It hurt, too." [laughter] I said, "Well, it could've knocked him out." Mother told him, "That is good enough for you. They ought to have hit you. Now see if you can't stop this foolishness." But they hit him pretty square with the rock right in the head. I think he was mad at the kids when he came to the house, and Mother said, "No, you're not! You're not going to say a thing to those kids. You're the very one that brought it on, and if they hit you again, well, the same thing again." It was funny anyway.

We had some children that lived on the place at one time that we knew were [abused], and Dad and Mother took care of that. And [another] old man . . . let his older boys abuse the girls, but they took them to the children's home.

Dad had a dairy and then raised corn and wheat when the weather was good. I said, "He marked me." I tell you, when it begins to get dry, I get upset. Our house had a porch that went all the way around it. Dad would start, "It's going to the mountains, going up the river, going to the mountains, going to the river. We're in the middle and we're not going to get any rain. Going to the mountains, going to the river." You know, when it starts to rain,

I've got to go see what direction it's going to see whether we're going to get rain or not. I'm still happy to get a rain. I can't stand dry weather.

At that time, and on up for a long time, eggs were nine cents and twelve cents a dozen. I remember selling eggs at nine and twelve; I was small then, but I still remember them selling for that. And even after I was married in 1935, we were still getting twenty-five cents a dozen for eggs. We sold butter. A colored guy, Mr. Bouley, came through once a week with his hack, and he bought the butter and eggs from everybody along the way, and he swapped it for whatever he had. And we swapped for salt and soda and the necessities. And he bought lard if you had any left over. And he bought their eggs and butter. And I remember Mother was so disgusted; she always worked her butter, and it always looked so pretty. She would mold it, and it was so pretty. And he'd take it out there and dump it in a lard can with all the rest of them that just put theirs into pats. And she'd come in so disgusted. He didn't have anything to do with it, but she was disgusted that her pretty butter was messed up. She spent all that time getting that butter looking like that.

From there up through '35, we separated it [milk] and made butter with it and fed the other milk to the hogs and the chickens. And whole milk—we sold a lot of whole milk for twenty-five cents a gallon. I look at it now, and I think, "Oh, here two dollars and a half [a gallon]." We separated our milk and sold the cream. Shipped it to Knoxville on the train. Have you ever seen a separator? Well, see that's what I got my arm cut off in. Got it caught in the back.

We raised about everything we ate. We raised our vegetables. We raised our meat. We canned our sausage. I've canned hundreds and hundreds of cans of sausage. I wish I had a can of it now. And hundreds of cans of tenderloin. On up until Henry [her husband] died, we still canned our meat to have for the summer, and it was good. But I don't can it any more. I don't need it in the first place.

People didn't have any money. Back then, it wasn't necessarily because of the Depression, it was just the fact that we didn't have it. They bartered for everything they possibly could. The quarry was running over there part-time.[3] And there was some money there. ALCOA was running, but it was not in full operation.[4] When I was a child, I never heard nothing about ALCOA. Of course, I was born in 1912, and it wasn't started yet.

Now, when I first started school at Holston [School], we carried our water from the spring to the hill, and we had a bucket with a dipper, and everybody had their own little cup. I had one of those collapsible cups that you put in your own lunch box. We just had one room, and we had a fireplace, and we had logs for the fireplace. I can remember Dad, the teacher letting me stand up in the chair and look out the window while Dad dumped off a load of logs for the fireplace. I guess that was to keep me quiet. Our blackboard was, the walls were plaster covered, been a college there, so shoe polish on the walls was our blackboard. Two sat in a seat and sometimes three, a little one in the middle. Arthur Hobbs's mother and his aunt were seventh and eighth grade when I was in fourth and the teacher put me in the middle of the two of them. That's where I learned all the physiology I ever learned. I think she put me there to keep me in my seat and keep me quiet.

I know over there at Zion's Chapel [School], the teacher I had in the fourth grade had sixty students enrolled. They weren't all there at the same time, but I remember things I learned in that class that I wouldn't have learned somewhere else. She [the teacher] lived with us, roomed with us.[5] They walked to school.

I remember the first [school] buses. The first bus that I remember, the boys and my sister took to Friendsville.[6] They had a bus that was like a truck—you know, long like a cattle truck—and it had seats, planks that they sat on. I remember the Morton boys and my brothers and all [the kids] going to Friendsville in that. When it was hot, they had sides that they rolled up, curtains that they rolled on top and tied up. When it was cold they let [the curtains] down. [The curtains] didn't do much but flop and make a noise and kept them entertained from freezing to death. [laughter] They didn't have better transportation than that for a long time.

There was a dirt road through Miser Station, [from] Maryville down to Friendsville.[7] At that time that was just a rock road, and there was a road up toward Zion's Chapel. But we lived on a dirt road. Now back then every year, the men got a card from the office of the road department or wherever, telling them the days they were supposed to work [on the road]. I know Dad always helped. They took their shovels and picks and wagons to haul rocks and all. There was always holes that when you got in the car you'd drag on them. So they always got big rocks somewhere and filled those holes up. Didn't help much; they was still rough, but they filled them up. Next year there'd be another somewhere, or that one would be there, too. But the roads were very, very bad. You come down that road now between Louisville and Friendsville and come down through there, you just sail down through there. And I can remember when a wagon wouldn't go up through there hardly. I was with Dad on the wagon up where the road forks to go down to Holston College and down that way, they was a blacksmith's shop there, and he'd go up there and get his wagon wheels fixed and things like that. Anyway, there just were no roads. There were roads, but they weren't car roads.

It was just hard times, there was no two ways about it. To get enough cash to buy shoes and whatever the children needed to start to school was something else. Mother used to come up [to town] and get material. We always had a bunch of kids that lived in the renter's house. Then she'd go to town, and she'd get material, and she'd make them all new dresses to wear to school. And they'd promise her if she'd make them the dresses, they'd go [to school]. Well, they went the first week until they got dirty, and then they didn't go anymore, and she'd go down there and try to get them to go and they wouldn't go. She'd cut their hair and get them all cleaned up and send them to school first day and then. . . .

There's one [person] . . . now that I know of that was living down there [on her father's farm], and I see where he's retired from the plant and got a nice home now and everything. Poor kid, he had a poor start. ALCOA has helped an awful, awful lot of people that were at the very bottom of the bucket there. I remember when they took his grandmother to the poorhouse.[8] They just took her in a wagon; they didn't have the money to take care of her. So they took her down to the poorhouse. They were there for years; and talk about somebody that was good to people. I don't know what the county would have done if they hadn't had the Marshes.[9]

Everybody got the colored chicken feed sacks. And there were certain kinds [patterns] we'd want. Lands, we all had dresses and aprons, and children had play clothes [made from feed sacks]. A lot of kids wore sack dresses to school. Pretty things. Some of the prettiest sack dresses. I used to make them when I sewed. That's OK; I don't miss that. I made bedspreads for the children's room upstairs with them. They were just real pretty. We also made dishtowels out of the sacks. I've still got some stuck around. I don't use them because I want to keep them to have.

Of course, if you had hogs, you did your own butchering and rendered your own lard and made your own lye soap. I've seen Mother make lye soap. They had an ash hopper. Did you ever see an ash hopper? Well, it was a container that was built in this shape [she draws a diagram of a funnel-shaped device on the back of an envelope]. This was an ash hopper that the top of it was square. You put all your ashes [in there]. Now at home, they wouldn't put in anything except oak; they wouldn't put in cedar or pine or anything like that.[10] When you cleaned out the fireplace, usually they didn't use the stove ashes. But you take it out and pour your ashes in there, and it would rain, and water would run in there, and it went down over the ashes, and then it'd come out at this point here into a container. It [the resulting liquid] was that red lye, and it was strong. And if it didn't rain enough, they'd carry water and pour in it. And when the water went through those ashes, lye came out strong.

And they saved all their [meat scraps], and when we cut a ham, we took the skin off it and kept the bones that we wouldn't use [for soap]. Any kind of meat, whatever kind—it didn't make any difference what kind—they put it in when they got ready to make their soap. They put it in a big old kettle and cooked it and cooked it and cooked it and cooked it till they got all that fat out; then they took the stuff out [bones and other solids] and put the lye in and it made a soap that look like molasses. Now, I tell you, that would suds up. It washed overalls, and it washed towels, and it washed everything. There were some [people] that didn't have the ash hopper; they bought the lye and put it with the fat that was rendered off. But they used everything—the ears and the feet and whatever else [from the hog]. They cooked it all and got all the fat out of it and then put this lye in, and they'd cook it down.

And they always stored it [the soap] in these some big old earthen crocks, and they'd put it in it. Mother used to take a cup and dip it out for whatever she was going to do with it. She'd put it in the wash kettle, and it'd just boil. They always boiled the white clothes, and they boiled the men's jeans and pants; they didn't have jeans then, they had overalls, whatever they had [they boiled in the lye soap]. And that saved a lot of washing on the washboard that they'd had to have done if they hadn't had that. That was our method of washing then we used that we don't have today.

My dear, I've done it. Your fingers would be sore. We used to have a woman who came every Monday and did our laundry, but we had to watch her because she went back through there and over to where she'd live, and she'd take all the eggs out of the nests in the henhouse when she went by. Dad said about the time he thought she was going home, he'd go pick his eggs up and bring them in. That's something I remember. And there's a lot of things I ought to remember, and I've forgotten now.

But back then, funerals were quite different. Anybody that died, they laid them out; people came in and washed them and bathed them and put clean clothes on them. We had this one old man that lived up there above us that never went out any. He had a brother that wasn't right bright that lived up the other way. And when this guy died, they came down—Dad had a country store—and they came down and bought him a clean, new set of overalls and shirts. The brother came by, and Dad come home just a-dying laughing, and said, "I tell you they was a sight to see them walk by; poor, old, all dressed up and nowheres to go." [laughter] But I've seen them go by with the wagon lots of times taking [dead] people from the chapel.

One thing that I remember during the Depression [was] when they were trying to find work for people. And they decided that they had a lot of cotton

—I don't know where it originated. They shipped in a lot of bales of cotton, and it came in. . . . That cotton came in, and Henry [her husband] delivered it. [He] took it out to different places on the wagon. And he did the same thing with hay for a while. And that was in 1937, I guess, somewhere along there. The cotton was government surplus. And the home demonstration agent taught the people in home demonstration clubs how to make mattresses with that cotton. You went in and ironed it and put it down, and they tufted it, whatever it took to make it. And whenever there was some broken bales [of cotton], Mrs. Lane[11] got to carding those. I don't know how many quilts we had that she made out of these scraps that were laying around. She picked up and carded them. She made the [quilt] tops out of chicken feed sacks. And I had several of the quilts made out of it [the surplus cotton and feed sacks]. I've given them to the grandkids, and they've got them scattered around, Brown domestic on the bottom, and sometimes chicken feed sacks on both [sides] and the chicken feed sacks pieced on top and then the cotton in the middle.

[During the Depression, the federal government] also shipped in hay, we had this one summer, I guess that was '37, that they shipped in a lot of hay from up north. That was mainly because of the dry weather rather than the Depression, I guess.

Another thing, during the Depression and during the time that times were so hard, we had [food commodities] at Alnwick [School] for our lunchroom. See Alnwick had the first lunchroom in the county. Lucy Edmondson started it. They started by bringing in [food from the farms]. The children would bring in some milk, and they'd bring some potatoes. And somebody would get in and peel those and make potato soup on top of the little pot-bellied stove in the library. But the government sent surplus food then. And I know we'd get great big one-hundred-pound sacks of carrots. Big carrots, about that big around [she indicated about an inch and a half in diameter]. You've never seen such pretty things. But those parents would come in and cut these carrots, and we'd can them on Saturday. And they'd can them by the half-gallon, and that's what we had all winter in the lunchroom. The PTA did that; we had a good PTA.[12] They [the federal government] also sent a lot of dried beans, which of course we didn't have to process. But they sent cabbage, and we made kraut, more kraut, more kraut, more kraut [sauerkraut]. And we made it in half-gallon cans and poured the hot water over it and then sealed it. And it made pretty good kraut. So one day we'd have dried beans and onions and cornbread and kraut. And then another day we'd have soup. And then another day we would have potatoes and onions again. We had a lot of onions. And slaw and whatever we had for lunch. We got a lot of butter, good butter [from the government]. We also got a lot of good cheese, the best grade of cheese. So with that they made the best macaroni and cheese you've ever eaten and also fattened the teachers and all the children. I never got mine off yet [weight].

I was teaching, and we had a real good PTA group. They came in and worked Saturdays and after school. And we had good lunches, very good lunches. We did hire a cook. [First] one, then we got so we had two. Then we got so we had what was considered the best lunchroom in the county, because everybody wanted to come to Alnwick [School] and eat lunch. And it was good. Aunt Kate Self made rolls that were out of this world. I said, "Aunt Kate, it's sinful for you to do me this way." Because she knew I loved them out of the corner [of the pan where they baked crispy-brown on two sides]. I'd be sitting there, and she'd come with a little saucer, and there'd be two hot rolls and that brown around it and that butter running out of it. You know what I did with it; you can tell by looking. But we had some good cooks, real good cooks.

I started teaching sixty years ago this fall. I taught my first year at Union, sixty years ago this fall.[13] I have a lot of kids that [I taught] have now retired. I lived and boarded in town and rode with somebody out [to school]. We had three rooms at that school at that time, and they built the fourth one on, enlarged it, taking the library. Course, we didn't have a lunchroom or anything. And from then on until '40, they had outdoor toilets. They [the students] always wanted to go and scrub them. I never knew. Anything to get out [of class]. They'd scrub a toilet, the boys and the girls both, to get out of class. [laughter] Out at Union, we had a pump. When I first went out there, course I was a little green and things. [I had just] graduated from college. I learned a whole lot more my first year at Union than my kids did. I'd go out and pump the water and bring it in, and everybody had different cups.

At Alnwick [School], we had the first toilets that had the holes dug and then closed.[14] And we also had the first drinking fountain. But they weren't on drugs; we had a few that drank. I didn't have a broken home that I knew of for a long time. I had two or three whose families were divorced. Now they say they have two or three that aren't [from divorced families]. That every child has four parents. I never heard sex mentioned back then. You'd get whipped if you said one of those four letter words. But anyway, ever time one of the girls said "Mrs. Lane," or "Miss Russell, he pinched me again." Every time they went by, he [a boy in the class] would reach down and pinch them on the leg or tail or wherever he could reach. So I told him one day, I said, "The next time you do that, I'm going to give you a whipping." "Miss Russell, he pinched me again." He was a great big boy, and I said, "OK, you're going to get a whipping." I got up and went back there where I had my paddle, and he said, "You're not going to whip me." And I said, "Then you better go home, and you can't come back until somebody comes with you and you take your punishment." Well, he stood there a little bit and says, "Oh, well, go on." So I did, I hit him a pretty good one. I didn't know if he'd hit me; I didn't know what he'd do. But he didn't do anything.

So I saw him years after, and I said, "Chris, do you remember the day that you literally scared me to death?" He said, "No, what did I do?" I said, "Do you remember the day that I whipped you?" "Yes!" I said, "I've never been as scared in all my life as I was that day." And he said, "Well, I wish I'd known that then." [laughter] I just knew he'd hit back. "Miss Russell, he's pinched me on the leg again." And now then what do they do; everything under the sun. Donna says, "Grandmother, you could not teach these kids with what they talk about among themselves and say that I can hear and all that I can't do one thing in the world about."[15]

I used to think that the fifth grade was the best grade. That's the one I always taught. I said it was the best grade to teach because they could read to a point, and they could go to the bathroom and get their pants and all that stuff and tie their shoes once a week or something, and they weren't crazy about the boys. They'd have their little girlfriends and twitter and carry on, but they wouldn't . . . In the upper grades, they'd get pretty heavy into being in love with somebody. Donna said, "Well, you're off your rocker now, because if they're in fifth grade they're into [love]." I believe I taught the best years; I don't know if I'd want to do that now.

They built the Great Smoky Mountains National Park the first year I taught school. I had something I could remember that year by; now I've forgotten what it was. It was along about then, because Roosevelt came and spoke up there. Grandpa Lane wouldn't go see him. Roosevelt was a Democrat and Grandpa was a Republican, and heaven help a Democrat if he got in his way, especially when they was putting the TVA and the dam in up there and building that up there, pulling wires across our place.

We always had a fair at Alnwick. That's where I met my husband was at the fair on the Alnwick campus. Sixty years ago this fall.

I taught one year, in 1934 and '35.[16] I got married that fall, and they wouldn't let [married women] teachers teach because the men had to have a job. So I finished out a school up at Old Chilhowee for somebody that got sick, and I had to finish out for her.[17] And then my son came along, and I think I started back in '43 or '44. And then I taught on after that always, but I couldn't teach when I was first married. And I needed to, and it would have been a good time and everything, but they just didn't want married women to teach. So I didn't teach then, but I taught on for twenty-nine years, and then I was on the school board for eight years, so I had thirty-seven years [of service to the county]. I still work in the elections and everything.

We lived with the Lanes [her in-laws] for quite a while, much to my regret and everybody else's, I think. I told my children when they married, they couldn't live with me for their sake and mine, too. Of course, people don't have to now like they did then. We were farmers and there was nowhere else. Absolutely nowhere else. We lived there twelve years.[18]

Henry used to raise to seed corn.[19] He'd plant the male rows and the female—I never did understand how you can have male and female corn, but you do. And he was supposed to take the pollen off every morning. We went to church one Sunday morning, and he came home and went out right after lunch, and they come and caught him, and threw it out [refused to buy the seed corn he had produced]. They said it was no good for seed corn. He couldn't see how waiting till early afternoon that one time would hurt that much, but it did. They came at the wrong time, or the right time in their eyes. So they [the seed company] are so strict on some things. I was just reading an article in the *Reader's Digest,* I guess it was, or *Progressive Farmer,* or I don't know what it was, and it was talking about where they use the pesticides and how they're going to have to be dressed [in protective clothing in order to spray dangerous pesticides].

Of course, machinery has changed completely from the Depression, because you had a wagon, team, corn planter, cultivator, rake, and a mower, all of them horse-drawn. We got our first tractor the day my son was born. 1937. Henry's dad come up to get it [in town], and heard that Henry had a baby boy. October 29, 1937. I sent it [the date] down to his teacher his first year as 1935, and she sent a note back and said, "Mary Evelyn, he wasn't born before you were married, was he?" [laughter] She knew better.

I was on the school board when we built Heritage and William Blount [High Schools].[20] I guess I got off the board in '82. We had such a hard time at Heritage with leaks because it rained, and I'm still preaching on that because nobody followed that job, and I begged them to put somebody on to follow the steps and see that everything was done right. "Oh, it'd be done right. They couldn't afford it. Blah, blah, blah, blah." I was a woman, and I didn't have any sense. When we got it done, the architect had left air conditioning out of the gym and cut down the pool. It was supposed to have been Olympic-sized, and it wasn't. And they built the planetarium, which we did not need. It was a nice thing. But it would never serve a purpose there. Somebody said the county court voted for it because it had p-l-a-n-t in it, and they thought it had to do with agriculture.

Anyway, we learned a lot on Heritage that made William Blount much more functional and an easier place to teach. A lot of things about it are much easier and better than Heritage. Heritage is beautiful; they'll never be a prettier school than Heritage because of the view from there and everything.[21] It's really a nice school. There's more wasted space in it than William Blount. There's not much wasted space in William Blount. Well, now Mary Blount [Elementary] is a good school. They finally learned not to put the flat roof on, and gave it a little bit of tilt. I tried to tell them, but I couldn't make them do it. I didn't know anything. I was a woman; I was a dum-dum. But anybody knows that if you put a [flat] roof on like that, then it gets hot and sinks in the middle, and the water's going to stand there. It's just common sense. Montvale [Middle School] leaked from the time it was built, and Middlesettlements [Elementary] leaked from the time it was built. I can't see why when we pay for it, we can't have so it won't leak.

[After the Depression, people felt] get us off the farm as fast as you can get us. Men and women both. Men liked to farm, but there was just no money to be made on it. You've got to have capital or you can't do anything on a farm. You cannot. There's no way in the world for a young man to go and buy a farm and start unless he's got capital or unless he's got a lot of machinery given to him or something. Well, you know what little old tractors cost and all. And you have to keep up; if you don't, you can't do it. And you have to do it by yourself anymore; you can't even get anybody to help load the hay even after you cut it and bale it.

An awful lot of people liked to farm. My family all loved to farm. My dad and one brother. But they didn't much because they never made any money, because they didn't have the money to farm. But they all loved to farm. Dad lost his farm during the Depression. He had signed some notes was the main thing, for somebody that was sick and couldn't pay, and he had to sell his cattle to pay that. And I'll never forget that.

Anyway, I don't know, when you look around, there aren't a whole lot of people on the farm today unless their parents began it, and they got their foot in the door like the Walker boys and your family.[22]

NOTES

1. The arrangement Mrs. Lane is talking about was a cross between a tenancy arrangement and day labor. The hired man and his family were given a home, a garden plot, use of the owner's work stock, and a milk cow. In return, they worked for the landowner whenever he needed them for a very low daily wage. The work was seasonal, and in the winter months especially, hired hands might not work every day. During the agricultural depression of the 1920s and 1930s, daily wages of fifty cents a day were more common. This type of arrangement was common in east

Tennessee. Workers under these circumstances could leave at will, but when they did leave a landowner's employ, they were also homeless.

2. She is making a distinction between the "renter" who worked as a hired hand and a renter who actually paid rent to live in a house on their property, rent he earned working at the local marble quarry.

3. John J. Craig and Company in nearby Friendsville, Tennessee, employed a fair number of men from the surrounding farming communities.

4. The Aluminum Company of America near the Blount County seat, Maryville, employed several thousand men, many of them farm people who commuted to their jobs. The company began production in 1914. See French Clark interview.

5. It was common practice for rural schoolteachers to board with local families who had large homes.

6. Mary Evelyn Lane's brothers and sisters.

7. Miser Station was the closest community crossroads of any size to Lanes' family home. Maryville and Friendsville were larger towns.

8. Like many southern rural counties, Blount County cared for its most destitute residents by housing them on a county "poor farm." See Peggy Delozier Jones interview for more details.

9. The family employed to manage the Blount County Poor Farm.

10. Certain types of wood ashes produced stronger lye than others. Oak produced an especially strong lye.

11. Her mother-in-law. Mrs. Lane carded the cotton fibers from broken bales and used them as batting or stuffing in quilts. She pieced the quilt tops from the cotton print fabric used to make feed sacks. The bottom layer or backing was usually made of an unbleached muslin cloth commonly called "domestic."

12. Parent-Teacher Association.

13. Union School was located in a rural community on the northeast side of the county.

14. Outhouses in which the waste holes were completely enclosed except for the opening at the seat. Mrs. Lane taught at Alnwick School after she left Union School.

15. Mrs. Lane's granddaughter is also a schoolteacher.

16. The 1934–35 academic year. Apparently she taught one term at Union and one term at Alnwick.

17. After her marriage, county officials allowed Mrs. Lane to finish a term for a teacher who had grown ill. Then she was not hired again until World War II. During the Great Depression, many local school boards instituted the practice of firing or refusing to hire married female teachers because of the belief that they were being supported by their husbands and would be depriving another man of a job he needed to support his family. Single female teachers were hired, and they were routinely paid less than males because of the common but often erroneous assumption that single women did not have families to support. See Korola Lee interview.

18. Mary Evelyn and Henry Lane eventually built a house on Henry's parents' farm.

19. Raising hybrid seed corn for seed companies was a good source of cash income for some farmers, but it was arduous work because of the daily effort required to

prevent any accidental cross-pollination. For hybrid corn to be useful and valuable to farmers, the strain had to remain pure.

20. During Mrs. Lane's two terms on the Blount County School Board, the county built a number of schools. In this section, she is discussing the challenges of building the new schools.

21. Heritage High School has a breathtaking view of the Great Smoky Mountains.

22. The "Walker boys" to whom Mrs. Lane refers are unrelated to the editor's family. The editor's family, however, also farmed until the early 1990s, and Mrs. Lane is referring to them when she says "your family." She is making the point that if young people do not inherit land, they will probably never be able to acquire enough capital to even begin farming. Historian Gilbert C. Fite has coined the phrase "equity head start" to refer to twentieth-century farmers who enjoyed an advantage over others by inheriting significant land, cattle, or equipment, reducing their need to go into debt as they launched commercial farming operations. See *American Farmers: The New Minority* (Bloomington: Indiana University Press, 1981).

Peggy Delozier Jones

Peggy Delozier Jones[1] was born July 6, 1899, in Loudon County, Tennessee. She was the sixth of eight children born to a farming family. Her family practiced general farming, combining subsistence production with the planting of small grains and raising livestock for the market. Blessed with fertile river bottomland, Loudon County featured a combination of small general farms and larger plantation-style agriculture. Apparently Jones's parents were quite prosperous for Loudon County because they had owned a few slaves during the antebellum years. A few of the former slaves remained on the farm as hired hands and sharecroppers into Mrs. Jones's childhood.[2]

Peggy Delozier Jones told a friend that she was the first girl in Lenoir City, Tennessee, to drive a Model T Ford. Her father bought the car when Peggy Delozier was fourteen, but he never learned to drive, so Peggy drove the car for him when he took trips to Knoxville and other cities on farm business. Mrs. Jones recalled that she and her sister had to learn to change the tires when the car developed a flat.

Jones's father valued education, and he insisted that his children attend school regularly. In addition, he sent several of the children, including Peggy, to college. She studied home economics at Mary Washington College in Virginia. After two years, she left school to teach home economics in a Loudon County public school. (At that time, the state of Tennessee required only limited college credit in order to issue a teaching certificate, and most colleges awarded education degrees after two years of college study.)

In 1922, Peggy Delozier married Homer Jones, the son of a local farmer. Homer had a job off the farm when the couple married, and that suited Mrs. Jones just fine. She had always sworn that she would not marry a farmer because the life was so difficult. Soon, however, Homer's father purchased additional land, and Homer and Peggy Jones moved there to begin farming it. She soon settled into the rhythms of the farmwife's life. The couple had two children: Joe, born in 1923, and Homer Vaughn, born in 1927.

Between 1920 and 1960, Loudon County, Tennessee, became a center for commercial dairy farming. From the beginning of white settlement in the eighteenth century until the dawn of the twentieth, the county's rich river bottoms supported successful grain farming. By 1910, the county was a mix of general farms and small industry. The Louisville and Nashville and the Southern Railways lines provided transport routes for farm commodities and for the products of local manufacturers, including chair factories, a candy maker, a brick company, and three hosiery mills. These rail connections proved crucial to local dairy farmers' ability to reach markets in Knoxville and Chattanooga. In 1927, a Wisconsin cheese maker came south to open a plant in neighboring Monroe County, providing another customer for locally produced raw milk. In the mid 1930s, the Tennessee Valley Authority began acquiring river bottom property in the county, acreage that would be flooded with the construction of Fort Loudon Dam. Although this project displaced some local farmers, it provided many with cash to buy additional land, to expand and mechanize farming operations, or to pay off debts. The number of farms reporting dairying as their major source of income doubled between 1939 and 1949 as World War II increased the demand for whole milk and spurred local production.

In the late 1930s, after the death of Homer Jones's father, Homer became manager of the Loudon County Poor Farm, and the family moved to a home on that property. Until the mid twentieth century, many rural southern counties provided for their most destitute residents by housing them on a county "poor farm." Here residents were provided with housing, board, clothing, and limited medical care. Able-bodied residents were expected to help tend gardens, livestock, and crops that helped feed the residents and provided some revenue to meet other expenses.

With the arrival of New Deal programs and the practice of paying welfare benefits directly to poor families who lived on their own, Loudon County decided to sell its poor farm. The Jones family purchased the farm. They farmed corn and small grains until younger son Homer Vaughn took over the operation and converted it to a dairy farm.

Peggy Jones reentered the work force when her sons were in high school. She worked first as a school lunchroom supervisor in WPA-funded school lunchrooms in Loudon County. Later she became a supervisor for the county welfare department.

After her retirement, she again took an active role on the farm, driving tractors and performing other farm work until she was into her eighties. By the time I met her she was ninety-five years old and mostly blind, but Peggy Jones still lived alone in the farmhouse she and her husband remodeled. She still cooked for herself and sometimes for her son and his wife, and she still canned and froze farm produce.

I interviewed her at her home on a hot July day. Ann Ross Bright, a friend of Mrs. Jones's who arranged the interview, was also present. It was the height of garden season, and Mrs. Jones made reference to the condition of her garden. She was unable to garden at that point, but her son, daughter-in-law, and grandsons worked it for the whole family's use. At two or three different points in the interview, Mrs. Jones seemed to be winding down. She would say, "And that's about all there is to it." Then she would pause for just a few seconds, think of another story, and resume talking. After we finished talking, Mrs. Jones gave us a brief tour of the living room and described the many beautiful antiques, most of which were family heirlooms.

I was born in a big family at Lenoir City, and I lived on the farm. I was born July 6, 1899. I'm ninety-five years old. And there was eight of us: four boys and four girls. My father was a farmer, and he did a good job raising eight children. I don't know how he did it, but he did.

We went to school. We never missed a day of school, and we lived two miles from the school. My father saw that we all went to school, and we never missed a day. Rain, snow, or anything, we had to go to school. My daddy [placed a high value on education]. We never missed Sunday school and church either. We had a two-seated hack or a surrey or something we drove to school. And then when Ford cars came out in 1911, we bought us a Ford. He [her father] always saw that we had a way to go to Sunday school and church and school.

I married in 1922. But I graduated from college . . . before that. It was a Methodist school in Virginia, Mary Washington College. I've always liked sports. I played basketball. I was on a basketball team when I was in college. And I like basketball and football and baseball. And my husband always liked sports. I was in the home economics department [in college], you know. We had a tearoom on the campus, and ever so often, they'd have food out there, and the girls would cook in the tearoom. They always had me a planning what they was going to fix for the tearoom. And I taught home economics after that [after college].

And I married in 1922. My husband didn't do too much working for public works.[3] He worked at a garage and sold cars for a while. He helped on his grandfather's farm, and then he worked for an uncle of his that had a farm there near Lenoir City.

My husband wasn't a farmer when I promised to marry him; I always said I wouldn't marry a farmer, but I did. His father bought a farm. It was his wife's old home, and he bought the other heirs out and put Homer on it farming.[4] And he [her husband, Homer] hadn't had too much experience. He'd helped on his grandfather's farm some.

So when the Depression hit, we had a right hard time. We had a little five-room house, and the Depression hit. We had a kind of hard time because we had to buy farm machinery [when] we started farming. And one year, we kept a record and we spent three hundred dollars cash, and the rest we just raised ourselves. I raised chickens and turkeys and had a nice garden and canned.

I sold some [of my turkeys], and some of them I'd dress for different friends of mine, they'd want them dressed.[5] And back then you couldn't buy a dressed turkey in the store. I sold eggs, [but] I didn't sell milk and butter. We had milk and butter [for family use], and we always had a nice garden. We didn't have any telephone or electricity for a while after we married. We had a time getting them to put the line out here, but there wasn't many people lived out here. But we finally got a telephone and then later got electricity. An ice truck would come about twice a week and bring us ice. And that's about all there is to it.

We had a lot of river bottom, and we raised corn. And wheat. And we had cattle and sheep, beef cattle. And we always had a milk cow or two or three, something like that. We bought a tractor about two years before we bought this farm, about 1937 or '38, somewhere along that. That was the first one we had.

I sewed and made my own clothes. And I sewed for the boys. Back then we didn't have no suits much when they were little. They wore little aprons with the straps on the back, you remember that, don't you, Mrs. Bright?[6] Till they got up a little bigger, and then they wore pants.

I canned beans and tomatoes, and [when] we killed our hogs, I canned sausage and tenderloin. I canned a little bit of everything. Now we freeze more than we can. Sue's [her daughter-in-law] got two or three freezers, and I've got two. We've had the nicest garden this year, all but the tomatoes. They're rotting. We put up corn all day Friday and all day Saturday and Monday.

We were lucky [in the Depression]. We had relatives that were doctors, and they didn't charge us anything. Homer had a first cousin in Knoxville in obstetrics, and then he had a relative here that looked after us. I had my babies at the house. We had a little hospital here, and I was supposed to have gone to the hospital with the last one [Homer Vaughn], and the doctor that looked after me, I told him when he was going to be born, and he said, "No, he won't be born that soon." And he was out of town. He [her son] was born the day I told him [the doctor]. Another doctor came. I was in labor for just a short time with either one of them. The doctors always told me I could have all the babies 'cause I had them so easy. I think it was because I took so much exercise and worked. The day my oldest son [Joe] was born, that afternoon we had a lot of cornfield beans, and Homer was going to turn the hogs in on the field where the corn was, and I picked cornfield beans all afternoon. He was born that night. And when the doctor came, I told him to hurry up, and he said, "Oh, we'll be here till daylight." It was about midnight. I said, "No, we won't either." And when he looked at me, he said, "Oh, the baby's almost here." I knew.

I had an easy time with my children. They say now they came up the hard way, but both of them, they're glad they did. They appreciate what they have.

Homer's father died, and the other son took over the other farm [the one they farmed at first]. We wanted to get out on our own. And we had two boys. By the time we moved here, both of them was well up in age—the oldest one was in high school and the younger one was in the eighth grade. This house was in terrible bad shape, but we fixed it up gradually.

This farm where I am now belonged to the county. The county owned it sixty years, and they kept paupers.[7] They [the county] didn't farm it much; they just kept the paupers. They could raise truck patches [small plots of vegetables] and things like that. They kept a cow or two to milk and things like that, but they didn't do too much farming. They didn't have any equipment. There were two little houses up on the hill where they kept paupers. They kept the men in one and the women in the other, and my husband was the overseer of it. And different families would rent it, and maybe they'd stay here four or five years, and then he'd have to get another renter. Then after the welfare department started, they all got out on their own, and the farm was for sale. And my husband bought it in 1939, and we moved here in 1941.

The county owned this farm for sixty years, and when we bought it, it was growed up so much till you couldn't see the road over there for the sprouts.[8]

I'll tell you one thing that's interesting. This farm belonged to the Indians years ago, and an Eldridge lived across the river. You see, the river's[9] all around us. It makes a bend here, and it cinches us on three sides, and an Eldridge family all lived on that side of the river. And their daughter married, and Mr. Eldridge bought this farm for his daughter and put his daughter and son-in-law on here. And they built this house, and it's close, I guess, to three hundred years old. And you know what he paid for it, to the Indians? He paid them what they wanted. They wanted a butcher knife, a pony, and a shotgun, and that's what he paid them with.[10] And their [the Eldridge's] daughter told me that, Miss Suzy Coffin. She's been dead, I guess, twenty-five or thirty years, but she was raised here as a little girl. It was a long time ago. Before the Civil War. I don't remember his first name, but the Eldridge family is still over there. It's been handed down for years and years. They still live across the river.

And then a friend of ours came to see me and said that he knew of a job that was available for a home economics graduate. And if I wanted it, he'd help me get it. So I went to work after that, and I worked for about thirty years. I went to work in '41. I worked for the WPA. I was the supervisor of Loudon and Roane and Monroe County, and they had the lunchroom program. And then after it closed, I went to work for the welfare department. And that's about all there is to it.

When TVA came, that's how we paid for this farm. They took our river bottoms. When Watts Bar was here, see it backed the river up on our farm, and that's the way we paid for this farm. Watts Bar [Dam] was built before Fort Loudon [Dam].[11]

My son started the dairy. My husband didn't want to start it, but Homer Vaughn started it. I don't know when it was; it's been several years. But Homer never did like to dairy. He liked these great big black cattle. Homer Vaughn, he let him do the dairying. He never did work at it. He said, "That's too much work."

My son farms, and he's turned it over to his two sons. He's kind of retired, and he's helping them get started. And one son's single and the other one's married. He [Homer Vaughn] bought a farm over on the edge of Monroe County and got one boy on it. And they all work together. And they're all good to me. These two grandsons, I never ask them to do anything that they don't do it willingly and just seem pleased to do it for me.

Gene Brady kindly[12] supervises the dairy, and Tommy kindly manages the farm.[13]

Homer Vaughn had a farm at Lenoir City that belonged to my sister. Her husband died and left her this, and he never did farm. He [Homer Vaughn] thought it was a bargain, and he bought it as kind of an investment. And after he died, she didn't want to fool with no farm and all, so she sold it to Homer Vaughn pretty cheap, practically gave it to him. But he paid her some on it; she said she wanted him to have it. It was the nicest place to keep cattle that you wanted to keep away from the bull, you know. He had it all fenced in, and it had a creek on two sides. It was just an ideal place to keep his heifers and things. Till Lenoir City decided [they] wanted to buy it for a school. And he told them he didn't want to sell it. And they'd come and talk and talk and talk. And they couldn't condemn it because it was outside the city. Finally they put it inside the city limits, condemned it, and took it. And he had two years to invest his money. They didn't want to give him anything for it. They knew what he paid for it, you know, and they were trying to get it as cheap as they could. And he had a time getting a settlement on it. The mayor used to come down here and talk to him and try to get him to sell it to them. And one night, he just kept staying, and Homer Vaughn said, "Now, mayor, you can stay as long as you want to, but I've got to go to the barn and do my chores." [Laughter] But they thought they ought to get it for what Homer Vaughn paid for it. He told them they was funny. So they put it in the city limits and took it.[14]

And he had two years to invest his money to keep from paying income [tax] on it. So he bought that farm over in Monroe County. It was up for sale. And it's a real nice place. And Tommy lives over there. It's fifteen miles from here, and Tommy comes over here every day. His wife works in Monroe County. Tommy lives on the farm. And they have cattle over there and a corn crop. That's the reason we had that farm because the government was going take so much money out of it.[15]

And Mrs. Bright knows what a good daughter-in-law I have, don't you, Mrs. Bright? She is so good to me. When I cook, they eat with me, and when she cooks, I eat over there. We never cook at the same time. Everybody ate with me yesterday, and now we're all eating with her today. I like to give her a rest once in a while. We get along fine. The worst part [of being old] is my eyesight is so bad; I can't see good. I can't read a recipe now; I told them, I just have to cook what I know. But I've always liked to cook.

And then I like to travel. After I got older and retired, I traveled some. I made two trips to California. I went to Alaska and Hawaii and took a boat trip and went to Canada and made several small trips around. I was a little disappointed [in Alaska]. I thought I'd get to see the Eskimos and go into the wild, but they don't take you on that. They just take you to places more like it is now. The other thing I liked about it, [although] they don't have screens in the windows, they don't have flies and bugs like we do. And they raise cabbage in flower beds for ornamental. They raise different colors of cabbage in their flower beds, and the bugs don't eat them up. If we raised them here, the bugs would eat them up, wouldn't they, Mrs. Bright?

My son goes to Alaska. He's going on a trip on Sunday. He goes up in the wild. He takes a plane to some place, then takes a smaller plane, and goes up to a fishing camp. And he sees the Eskimos. And they have guards at this camp that cook for them and everything. They carry guns on account of the bears. He's been once, and he's going again Sunday. His wife wouldn't go on a trip like that. She goes to Myrtle Beach while he goes. She likes to go to the beach. But they have a good time. They [the staff at the fishing camp] cook their fish for them and everything. He says they have wonderful food at this lodge where he is. He and a friend of his are going. His son went with him one year, but he says he can't get off this year.

This is my son who was a forester and worked for Bowater.[16] For thirty years he worked for them. He was president of one of the timber companies that kept the lumber to the plant. He never did farm. His daddy wanted him to farm, but he never did farm. He was in World War II, and when he came back, he went to college and took up forestry. He never has farmed much. He helped on the farm when he was growing up.

The younger one [Homer Vaughn] likes to farm. And my husband used to go off and tell the oldest one what to do while he's gone, and the younger one would do it. He just likes to. Homer Vaughn likes to farm yet, but he's not able to do much. He can drive a tractor and help the boys a little, but he don't do too much.

I didn't do too much out in the fields. . . . But after I retired from my job, I helped my son. His youngest son was in college. [The grandsons] and Homer Vaughn and I filled four silos that fall. I'd drive the empty wagon to the field and bring a full one back, and the other son would unload it. And I'd work from daylight to dark with him. I like to drive a tractor, and I'd help him. I'd even load the hay and drove a tractor to pull a mower and haul the hay. One time I was coming in with a load of hay, and my husband was sitting out here in the yard. He was disabled.[17] And the preacher was sitting there talking to him. And I didn't want to come right by the house to go to the barn with a load of hay, and I went through the field. And when I come to the house, Homer says, "What'd you go down in the field with that load of hay for?" And I said, "I didn't want the preacher to see me with shorts on." [laughter] But I've helped Homer Vaughn a lot. I never did the real hard work. I'd just drive the tractor and do things like I was able. Sue's cooking, and I'd work with the boys. I'd rather work outside. I'd pay a woman to come in and clean up my house and then go out there and help them. But I've always, after I retired, helped him. Anytime he needed an extra tractor driver, I'd help him.

Another thing, you asked me what I did for recreation. I belonged to a bridge club. They was eight of us that went through high school together that had a bridge club for years. We played bridge at different times. I'm the only one living now. There was eight of us that played together. I was in the

Farm Bureau. I used to help feed the Farm Bureau, didn't I? I always, I tried to do a little something. My brother saw that I was a big Farm Bureau member.[18] They used to have a picnic, and I fixed the food for the picnic for the Farm Bureau. They usually put me on the cooking jobs.

I didn't take too much active part [in home demonstration clubs]. That was when I was working, and I didn't work at it too much. I went sometimes, but I was working most of the time. Everybody asks me, to what do I attribute my long life, and I tell them hard work and clean living.

I always kept my garden clean. One year I had a pretty strawberry patch, and I had more strawberries than I could use, and my friends came out and helped me pick them. But I've always worked. Even had a garden when I was working, I'd work it when I come home. It's just been three years that I don't have one [a garden]. When they got a dairyman[19] to work in the dairy, he wanted a garden. Homer Vaughn said, "Mother, you're getting too old to work in the garden. Let [the dairyman] have your garden." And so I did. And he comes and brings me things and puts on the porch out of the garden. Real nice. They know I can't see to string my beans, and they're afraid they'll have a bug bite on them or something, so he takes them home, and his wife strings them and breaks them and brings them back to me.

But I had a good life, and I've got a nice family. I've got two sons and five grandchildren and eight great-grandchildren.

Notes

1. The name has been changed at the narrator's request. All other family names within the interview have also been changed.

2. This information was gleaned from an interview with Mrs. Jones's brother and from notes on a phone conversation between Mrs. Delozier and Ann Ross Bright. See Arthur Delozier, interview by editor, July 1994, McClung Historical Collection, Knoxville, Tennessee, and Peggy Delozier Jones, phone conversation with Ann Ross Bright, July 1994, notes in editor's possession.

3. "Public works" is the term most rural Southerners used to describe an off-farm job.

4. The farm had belonged to Homer's maternal grandparents.

5. To clean and eviscerate the fowl for cooking.

6. Early in the century, it was common to dress little boys in garments shaped like dresses or pinafores until they were potty-trained. The garments simplified the process of changing diapers.

7. The Loudon County Poor Farm.

8. Saplings.

9. The Tennessee River.

10. I have been unable to confirm any of the details of this story. Indeed, in the seventeenth century, Loudon County was a center of Cherokee Indian civilization, but

whites pushed most of them out of the area by the time of American Revolution. It is, however, unlikely that Mrs. Jones's house was three hundred years old. Given its appearance and the vernacular farmhouse architecture, my guess would be that most of the house was no more than one hundred years old in 1994.

11. The Tennessee Valley Authority began construction on Watts Bar Dam in Loudon County, completing it in the early 1940s. The floodwaters from the dam covered some of the river bottoms on the Jones farm. With the money they received from the sale of the river bottoms, the Jones's were able to pay off the mortgage on their farm.

12. Local dialect for "kind of."

13. Gene Brady and Tommy are Mrs. Jones's grandsons, the sons of her son Homer Vaughn, who turned their farm into a commercial dairy farm.

14. The city annexed the farm. Once it was within the city limits, they could claim the land by right of eminent domain and force Mr. Delozier to sell the land for a sum the court determined was a fair price.

15. Apparently the sale of the previous farm to Lenoir City had generated enough capital gains to leave Homer Vaughn Jones with a significant tax liability unless he reinvested the proceeds elsewhere.

16. Her son Joe worked for Bowater Paper Company.

17. Apparently this story took place in the mid 1970s, after Mrs. Jones's retirement. Her husband was unable to do much physical labor by this time.

18. Mrs. Delozier's brother was a founding member of the Loudon County, Tennessee, chapter of the Farm Bureau.

19. A worker responsible for milking the cows twice a day.

Ethel Davis

ETHEL DAVIS[1] WAS born in 1905 on a general farm in Loudon County, Tennessee. One of seven children, she attended a local two-room school until the upper grades when she moved to a secondary school in the nearby village of Philadelphia. In 1926, she married Earl Davis, a local dairy farmer. The couple struggled to survive the Depression. Mrs. Davis's husband's brother, John, lived with them until his marriage. Ethel and Earl Davis had one son, Sam, who went on to expand the family dairy into a large commercial operation that he still runs today. As the Jones family did at a later time, the Davis family took advantage of expanding markets to enter commercial dairy farming. Mrs. Davis died in 1999.

Eighty-nine years old when she was interviewed, Mrs. Davis's memory of farm life was fragmented. She remembered the details of daily life quite clearly, but she was foggy on some events. In old age, she lived with her son and his wife at their ranch home on the farm. I spoke with Ethel Davis on July 19, 1994, at the Davis home. Also present was Mrs. Davis's daughter-in-law and her sister-in-law, who had arranged the interview. They occasionally jogged her memory about the past. Mrs. Davis's daughter-in-law helped Mrs. Davis review the transcript and sent the editor hand-written corrections on May 30, 1995. Together, the Davis women answered my additional questions in writing. I have corrected the edited interview and added details based on their written corrections and comments.

I was born in nineteen and five. Been here a long time.

We was poor and all of our neighbors were. [laughs] There were seven children in my family. I don't know how they raised that many. We raised our food. We always fattened our hogs and had hog meat all the time. We had chickens all the time and eggs all the time so you didn't have to go to town for anything but soda and salt. [laughter] My father was a miller. He made the cornmeal and the flour and had a sawmill. We were never hungry.

One year we didn't have any shoes all year. Because of hard times, I reckon. They [her parents] said we couldn't get any money for them. Everybody got their shoes by trading in their corn and peas. Most of the time we bought them [the shoes] from a peddler. We sold chickens and eggs. Then we did sell some butter and a little milk from time to time.

I went to school in two different places. I went to Paint Rock [School] a few years. That had two teachers. Then I went to Cook School, which was one room. Cook School was in Philadelphia.[2] Back then in my younger days, we just had five or six months [of school]. But then when we went to Philadelphia it was longer. We walked to school. Now we always helped the teachers. The teacher might be in the back with one group and we's up front with the little ones. The older girls and boys helped. My father taught school for a while. I don't remember how long. He didn't like it much.

I married in 1926. We had it kindly rough. My husband's daddy was a dairyman,[3] but he died when we had been married about two years. John, my brother-in-law, lived with us then, and he helped us [on the farm].

After times had gotten better, it was worse with us.[4] Yeah, hard times before for everybody else. We thought we was going to lose the farm at one time. One of the neighbors loaned us money. I don't know where he heard it [that they were about to lose the farm to foreclosure]. He just had money and he wanted to loan it so we could hang on to it [the farm]. [laughs] I said a dollar was worth a dollar and fifty cents then. But them was the hardest times for us.

I just had one child [son Sam], but he was a good one.

We had dairy cows there on the farm. I don't know how many we milked. It varied. We would have to cull out some sometimes, and sometimes we'd get a new bunch.[5] I had once fourteen that I milked, and that was my biggest amount at one time. Milked fourteen by hand. I don't remember how long it took. But I didn't do that many most of the time. My husband milked all the time in the morning, but sometimes he'd come in late after working on the farm, so I would milk at nights a lot of times. At first, we started selling our milk in Chattanooga. We took it to Philadelphia and put it on the train [to send to Chattanooga]. And we made some money in the dairy. But it's got so now you can't make money at it.

For a while, Earl drove a milk truck,[6] I guess whenever Sam was a baby. My husband would come home late and do the farm work. And I think John drove the milk truck, too, sometimes. I remember John telling about one of his customers [whose] baby had lost its shoe, and they couldn't find the shoe anywhere, and then John poured out the milk, and the shoe came out. [laughter] They [the milk processing company] took the milk right on, though. Pasteurized it.

I always had a garden. I canned a lot, but I haven't canned any in, oh, four or five years. There's still some down in the basement that we haven't used yet. We still have beans, apples, pickles.

And we had Sears Roebuck catalogs to keep us warm, too. I'd take a Sears Roebuck catalog and open it up about halfway and lay it up on the stove . . . and I'd warm it and put it [the catalog] on their chest if they had a cold or something. And I've heard of people putting their irons in the fire and wrapping them up and taking them to bed.

I made all of my clothes. I didn't have many, but I made them. The men bought their overalls. I made their shirts. They maybe had one Sunday shirt. Sometimes my clothes was awful ragged, and I'd complain. I didn't have probably but one Sunday dress. When Sam was little, he went with his uncle and his girlfriend when they were dating, and the girlfriend had on an eyelet embroidery dress. And when he came home he said, "Mother, don't worry your clothes. Tammy had on a dress and it was just full of holes." [laughter]

I never knowed anything else but farming. A lot of the women around here got jobs at Philadelphia at that hosiery mill, but I didn't.[7]

We didn't have much . . . spare time. Sometimes we'd go to the mountains. Now during the Depression times, we had some corn shuckings, and the one who got the red cob got to kiss the pretty girl. I never got it. We had a lot of church revivals. And I quilted. I thought I had to quilt every winter for our covers.

We had the only telephone in the community for a long time, and people came to us to call the doctor. I guess we got the phone when Sam was about four. It was a private line, and the ones who had it had to keep up the line. We didn't put up the line, though.[8] I think my husband outtalked somebody on that one. He never did hang the line.

When they had all those government programs in the Depression, I don't know whether it helped or not. I know we got some work done on the farm and got fertilizer. That was the test demonstration program run by TVA.[9] You had to follow their program. You followed their directions and got their fertilizer. They taught that type of plowing that made cuts across ridges. What do they call that? Contour plowing. Still in Loudon County you can look at ridges and see the contour marks. It kept the Tennessee hills from washing away. Shortly after the contouring of the hills, they brought in fescue into Tennessee. And that kept our hills from washing away, too.

NOTES

1. The name has been changed at the narrator's request. All other family names within the interview have also been changed.

2. Philadelphia was a small town in Loudon County. Because it boasted a railroad depot, Philadelphia became a small trade center and home to a hosiery mill.

3. Dairyman is a term used interchangeably by many rural southerners. In some cases, the term refers to the hired man responsible for milking the cows (also called a milker), but in this case, Mrs. Davis was referring to a dairy farmer.

4. Apparently times were hard for the Davis family because they had gone into debt to pay for their land, and they were having trouble making the mortgage payments.

5. Periodically dairy farmers "cull" or sell old or infirm cows that are no longer producing at optimum levels because they cost more to feed than they can produce.

6. A bulk milk truck, which picked up production from individual farms and hauled it to a processing plant.

7. Like many small southern communities, Philadelphia boasted a small textile mill that took advantage of the availability of surplus laborers from local farms, usually women.

8. Early telephone service in the countryside was usually the result of the cooperative efforts of neighbors who convinced a phone company to provide service if the local residents installed the phone line and maintained it. In this case, the Davises did not install the line, though Mrs. Davis is unclear on how they avoided doing so.

9. The Tennessee Valley Authority ran a test demonstration farm program that provided farmers with expert advice and fertilizer to improve soil conservation and production on their farms. Participating farmers had to be willing to allow other farmers to tour the farm to see the results of using improved agricultural practices. The Soil Conservation Service ran similar educational programs for farmers all over the South.

Mabel Love

MABEL LOVE[1] was born in 1910 in the farming community of Philadelphia, Tennessee, ten miles from Loudon, seat of the county with the same name. Her birth family worked as tenant farmers except for a five-year period when her father moved the family to Montana, where he managed a grain operation. Mrs. Love married into a landowning family and had two sons.

In the middle years of the twentieth century, many farmers in the Philadelphia community and throughout the county built commercial dairy operations.[2] Mrs. Love and her husband began large-scale dairy production in partnership with his brother. During World War II, the Loves bought the brother's share of the land they inherited from his parents and began to expand their herd. Gradually they accumulated additional acreage. Mrs. Love considered herself an active partner in the farming operation and participated in decisions to expand and to mechanize. The farm is still operated by Mrs. Love's son and grandsons and is one of the largest dairies in the county.

In the 1980s, Mrs. Love retired. She moved to Florida, where she lived in a travel trailer near another son. She brought the trailer to Tennessee each summer. She parked in a son's yard, visited with family, and worked the vegetable garden for the warm months, returning to Florida as the leaves began to turn in east Tennessee. Mrs. Love died in 1996.

This interview took place on July 19, 1994, on the lawn outside Mrs. Love's travel trailer. A friend of Mrs. Love's who arranged the interview was also present, and occasionally she jogged Mrs. Love's memory. The editor sent Mrs. Love a transcript, but she made no changes.

Well, I can tell you about my life if I don't get tangled up a-trying to. [laughter] Sometimes I have problems with that. I was born in 1910, May of 1910. There was about two in my family, me and my sister. And of course my mother and dad; long back that time they was still living. Our family never knowed nothing but farming. Our farm had crops; they never dairy farmed.

You had to sell eggs and stuff. You sold your chickens and eggs and bought your groceries. That's how my mother bought her sugar, salt, and coffee. We had lard. Makes you sick. I mean makes you sick to think of lard now. Well, there's altogether difference in cooking now from the way we cooked back then. We didn't know any better. But, law, we had good food.

I never have been too good about remembering dates or anything. When I went to school that was my worst subject, remembering dates on anything. I went to school right out here at Philadelphia; I went there the first year I went to school. Then we moved to Montana, and I went to school out there. This man was wanting my dad to come out there to his farm and work for him out there, and we spent, I think it must have been about five years that we was there, and I went to school there. Then when we came back, he decided he wanted to work over here in Sweetwater, and we lived there a year or so, and then we moved back down here to Philadelphia.

I never did like to go to school out there at Philadelphia. I was just a little kid; well that was my first year in school. And I didn't like it out there, I just didn't like the people, and I guess they didn't like me either. But anyway, I'd do everything I could to keep from going to school, and they finally let me quit school before I finished the eighth grade. I was still going to school in the eighth grade. And they let me quit. I didn't like to go to school there, I didn't like it one bit. And it's funny because the people I know out there now, I like them, but I didn't like any of them then.

We married about 1927. Now these dates, I may get them wrong. We set up housekeeping across the road over there. That was the first place we lived. Then we moved down here to the house down here. It was a story and a half high.

I married into dairy farming. We was in the dairy business practically all our married lives. When we got married, his family was not dairying. Not when I got married. My in-laws was still living at first. Then the two boys [her husband and his brother] kindly took over the farm, and they started to milk cows. That lasted fifteen years, I guess. I can't remember how long exactly. We went through some pretty hard times, long back in them days, why it was pretty rough. But I guess we's pretty happy.

When we went into the dairy business, we bought out the rest of his brothers. Then we got this place here. Then we just kept on buying a little bit more land. [laughter] The first one I guess that we bought was this area right up where you go around the curve up there, there's a field right there that runs out through there. And we bought that and paid on it a while and then decided to try to buy some more. Then we bought where the grandson lives, right this side of the interstate,[3] and we bought that. Then after we got that paid for, which was quite a job to get that done, then we bought where that field is right over there on top of that hill. It come down to the creek there. We bought that. I guess that's all we've bought.

We got our first tractor after the war. I remember when we got it, but I don't remember how long ago that was. But it was a Farmall H, I believe it was.

You know when we had threshing and things like that, we'd have our great big table put together. The women did the cooking, and the men done the work. I'd have at least two big tables. But everybody helped everybody else. It was real good. It didn't seem like work. We just had such a good time being together that it didn't seem like work. You'd feed the men first. [laughter] We'd have buckets and buckets of green beans, corn, fried chicken, some kind of greens, cornbread, biscuits, rolls, some kind of pies. We had a lot of pies. We always had iced tea and coffee. We generally had coffee, but they didn't drink that much coffee. I guess it was just too hot. We had plenty of iced tea. We'd have two different kinds of potatoes. And coleslaw. We did most of the cooking at whichever house you was at. I had a pretty big stove, and I could cook several things at one time.

I always had a big garden, but I did help on the farm some. I would drive the tractors. I milked. When we started, I was hand milking. Then it wasn't but just a little while till we got milkers you've seen,[4] and that's just a small thing to what they've got down here now. They stick 'em on the cows, and they just drop off when they're done milking. It's a lot easier now than when I did it. Faster, too. They're probably milking four or five to my one. Can you imagine me sitting in there milking all those cows by hand? I never have been a real good milker.

My husband died in 1974, I believe. My son, Doug, runs one farm, and Jimmy, my grandson runs the other. The other son—he's the one who lives in Florida. He has been living down there for years, and me and him comes back up here and then goes back down there ever year. He never did go into farming very much. He never did like farming. I had four sons. I love my boys, but I'd dearly love to have had a girl.

Notes

1. The name has been changed at the narrator's request. All other family names within the interview have also been changed.

2. Philadelphia is a small town in London County. Because it boasted a railroad depot, Philadelphia became a small trade center and home to a hosiery mill.

3. Interstate 75 runs near the Love farm.

4. She is referring to an early type of electric milking machine that had a milking unit attached to a lidded bucket that held the milk. After milking a couple of cows, the bucket would be full and would have to be carried to some kind of cooling tank and emptied there. Today milking machines deposit the milk in a pipeline system that carries it directly to a bulk cooling tank.

Kate Simmons

KATE SIMMONS[1] WAS born in 1913 in Sneedville, Tennessee. Soon after her birth, Mrs. Simmons's family moved to a farm near New Market, in neighboring Jefferson County. Jefferson County offered rich, river bottom farmland, and her family engaged in general farming, growing subsistence crops for family use and raising tobacco, truck crops, and livestock for the market. The middle of eleven children, Kate Simmons recalled that she had always enjoyed life on the farm.

After a few years working in a local hospital and then as a cook for a Jefferson County family, Kate married Mack Simmons and moved into his family home. There, Mack Simmons continued to farm with his father, and Mrs. Simmons did the traditional work of a farm woman alongside her mother-in-law. The couple had two children, a son and a daughter.

A few years after the Simmons's marriage, the Tennessee Valley Authority began acquiring land in Jefferson County for its Cherokee Dam project. Part of the Simmons farm fell within TVA's "taking" line; the family decided to sell the entire farm.[2] Mack and Kate Simmons decided to look for their own land elsewhere. The couple purchased about fifteen hundred acres of prime land on the Little Tennessee River in Loudon County and moved there with their two children and with Mack's brother, Sam, in the early 1940s.

The farm the Simmons family purchased was known in Loudon County as the old Davis farm or Riverview. The Davises had been slave-owning planters in the antebellum years. The property included a log house that had been expanded and improved over the years. Mrs. Simmons's daughter remembered a huge dining room and a parlor with aqua plaster walls.

As they had in Jefferson County, the Simmonses engaged in general farming at first. They grew and sold watermelons, raised sheep and sheared them for wool, and grew peas that they sold to canneries in east Tennessee. They also raised tobacco and a few cows. After a number of years, they began to specialize in dairy farming, and eventually the Simmonses built a large commercial dairy farming operation in Loudon County. They raised and educated two children, and their son, Jim, joined the family dairy.[3]

Mrs. Simmons was active in the local Farm Bureau and in home demonstration work. She engaged in many crafts activities she learned through home demonstration work. In September 1954, Mrs. Simmons's Loudon County farm home was featured in the homemaker's column in *Progressive Farmer* as a model farm home. The article featured many of the inexpensive home improvements she had made using ideas garnered from home demonstration work and from the pages of *Progressive Farmer.*[4]

Ironically, the Simmonses also lost the Loudon County farm to TVA. Fort Loudon Dam had been built on the Loudon County section of the Tennessee River in the 1940s. In the 1970s, the federal agency began acquiring land for another dam in the county, this one on the Little Tennessee River, a tributary of the Tennessee. The latter project was known as Tellico Dam. The project's aim was to make the Little Tennessee navigable further upriver and to provide recreational development in the region. Tellico Dam proved to be far more controversial than earlier TVA projects, in part because flood control and the generation of hydroelectric power were not goals for the project and in part because the agency condemned and purchased entire farms, not just the portion of the land which fell below the water line as they had done in earlier projects. Mrs. Simmons complained bitterly that much of the best farmland was covered up by water or taken for fancy housing developments. She noted that Tellico Lake only covered about half of her family's acreage, yet TVA took all the land and later sold it for pricey residential developments. As she put it, "There was no need for them to take all this land down here. Now they sell a little old yard for a hundred thousand dollars."[5]

By this time, Mack Simmons had died. Kate Simmons's son took the proceeds from the Tellico sale and bought an eleven-hundred-acre river bottom farm in Newport, Tennessee, where he still dairy farms with one of his sons.

Kate Simmons bought a ten-acre property in southern Loudon County. The property contained a lovely old farmhouse, which she filled with the Victorian antiques she had collected over the years and with a large doll collection begun during her childhood. Yet she could not seem to stay out of the path of federal development projects. In the late 1970s, U.S. Interstate 75 through Loudon County came right through Mrs. Simmons's property. She recalled, " I almost got moved because of the interstate. My yard went right down to the bridge. They took five acres for that."

I interviewed her on August 5, 1994, at her home. Her friend Ann Ross Bright arranged the interview and accompanied me. Kate Simmons was a gracious and charming white-haired woman. She showed Mrs. Bright and me her dolls and told us the stories behind many family antiques. She also showed us numerous examples of the various crafts that she makes and lots of family photographs. She was particularly proud of a grandson, her daughter's son, who played football with the Dallas Cowboys. Many portions of the interview with Mrs. Simmons were inaudible, and I reconstructed some of the above history from my notes and from a news article. Most of her interview focused on her childhood and young adult years. Mrs. Simmons died in 1996.

You want me to talk about how old I am and all that? I was born in 1913 up in Sneedville, Tennessee, in Hancock County. My father moved to Jefferson City in Jefferson County near New Market when I was a baby. I was about six months old. There was eleven children in my family, six boys and five girls. We farmed. We bought a farm there [in Jefferson County]. He had a sawmill and cut lumber. We had a peach orchard and an apple orchard. We always had raspberries to sell. And he sold a lot of vegetables, too. We had people who would come by to pick them up.

He [her father] would take his tobacco to the market in Knoxville. Then you could raise as much [tobacco] as you wanted.[6] Boy, that was a lot of work [tobacco cultivation].[7] Then later he had an allotment for about fifty acres. I guess he bought some of the others' [allotments in order to have such a large allotments]. We kids always worked in tobacco. I liked working in it.

My mother raised chickens and had four cows. She sold buttermilk, milk, and butter. She had about a hundred hens, and she sold eggs for ten cents a dozen. Ain't that awful? We took them to the store in New Market and exchanged them for groceries. We were about two miles and a half from New Market.

We went to school at Rocky Valley. It was one room until they consolidated, and we went to [school in] New Market when I was about fourteen. I didn't finish school. I went to Jefferson City and helped a nurse for five years. There was a hospital in her home, and I helped her. Seems like I worked for her for five years. We didn't get wages; we got room and board. There was about three of us girls who worked for that family. I have an old Bible from . . . the family I took care of. The lady, Elizabeth Toller, willed her Bible to me. Then after a while I got tired of it [working for the nurse]. It was hard work. She took good care of her patients. Then later they built the hospital.[8]

Then after that, I went out to Flat Gap taking care of a family, and I took care of them for about two years. And there was four in the family, four generations that I took care of. I didn't do too much housework. I just waited on them, cooked for them. I got their meals for them. My husband lived on a farm nearby to the . . . family that I lived with. He told everybody that he courted all around and come back home and married the girl next door. He was thirty-two years old when we married in 1934.

My husband was Mack. We set up housekeeping there on the Simmons farm. There was a house that they had just built to rent, and we set up house-keeping there. We had chickens. We raised most all the things we needed on the farm. And if we had anything to sell, we took it to the store and ex-changed it for what we needed. A lot of things we done without. You could sell your wheat, corn, and barley, or whatever. Farm crops wouldn't bring anything. Wheat was bringing fifty cents a bushel.

[In the Depression] I knew about six or seven families that lived there close to us that were on the welfare. They didn't have any money even to buy clothes with. I know I helped two families—helped support them. It was hard to pay the preacher [in the Depression]. A lot of times we'd give him what you'd call a pounding.[9] I don't know how we managed to pay him. Sometimes we'd give him a dollar anyway.

And then Cherokee Dam, you know when they built Cherokee Dam, we sold it to them and moved out here on the river.[10] People just thought it was terrible for them [TVA] to come in and take their homes. Some of them had been there so long. My son was about six years old when we sold it, and my daughter was two years old.

We moved to Loudon County in 1936.[11] TVA sent people around who helped you find new farms and places to go. There was about two or three [TVA employees] that helped locate farms. My brother-in-law was in real estate then, and he did some of that.

I don't remember [when it was], but we had the first tractor in Loudon County. Electricity? Law, when was that? I believe it was early in 1945. My husband helped build the telephone line. I can't remember when that was.

It seemed like things kind of got moving in World War II; [they] got bet-ter. We had trouble getting gas for the tractors. They rationed gas and tires. And then we had that sugar ration, an emergency on sugar. I had trouble getting enough sugar for canning. And there was something else that was rationed, but I can't think what it was. We had our own meat we killed on the farm. We couldn't buy any. I remember my first pressure cooker we canned with. I blew it up. The first thing I bought [that used electricity] was a stove, which I loved. I was ready to give up on that wood stove.

Did you see my dolls? I got started collecting them years ago. At New Market there was just an old store; they called it Henderson's Store. And they just had everything piled up in there. And the man that worked there, he was a lot older than me. I guess I was just about twelve or thirteen years old. He thought I was the grandest little girl there was. And he gave me these two dolls. And I've got them in there. So that's the way I got started. You know they broke in my house once, on my back porch. And they got about thirty-two dolls on the back porch.

Now my brother lives at the old home place [near New Market]. I was in the middle [of my brothers and sisters]. One of my brothers had a chicken farm; he served in the army, and he had a chicken farm. And then one of them worked at the Cherokee Dam. And then my other two brothers, they never did farm for a living. My sisters couldn't wait to get away from the farm. I loved it. None of my sisters liked the farm. I guess they thought it was too hard or something, I don't know.

NOTES

1. The name has been changed at the narrator's request. All other family names within the interview have also been changed.

2. For its early projects, TVA purchased only the acreage expected to fall below the anticipated high water mark, plus a small buffer zone beyond. Occasionally it purchased entire farms if the families were agreeable.

3. Much of the background on the Simmons family's move to Loudon County comes from two news articles. See "Loudon Ferry Boat Remembered," *Loudon County News Herald,* July 21, 1994, sec. A, p. 12, and "Silos Site of Riverview," *Village Connection,* May 1, 1998, pp. 16–17.

4. "The Ideal Farm Home," *Loudon (Tennessee) Progressive Farmer* (September 1954).

5. Indeed, after some abortive attempts at developing the property for recreational use, TVA sold most of the acreage it seized for Tellico Dam and Lake to Arkansas-based Cooper Communities and to other speculators. Today, Cooper Communities' Tellico Village housing development and the gated neighborhood Rarity Bay developed by east Tennessee investors occupies much of Loudon County's former farmland. These pricey developments have drawn retirees and other residents from all over the country.

6. Her father's early tobacco farming took place before government tobacco allotments limited each tobacco farmer's production.

7. Tobacco is one of the most labor-intensive crops. It requires twelve or more months of intensive cultivation.

8. Mrs. Simmons is making a distinction between the small facility run by the nurse in her home and the formally organized community hospital that was built later.

9. An old rural tradition in which farm people present someone with gifts of food, including meat, flour or cornmeal, home canned goods, and fresh garden produce. In addition to compensating ministers—usually part-time lay ministers who made their living in other ways—rural people held poundings for newlyweds and for people who might have lost a home to fire or might otherwise be in need.

10. A Tennessee Valley Authority project constructed in the 1930s.

11. Mrs. Simmons may have been mistaken about the date of the move. The family purchased the land in 1933.

Evelyn Petree Lewellyn

EVELYN PETREE LEWELLYN was born in 1923 in East Chicago, Indiana. Her parents, natives of east Tennessee, had gone north to seek work, but they soon returned to Knoxville. Knoxville was a commercial and industrial center on the Tennessee River in central east Tennessee.

In Knoxville, Evelyn's father, Isaac Columbus Petree, made a living as a musical evangelist. He directed church choirs, sang anthems, and organized musical programs for revival meetings all over the area. This occupation offered little financial security, so twice during Evelyn Petree Lewellyn's childhood, the family left the city to live rent-free in an empty log cabin on Mr. Petree's childhood home place in rural Anderson County, Tennessee. The Petrees' strategy was a common one during the Great Depression. All over the South, town dwellers with rural roots returned to the countryside and their family's farms when they found themselves unable to pay rent in the city. In the country, families could be assured of housing and food, at least. Nonetheless, they usually found their quality of life reduced. Whether they doubled up with family members or moved into empty housing as the Petrees did, families usually found themselves in overcrowded quarters that were far inferior to the homes they had enjoyed in town.

As it was for most families, returning to the country was a mixed blessing. Here the children reveled in the pleasures of rural life while their city-born mother struggled to cope with poverty and primitive living conditions. Anderson County was an isolated rural location northwest of Knoxville on the edge of the Cumberland Mountain range. During the 1930s, Anderson County would become the site of the Tennessee Valley Authority's first project, Norris Dam. Before the arrival of TVA and the coming of World War II, most of the county's residents were general and subsistence farmers.

During high school, Evelyn Petree clerked at a local dime store and a department store. She graduated from Knoxville High School in 1941 and went to work at Standard Knitting Mills in Knoxville. Then wartime mobilization opened new job opportunities for women. Evelyn Petree and her cousin Wilma were able to secure jobs at the Aluminum Company of America's (ALCOA) fabricating plant in neighboring Blount County.

Because of her high scores on a mechanical aptitude test, Evelyn Petree was assigned a high-paying position as a tool room attendant in the machinists' shop.

While working at ALCOA, she met and married Bill Lewellyn, a Blount Countian who was a machinist at the plant. Bill enlisted in the navy, and Evelyn returned to her family's home in Knoxville to await his return from the war. Her daughter, Rachel, was born there in 1944. After Bill Lewellyn returned from service in the Pacific, he resumed work as a machinist at ALCOA. The couple lived in company housing in the town of Alcoa for a brief time before purchasing their first farm. After this, Bill Lewellyn farmed part-time while working at ALCOA, and Mrs. Lewellyn devoted her time to raising their three children (Rachel, Walt, born in 1947, and Bobby, born in 1952), tending an enormous garden, preserving her produce, and doing church work. Her devotion to family is evident in her oral history that emphasizes extended family ties and the complications of family relationships.

This interview took place at the Lewellyns' home in Greenback, Tennessee, on August 10, 1993. Evelyn Lewellyn annotated and corrected the transcript on September 13, 1994. Although much of her narrative focuses on city life during the Depression years, I include her narrative because it illustrates the fluid boundaries between rural and town life and the rural coping strategies that city families used to survive the hard times.

The Depression was pretty rough, no doubt. I've got my parents' marriage date, here. I was born in '23. I think they were about twenty-nine or thirty when they got married. They married July 1, 1922.

Mama was a member of the first women's quartet in Knoxville at the time she got married to Daddy. I believe she told me how they met. Her family lived over there on—I can't remember the name of that street; it's there right across from the old General Hospital. The house, I think is still there. Mama's daddy had left. Mama's dad was a roving photographer— gone most of the time—a ladies' man, Mama said. He left when the children were all small, and her mother had raised all of the family herself. And they went to work when they were about twelve years old, the boys did. I don't know if my grandmother took in washing or what. I believe Mama said she did do washing and ironing for people. I don't know how she did it [raised her kids alone]. I think she took in washing. And the girls all went to work when they were a little older. Back then they could work in factories. They won't let them now, but back then they could.

And Mama lived there, and Daddy drove the little laundry wagon down her street. He came by the house in that laundry wagon, I believe she told me. But then they got into church work. She was in the quartet. And he was a choir director and a singer.

My daddy had earlier attended Moody Bible Institute and later Carson Newman College. He got the mumps and had to drop out of school. He went to war, too. He was in World War I. Growing up out there in the country, he learned to shoot well [by] squirrel hunting.[1] And when he went to war, he was so good at it—a good marksman—his job was to keep teaching the soldiers how to shoot. And he went to France, but they kept him off the front lines because he was teaching them how to shoot.

Anyway, they got married. And then after that, Daddy did evangelistic work quite a bit. He went away from home a lot to revivals. For years and years he directed church music.

I was born in Indiana. They moved up there to get work, I reckon. He had a sister there. We lived with Dad's sister. He worked in the steel mills in Chicago. I was born up there, but we came back here when I was a baby. Then we came back down here. We moved from place to place—never did have the money to buy a place.

There were six children, and the sixth one died. I had it written down who we were named after. Bud is Isaac Conwell. Daddy is Isaac Columbus. But they always called Bud I. C., Jr. Bud was named after a great orator. Richard Crusoe, he was named after a tenor singer. We called him Dude. Joann Evangel was named after Evangeline Booth. We called her Boots. Theodocia Winifred was named after Mom and Dad's mothers.[2]

When we'd come and get without money to pay rent, he'd move us back to Anderson County.[3] We did that twice, in the log house. We moved out there [when Evelyn was] in the sixth grade and eighth grade. And the CCC [Civilian Conservation Corps] come along at that time. And the WPA [Works Progress Administration], I guess it was along about that time, maybe it was after that. Uncle Moss Dew, my Aunt Babe's husband,[4] worked for the WPA; he was a road foreman. Daddy'd get a little help from them when he needed money.

The first place I remember living was, ah, do you know where Harve's Rug place is now out on Broadway in Knoxville? There was an Edlen Furniture Company across the street. On the corner of Broadway and, I believe they called it Folsom Street or Tyson, I'm not for sure which one it was. There was a little Jewish grocery store, and there was a house behind that store. And we lived in the house. Other people lived in it, too. It was a big house. And the Jews and my mother, they really liked each other; they were good friends. And she finally had a child of her own, the Jewish lady did. Goodstein was their name.[5] She finally had a baby of her own, and I know she wouldn't let us see it on Saturday. That was part of the Jewish belief, I think—"No see baby on Saturday," she said. [laughter] I can remember that, she wouldn't let us see her baby on Saturdays. They're related to the Goodsteins in Knoxville now.

When we lived in town, we couldn't afford to buy milk. And I remember Mama would buy a quart of milk once a day and divide it between five children, six children. And Mama didn't get any. She'd just buy a quart of milk once a day. She'd say, "Now put you some bread in it and make it go a little further." [laughter] No wonder we had bad teeth.

We had it rough, I know that. We didn't have a lot to eat. I think we would get bread about a nickel a loaf. I remember Mama sending us to the store one time, me and Bud [her younger brother] with a little wagon with, I can't remember if it was a sack of potatoes. Seemed to me like it was a sack of potatoes. Daddy must have gotten them on the farm. I can't remember all about it. She sent us to the White Store[6] on Broadway with that bag of potatoes, and we were to ask the grocery man if we could swap that bag of potatoes for a loaf of bread. And he wouldn't do it. That's about all I remember about it, but he wouldn't make us a trade. I guess he had more potatoes than he could use. I remember I was kind of embarrassed about it. [laughter] Bud and I, pulling that little wagon.

My Uncle Henry Miller had a fairly good job. Uncle Henry, Aunt Ora's husband, worked at the car barns there in Knoxville, and it was a fairly good job.[7] They made a fairly good living there, he did. At least they had more than what we had. Aunt Ora was Mama's oldest sister. And their daughter Wilma was the same age as me but larger, and Aunt Ora would hand me her [Wilma's] dresses down. And I was glad to get it. Because she'd [Aunt Ora] made them, and they were pretty.

And Uncle Ernest[8] worked at the railroad. . . . And they had it a little better than we did because he had a job. They fared a little better than we did. Uncle Sherm[9] run a used furniture place there on Broadway. His wife died. And he had a little old secondhand store there on Broadway on the right, just this side of where Broadway Baptist Church is there. He didn't make much. He'd fix things, buy and sell.

We moved from there off Broadway to 204 Hazel Place. It was a big, two-story house. It was about two blocks behind Broadway Baptist Church. Dad led music there then. I think rent was eighteen dollars a month. It was a large, two-story, eight-room house. Mama's mother and sister Nar lived with us on Hazel Place. Mama's mother died there.

Mama's sister, Aunt Nar [Narcissus], didn't have any children. She worked before she got married, and she would buy us stuff. And some of her words she couldn't say real good. And Boots and Dude[10] were so close together they were always like twins when they were babies, and she called Boots "Bootchie." She couldn't say Boots. Bootchie and Dude. She called Dude "Big Boy." Aunt Nar married Uncle Sterling who owned S. L. Salling Funeral Home. She didn't have any children. She'd take Bootchie and Dude and keep them all night with her and Uncle Sterling when they lived in a house before they moved into the funeral home on Baxter Avenue. And she'd take them to spend the night with her. But she'd buy us stuff. She had a little money, and she'd buy us stuff.

The funeral home was across from old Knoxville High School on the corner. I used to go there and stay all night with them. They lived there in the upstairs. Well, first it was down on Magnolia near Gay Street to start with, then they moved it up there. Uncle Sterling was getting old then, and he'd hired his niece and her husband to help him there in the funeral home. And they neglected the bills in some way; some way they got him in debt, and the bills weren't paid. And I don't know if they took some of the money or if they just didn't take care of it right or what. But they got him all in debt, and people owed him, and Aunt Nar would have me come there and spend the night and work on statements to send out. She'd pay me a little. All he had for book work was just cards, index cards in a box. He didn't hardly even know who owed him. That was the only records he had. They lived there. And she let me go in there and help her fix a dead woman one time. She said, "Now don't tell anybody because it's against the law."[11] And she let me go in there with her and see the woman and fix her hair and all that. But it didn't scare me. They'd have the bodies there in that part of that house.

Little Rachel, my youngest sister, also died when we lived on Hazel Place. She got diphtheria. She was two and a half when she died. They took her to the hospital. And she cried all the time she's at the hospital. Dr. Bill Wallace, he was the one who admitted her. Dr. Wallace was a missionary who was killed in China. They were our friends and neighbors. They went to Broadway church where we went. He was our family doctor when we got to see a doctor. She [Rachel] stayed in the hospital several days and cried all the time she was there. And they brought her home, and she died after they got her home. And they thought maybe it had weakened her heart from crying. They wouldn't let Mama in to see her when she was in the hospital. Mom and Dad could look at her through the window glass but couldn't go in to see her. And then she died after they brought her home.

I was so young when little Rachel died that I don't remember very well, but I remember going to the funeral. It was a private funeral, you know, it couldn't be a public funeral because of the diphtheria. Had it there at the house. I guess most of the time they had funerals at churches then.[12] We had Rachel's at home. It might have been 1935. Uncle Sterling handled the funeral. He was Aunt Nar's husband. I always said if I had a little girl, I'd name her Rachel.

And we were quarantined [because of the diphtheria]. I know we had to miss school. We were quarantined long enough to make us miss out on a half term of school. Back then you started school in September or January, depending on when your birthday was. And I graduated in June, but I would have graduated in January had I not had to miss that school. Yeah, they come out, the health department come out and swabbed our throats. I can't remember if it was every day or once a week or what. But every so often, they'd come out and swab our throats. And as long as we any of us had a diphtheria germ in the throat swab, we were quarantined. Nobody could come in; we couldn't go out. They had a quarantine sign up on the front of our house.

Daddy worked, I suppose. I can't remember. But they wouldn't let us kids go out or go to school. And we couldn't have visitors. And finally when the last one of us came back negative, they took the quarantine sign off. And she [Rachel] was the only one that had it [diphtheria]. None of the rest of us got it except her. She died of it.

Bud and I both had scarlet fever real bad! We were quarantined then, too. But we survived it. But we didn't have it at the same time. Nobody else had it when he had it; nobody else in the family had it when I had it. My scarlet fever as a child caused this problem I have now, mitral valve prolapse. I had it [scarlet fever] when we lived at Hazel Place. I was about eight or nine years old, I guess. I had the awfulest sore throat. Back then, scarlet fever, if you got it, it was bad. Now I don't think it's very bad if you get it. Back then if you got it, you had it bad. And I broke out all over, and as I was getting well, my hands all peeled off. I could pull big old pieces of dead skin off my hands. Like to died. But I lived through it. And Bud had it bad, but I don't think he had it as bad as I did. Wasn't much you could do for it that, I remember. But I guess the Lord took care of us.

We did have water and a bathroom in that house on Hazel Place. We had to go out on the porch, through the porch to the bathroom. No heaters in the bathroom, but we did have a bathroom.

And that was during the Depression. And Daddy didn't have money to pay the rent half the time, but the lady never did put us out. He finally had to move. I guess that's when he moved us to Anderson County. Probably because he didn't have money to pay the rent. And that's where we lived [Anderson County] when I was in sixth grade and eighth grade.

When we moved to Anderson County, that was a big change for us. Just a two-room log house. Mama grew up in Knoxville. I think she was born in Knoxville and grew up over there. That's the reason it was so hard for her to go to Anderson County, but we had to. Didn't have much choice. [laughter] Just two rooms. All of us slept in that one big old room. We had a kitchen on the back. Mama had a little step-stove.[13] There was a little table, and there was a little stove set right up on top of that table. It was a wood stove. And that's what we cooked on. Fire in the fireplace. It's a wonder we didn't freeze to death. The chimney was made out of rocks and wood.

When we lived in the old home place in Anderson County, Daddy was a choir leader, and he didn't make much money. And when we lived out there, he'd come back over to town to churches to sing. He'd get revivals sometimes. Mama never did go with him much; she couldn't because she had too many babies to take care of. She couldn't even go to church with Daddy on Sundays and Wednesdays except occasionally in Knoxville. Because there was too many of us to get ready. And half the time, Daddy would spend the night [in town] when we lived out in the country [and he worked in town]. And who wanted to keep a family of six children overnight? [laughter] Or even for dinner much?

I remember carrying water—after living in town and having water and an inside bathroom, we'd have to carry water, I guess about an eighth of a mile we carried our drinking water. There was a branch right below the house that was our washing water. And [washed with] lye soap, which Aunt Babe made. Mom used a washboard. Our outside toilet was built over the branch—below where we got our wash water. The spring was not deep. It was good water, but it ran off very slowly. And if you'd get two buckets at a time, the spring would be about empty. When you run out and had to go back, why the spring would be full again. A lot of folks got typhoid fever,[14] and a lot of people died. And them that didn't die almost died. It's a wonder we didn't have it, but we didn't.

I went to two-room school out there, four grades in each room. Eight grades in two rooms. We kids had a ball, but I know Mama didn't. Carry water, heat water. She was afraid of snakes, and there'd be snakes in between the logs of the walls.

My brother killed a copperhead one morning. Daddy was in Knoxville. It was in the house, between the logs. I woke up that morning, and I could see that snake between those logs; you could see the daylight out through the logs. And there's that snake crawling. And I got up and told Mama, and Bud got the rifle. Daddy had taught Bud how to shoot the rifle. And he went outside and shot that snake and killed it, although we didn't know he killed it at the time. And after Daddy came home, we told him about it, and he got the snake out. Bud had killed it, and it was a copperhead.

We got bedbugs out there one time. And we had an awful time getting rid of those. We had to take the mattresses off and clean them. I don't remember what we put on them. And the seams and all, you'd have to rub stuff in them and wash everything. I guess they were in the log house. I think we used kerosene to kill them. They bit, and you'd itch. And we got the itch one time [scabies]. I guess we got that at school. We all got it. And Daddy got some medicine, a big jar of medicine, old black medicine that you rubbed on it. You rubbed that on all of us at night and had to leave it on there two or three days. Then you'd take a bath, a pan bath and wash it all off. And we finally got rid of the itch. It was pretty miserable. We kids had a good time [in the country]. Poor old Mama didn't. [laughter]

We went to church at Mount Olive out there in Anderson County. And they had Sunday school on Sunday afternoons at two o'clock. Mama played the piano. And she taught some girls out there to play the piano. And one of them is still at that church playing the piano. I went to a reunion last year out there, a homecoming, and she is still taking some music lessons. She'd been taking them last few years. But she played the piano last summer when I went to the homecoming. I felt proud of that. I said Mama would have felt proud of it because she was still playing the piano.

Then [when we moved back to town] we moved to the Burlington area [an area of northeast Knoxville], and we lived I don't know how many places out there. Up on French Avenue and Speedway Circle and McCalla Avenue and Seahorn Avenue.

Then a friend of my dad's came to my daddy and said, "Pete, I know you need a place to move, and you don't have a place to go."[15] He said, "I've got a house that I'll sell you, and you can just make me monthly payments, like rent on it." Seemed to me like it was about eighteen dollars a month; I don't remember for sure. I can't remember all of it. The man said, "You need a place to go, don't you, Pete?" Daddy was singing at McCalla Avenue Church then. Maybe he made twenty-five dollars a week; I don't remember what he was making. The man said, "I've got a house that you can buy. I'll sell it to you if you like it. You go look at it." Said, "You can pay me monthly." Didn't have to make any down payment. "You just pay me like paying rent." So Daddy took it. And that's the way we lived. That's where we lived when Rachel [her daughter][16] was born. They paid for that house with monthly

Ike and Joe Retta
Petree, Evelyn
Lewellyn's parents,
in front of McCalla
Avenue Baptist Church
in Knoxville, July 21,
1943. Mr. Petree was
choir director at the
church at the time.
*Photograph courtesy
of Evelyn Lewellyn.*

payments. Seemed to me like it was eighteen dollars a month, I can't remember. But he paid that like paying rent. Daddy always remembered that. Might have been twenty-five dollars a month, I don't remember. But they always really appreciated that man. That was the first time they ever owned a house. He paid it off that way. It was 324 Lakeside. Daddy never had money—he wouldn't go in debt.

Then the house next door to them got for sale, and Daddy bought it then. We moved in it then, and rented the other one. And Daddy decided he liked the other one better, so Mama started moving back into 324, and Dad changed his mind. And it is tore down now, but 328 Lakeside is still there. That's the one that caught on fire in the kitchen.

When we moved back to town, Mama started cooking in the lunchroom at Fairgarden School. We lived on French Avenue right near there; I was in high school when we lived there. When the youngest one [Petree child] got big enough to go to school, she started cooking in the lunchroom out there. She started to wash dishes. Then she was a lunchroom cook for years, and then was a manager until she got down sick with neuritis and got all crippled up. Neuritis is similar to arthritis, but it's in the nerves. She couldn't stand

Evelyn Petree at the time of
her graduation from Knoxville
High School, 1942. *Photograph
courtesy of Evelyn Lewellyn.*

up. That's about the time I got out of high school when she got down with
that. It just took time [to get well]. She went to the doctor and took some gold
treatments, and we prayed. And she finally got over it.

But the house caught on fire one year when we lived on Lakeside. It
burned the kitchen. It didn't destroy the house; it damaged the kitchen. And
Mama had such a mess there to clean up, all that smoke; and she was trying
to work and raise five kids. And she thought that maybe it [stress] was what
caused the neuritis.

After working in school lunchrooms, Mama worked in Knoxville City
Hall kitchen. She liked that kind of work. She worked at Maryville College
one or two summers at a children's summer camp.

Oh yeah, Daddy used to fix our old shoes. He had a last.[17] He put our
shoes on there and got leather to patch our shoes with. And you could buy a
pair of shoes for fifty cents or a dollar then. And lots of times the soles would
be out of my shoes, and he'd put cardboard in our shoes. Line our shoes with
cardboard. Till that cardboard would wear out, and then he'd put a new piece
of cardboard in it. Sometimes he'd fix our shoes; if he could get the leather,
he'd fix them. Leather and nails and hammer. Sometimes we wore our shoes
with holes in the bottom of them. But it didn't hurt [their feet] then. It would
kind of hurt now, wouldn't it?

Evelyn Petree Lewellyn
enjoys a family Christ-
mas gathering at her
home, 2001. *Photograph
courtesy of Rachel
Lewellyn Walker*

I guess that's the reason they were so close with their money. Whenever Daddy would get any money, he'd save it; he wouldn't hardly spend it. I'd say, "Daddy, buy yourself a new car." He said, "I've been so used to not spending money, I can't. I don't need a new car." He was just not used to spending money; he'd save it. I guess it was a good thing. When he died, [he had] the money from selling the farm in Anderson County and what little money he'd saved up, and he drew a veteran's pension from World War I. And Social Security. Mama had got all the papers and information together where he could draw his Social Security; she already drew Social Security. With the Social Security check and veteran's pension check and what income he had saved coming in from selling the farm, we had enough to take care of him for as long as lived and had a little left when he died. And he lived a long time after he got sick.

Daddy always did put a tenth in church. They did, no matter how little they had, they put a tenth of it in church. So when I started taking care of his money, I continued to do the same thing. And I felt like that was the reason he had enough to last him. I just thought there'd be enough there to last him. I'd give it to some church: our church or wherever he belonged. When he was in the nursing home, he wasn't capable of knowing what went on with his money. He didn't realize I was doing that, and I didn't ask him because he wouldn't have understood. But I did that, because I knew he always did that. And when I started to work for a dime an hour, I put a tenth of it in church. Just always did that; we still do it.

The first place I worked was Easy Way Dime Store. I made ten cents an hour. I'd work after school and during Christmas when I got sixteen. I went from Easy Way to Miller's.[18] I was in high school then. I took retail training in school. I could go to school half a day and go to work half a day. I could walk out to Miller's from Knoxville High School. I usually rode the streetcar home. Car tokens were four cents a piece for school, a ticket, four cents a trip. Someway I managed to have enough, I guess I bought them myself at least part of the time, tickets to ride the streetcar. I did walk a few times. But that was mostly because I wanted to. But I'd walk from the high school to Miller's. It was about four or five miles to where we lived then. Tokens were six cents except for school. Worked till closing time and during Christmas. I'd make twenty-five cents an hour then. Bought my clothes and had my spending money. Bought my high school ring, which was $6.72. I still have the ring. And I couldn't go to the prom. I didn't have the money or know how to dance. Then I went to Standard Knitting Mills, and I went to work at forty cents an hour. I worked there a while.

Then the war started, and I got on at ALCOA and I started out at sixty cents an hour there. I took tests, and I made good on a mechanical test. I first worked in layout; that was also in the machine shop. Then I transferred to the machine shop toolroom when the job became open. I rode a work bus from Knoxville. You went down to the bus station and caught it every night. I worked the night shift, and I'd ride the bus to ALCOA. And then cousin Wilma and I got us a room over there in Alcoa. Lived in that together and walked to work or sometimes rode the bus. She got on at ALCOA, too. She got on before I did. And she worked longer than I did. She worked out at the plant for years. And I haven't worked out since. [laughter] Been working, but not public work.[19] Wilma's sister, Thelma, worked, too.

Of course, [the Anderson County house] was my daddy's, the house Daddy was born in, but there was eight of the children [his brothers and sisters] still living, and he bought all of their parts out, except Mary's. It was just not much money, because he didn't have much, and nobody else did either. But he bought all the parts of it except one, Aunt Mary's. She lived in St. Louis. She married a serviceman. I don't know how, but he died young. And she would not sell hers. Daddy offered to cut it off, measure it off for her and give her what she wanted, and she wouldn't do that. She would not pay taxes on it. She would not do anything. She wouldn't even answer his letters. So, she still owned her eighth of it, but he bought all the other parts. And Mama got to worrying about it when she got down sick with cancer in the late '60s. She worried there would be a problem with selling it after they died. So she got Daddy to sell it. The only way he could sell it was to do it through court, because Mary wouldn't sell hers. The court, they auctioned it off. And he took one-eighth of the money, subtracted for taxes down through the years and sent her a check for the rest of it. I don't remember how much it was. She never did write him or acknowledge receiving the check. We's afraid she'd write a letter and have a fit you know, but she never tried anything. Well, they'd write each other letters once in a while. Or she'd be complaining about something. He'd get mad and wouldn't write her for a while, and then he'd write again.

But she died up there in Missouri. She died up there all alone. She had one son who was a diabetic and an alcoholic who died before her. Mary and husband and son are buried at Mount Pleasant [Cemetery] in Anderson County. I suppose she died of old age. Aunt Mary lost both legs before she died in the nursing home. And then her oldest son died. The only time I remember seeing him, I guess, maybe not the only time, but the last time I saw him was when she and her son came down and stayed with us in the log house. She was so particular with him. And she wouldn't open the windows in her apartment in St. Louis, afraid the germs would get in the house. I guess that's some of where Winifred[20] gets it. She's all the time worrying about the pollution and stuff.

Daddy's brothers and sisters all died according to their age. Daddy was telling me, "They all died according to age, and I guess I'll be the next one." And he was. I've got all of Aunt Pearl's[21] letters. I've got stacks of them. And she tells about how it was out in Anderson County. I've saved them. Now they're funny. You may have read some of them. And I had saved them. I've always wished she could've written a book. 'Cause she could write. She could've written a book about how it was out there [on the farm in Anderson County]. It was funny but interesting, too.

And then, [I remember] Daddy telling about some of things that happened in the log house before he went to Knoxville. When he got old enough, he went to Knoxville and started going to school and trying to study and get some work at whatever he could get to do. And he said he came home drunk one night, and when he come in—and they didn't have electricity, you know —and he stumbled over the churn. And he told it lots of times. And his mother said, "I thought I brought you up for something better than that." I guess she knew he had been drinking. [laughter] Daddy never drank, but I guess [he did] when he was young. He stumbled over the churn, and she said, "I thought I raised you for better than that." They [the brothers and sisters] all left, about all of them did except Aunt Alice and Aunt Babe,[22] who remained in Anderson County. The others went to the city or north to find work.

Aunt Babe was the one that was married to Uncle Moss who worked for the WPA. Aunt Alice lived on the other side of the ridge. And she married Uncle Brad. She didn't get along with the rest of the family. I never knew exactly all the details of it, but they didn't have nothing to do with Aunt Alice. They said she put on a washing on the day of her mother's funeral and didn't go to the funeral.[23] Didn't go to the funeral.

We recently found out that her son, Orrin Long, lives in Andersonville. And when Bill was over there a few weeks ago, Orrin showed him an obituary out of the paper, and he said, "That's my half-sister. I've been to her funeral." We didn't know he had a half-sister. The family didn't like it because Aunt Alice married Brad, who had a child by an unwed mother. All these years we didn't know about it. And of course, when I talked to him again, I asked him about it. He said, "Yeah." He didn't know it till they were old. But the family knew it, I guess, but nobody ever told him. Finally somebody told him. Some girl had a baby by his daddy before his daddy married Aunt Alice. He never married the girl. So I wonder if that's maybe the reason that Aunt Alice's mother might not have liked Uncle Brad and didn't want her to marry him. That might have had something to do with it. But, finally somebody told Orrin about it, and he went to see her [the half-sister]. She was in the nursing home. They would talk and visit, and she died recently. And he said that they [Orrin's family members] told him that Aunt Alice and Uncle Brad went and tried to get this child [the half-sister]. They wanted to have that child and raise it. But the mother wouldn't give it up. . . . Thinking back, I wonder if that might have had something to do with it. Maybe Aunt Alice's mother didn't want her to marry Uncle Brad. And Aunt Alice and Uncle Brad just farmed out there. The house is there. It's falling down. If you'd like to go out and look at it, I'll take you out there.

But the house Daddy bought, the old log house, was at one time a church. That's what Aunt Babe told us. Now I don't remember that. She said before the Petree family lived in it, it was a church. It might have been while they were living in it. Maybe they had church there when they were living in it. I didn't know about that. There's nobody left to ask. But they called it Green Door Church. And you could still see patches of green paint on that door. I can remember that paint being there. It might have been while they were living in it, or before, I don't know which. And then, Daddy's daddy gave the land that Mount Olive Church is now built on. It joined the Petree property.

I wish that some of our family could have bought that. That house, I've been told, was reconstructed. The people that bought it reconstructed it near

Oak Ridge. I never did look it up. I thought I would, but I never did. I thought it might be at the Appalachian Museum. But Orrin Long knows that John Rice Irwin, director of the Museum of Appalachia.[24] He called over there and talked to him to see if he had bought it. Thought it could have been reconstructed there, but he said it wasn't. He didn't buy that one.

Aunt Babe was Dad's oldest sister. Her real name was Martha, which she never liked. Aunt Babe lived out there, the property's still there, but the house isn't. Aunt Babe and Uncle Moss farmed. Well, mostly Aunt Babe farmed. Uncle Moss, he sat on the porch. Apparently Moss wasn't much on manual labor, so Babe did most all of the farmwork.

And she got down sick, and her husband, Moss, died. Her daughter, Zelma, said, "Mama, how would you like for us to sell this and go to Norris[25] and buy us a little house that's got electricity and a bathroom and conveniences?" And said she just knew her mama would pitch a fit and say, no, she'd never leave that place. She said, "I think I'd like it!" So that's what they did. They sold it. They bought her a little house in Norris. And she took care of Aunt Babe until she died. Zelma is dead, too. Zelma willed that house to Uncle Lonz.[26] He sold it later.

And Babe's hair: she said she never washed it in her lifetime that I know of unless they did it when she got older. She had long hair. She'd let it down about once a week. Comb it. And she cleaned it with meal some way. Put meal in it. Somehow she did it. And it was pretty hair. Had little waves in it. And about once a week or ever so often, she'd let that hair down and comb it. And we kids would watch her. And she'd clean it and put it back up. Put it up in a ball here in the back of her head. And can you imagine her working in the garden and farm and the cornfield and the barn and the cattle, never washing her hair? I don't remember smelling it, but I was a child then.

But anyway, I started to tell you about Loss. Aunt Babe's other son was Loss. He married, and they didn't have any children. And he disappeared two or three different times. He'd be gone for several years, and Aunt Babe wouldn't know if he died or what. He never had kids, but his second wife had a child [from another marriage]. He had a stepchild when he got older. But he'd disappear for a few years at a time, and Aunt Babe wouldn't know where he was. She wouldn't know if he was dead. I know she wondered if he was dead. And he wouldn't contact her. And all at once, he'd show up. Stay on for a few years. They'd think he was going be all right, and he'd leave again. Wouldn't know if he was dead or alive, and he'd show up. He did that two or three different times, I remember that. His first wife finally died. And finally he married somebody else. And she had a child, and Loss died.

He's buried out there where they are. His [second] wife had no interest in the family whatsoever; she was a wife he married in later years.

She [Aunt Babe] had the old family Bible. I've got it in there now. And I assume that Loss had it. Anyway, after he died, his second wife had it. And Uncle Lonz wanted it, Daddy's brother. But she [the second wife] would not part with it. I don't know why, but she wouldn't part with it. And Uncle Lonz had a picture of Loss, that was my cousin, that she wanted. So finally, Uncle Lonz made a deal with her. That he would give her that picture of Loss, it was an eight-by-ten, if she would let him have that family Bible. Well, they did. So he got the family Bible. And he gave it to my daddy. And he said, "Now when you're gone, it's Evelyn's." And Daddy took it, and now I've got it.

NOTES

1. I. C. "Ike" Petree had grown up on a farm in rural Anderson County.

2. These brothers and sisters were named for various relatives and famous people admired by Ike and Joe Retta Petree. Evangeline Booth was the fourth general of the Salvation Army. Enrico Caruso was an opera singer.

3. Her father would move the family into his childhood home on the farm in Anderson County. By this time, I. C. Petree's parents had died, and his brothers and sisters had all moved away, leaving the family home empty.

4. Her father's sister. The Dews sometimes gave the Petrees financial assistance.

5. The Goodstein family was part of Knoxville's small but thriving Jewish community. In the 1920s and 1930s, most of them were merchants and businesspeople. Most lived on the east side of Knoxville, many in the same neighborhood as the Petrees. For more on Knoxville's Jewish community, see Wendy Lowe Bessman, *A Separate Circle: Jewish Life in Knoxville, Tennessee* (Knoxville: University of Tennessee Press, 2001).

6. A Knoxville grocery store chain.

7. Evelyn's uncle Henry worked in the "car barns," the maintenance facility for city streetcars.

8. Her mother's brother.

9. Another of her mother's brothers.

10. Boots is Evelyn's younger sister, JoAnn, and Dude is her younger brother, Richard.

11. It was against the law for someone who was not a licensed funeral director to work on the bodies.

12. In contrast to the countryside where families brought the deceased home to lie in state and to receive mourners, in southern cities families generally received friends at a funeral home before the funeral and held funerals in churches.

13. A cast-iron cookstove that sat on a tabletop and burned wood.

14. Typhoid fever was caused by drinking contaminated water.

15. "Pete" was another of I. C. Petree's nicknames.

16. Evelyn and Bill's daughter, Rachel, was born during the war in 1944.

17. A last is a cobbler's tool. It is made of cast iron and resembles an upside-down foot. A cobbler, or an amateur like I. C. Petree, can place a shoe over the last, sole side up, to work on it.

18. A Knoxville department store.

19. Farm people frequently use the term "public work" to refer to jobs away from home and farm.

20. Evelyn's sister.

21. Evelyn's father's sister.

22. Evelyn's father's sisters.

23. To "put on a washing" was to light a fire under the outdoor wash kettle in order to begin the wash, an all-day job. Putting on a washing the day of one's mother's funeral would have been an extremely disrespectful act, indicative of deep estrangement.

24. The Museum of Appalachia in Norris, Tennessee, is a living history museum that seeks to recreate and preserve aspects of Appalachian rural life. Museum director John Rice Irwin purchased many log buildings in east Tennessee and reconstructed them on the museum site.

25. Norris was the model town built by TVA near its Norris Dam site in Anderson County.

26. Evelyn's father's brother.

Martha Alice West

MARTHA ALICE WEST was born into a tenant farming family in Loudon County, Tennessee. Her family raised tobacco, corn, and a subsistence garden. She remembered farm life as hard and never wanted to go back to it once she was grown. In fact, she devoted little of her interview to describing her childhood on the land.

She married in 1937, and her husband worked at the John J. Craig and Co. marble quarry in Friendsville, Tennessee. They had two sons, Wayne and Bill. When Wayne was ten and Bill was fifteen, Martha Alice West's first husband died. Using the proceeds from her late husband's life insurance policy, she paid off the small house the couple had bought in Friendsville. Mrs. West supported her sons and her widowed mother with Social Security plus a job at a dry-cleaning establishment in Alcoa, Tennessee. The dry-cleaning business where Mrs. West worked was near McGhee Tyson Air National Guard base, and here she met her second husband, a career air force man, "Sarge" McDaniel.

McDaniel died in the 1980s, and Martha Alice married a third time—to John West, a retired farmer from Blount County. The couple lived in Mrs. West's Friendsville home where they raised huge gardens. Until very late in life, John West continued to raise and sell garden produce, and Mrs. West assisted him.

I interviewed the Wests together at their home, and John West dominated the conversation.[1] Martha Alice West's story is interesting both because of her family's tenant farming status, her conscious rejection of farm life, and her experience as a single mother. We spoke on August 12, 1993. In the summer of 1994, I sent the Wests a transcript of the interview. Mrs. West made a couple of corrections and returned the signed release forms but not the family history forms.

My husband don't like to talk about [the Depression] too much because he's a Republican. [laughter]

I grew up in Loudon County. The Depression didn't hurt us, because we made everything. We rented, you know.[2] We got a fourth [of the crop]. Now we made it all right ourselves. But I did see people that would just brown their flour in a skillet. Just dry. They didn't have any grease, but they had milk from the cow. They'd brown it and then pour their milk in and make gravy out of it like that. We didn't [lack for food]. Even our chickens and eggs, we had on the farm—we got half of those.[3] If it was tobacco or something like that, they got a half of it. It was 'cause of they way you had to hand it off.[4] You made good money out of tobacco. Well, it was good then according to what everything else was. Overalls was just ninety-eight cents a pair. And what you called a jump jacket [denim jacket] to go with them was ninety-eight cents each.

Then the days the men weren't working in the crops, they worked in town for fifty cents a day from daylight to dark. They brought their own meals.

We raised everything. There was no use of wasting anything.

The type of soap you made was according to what kind of grease you had to make it with. We had hog scraps. But it was good soap. We washed on a board. We just had two cisterns, one at the house and one at the barn. And then we had barrels we'd catch rain water in, and if it wouldn't rain, we'd be out of water. You see you had to heat your water in the wash kettle. You know all that. And scrub them on the board. First you'd boil them and take them out and scrub them and then rinse them through two waters, a clear water and a bluing water. And that's what you did to do your laundry. Every time you got a bunch dirty.

I married the first time in '37, August 14 of 1937. My husband, Bill and Wayne's dad, worked at the marble quarry. Here's some I had saved [displays some of her husband's check stubs]. Here's where he had worked fifty-two hours for $15.42. That was 1940.

I never did like farming much. When we married in '37, I said, "I never aim to farm again." And here I am. Well, I'm not married to a farmer, but we've had some big gardens. See, he's my third husband. [laughter]

Now I've not been divorced, you know. Well, see Bill and Wayne's daddy, he was just thirty-nine when he died. Wayne wasn't hardly ten and Bill was fifteen. I got by because of that man right over there [points to a picture of a man in uniform on the wall]. That was my second husband, Sarge. He was in the air force, and he was stationed out here at McGhee Tyson, and I was working down there at the dry cleaners, and he'd bring his dry cleaning in. And that's where he met me. And he helped me. I guess I raised them some way or another.

Well, we had Social Security back then. Both of the boys drew and got, well, a little over eighty dollars a month. You would think it was a lot then, but it don't amount to much to live on with boys in school. And my mother, of course, she lived with us. But, well, back then, you'd go on welfare they called it; it wasn't Social Security.[5] She drawed a little on that. Of course, we made it. Of course, when I married him [Sarge], that helped me a lot.

I got some insurance on their daddy. And I paid the rest of the second and third mortgage that was on this house. Now you've got to have something to live on. I divided the rest of it; I gave Bill half of it, and Wayne half of it, and I didn't keep any for myself because I wanted them to have it. And Bill used his about going to college, but Wayne got a car with his because he said he couldn't go to college; he just couldn't make it and no use in trying. He was the only one that drove a car to school.

NOTES

1. For more on my interview with John West, see "Culling Out the Men from the Boys," *Oral History Review* (summer 2000): 1–20.

2. Mrs. West refers to her father as a "renter," but she actually describes a share-cropping arrangement. Renters were landless tenants who paid cash to rent their farmland. Renters usually possessed some savings to carry them from year to year, and they usually owned their own tools and livestock and provided their own seed and fertilizer. Sharecroppers, by contrast, were landless tenants who owned few or no tools, no livestock, and could not afford to provide their own seed and fertilizer. The landlord provided them with seed, fertilizer, tools, the use of livestock, a house, and sometimes a barn. In lieu of rent, they returned a share of the crop to the landlord.

3. Apparently the arrangement with the landlord was that the family would give him half of its produce in return for his providing land, house, barn, livestock, and supplies.

4. Tobacco was an unusually labor-intensive crop. Because it involved more labor, the tenant family was entitled to keep a larger share of the crop. "Handing off" tobacco referred to the process of separating the leaves, "grading" them for quality level, and packing leaves of the same "grade" or quality together for sale. The process had to be completed by hand.

5. Probably Supplemental Security Income for the elderly.

Ruth Hatchette McBrayer

RUTH HATCHETTE MCBRAYER was born on the South Carolina side of that state's border with North Carolina. Her family made a living as general farmers in this rural community known as State Line. McBrayer's mother died when she was seven. Since the older children were in school or working, her father sent young Ruth to live with an older married sister in Spartanburg, South Carolina, throughout most of her childhood. Here she attended school, visiting the farm and her family on weekends and in the summer.

Mrs. McBrayer attended college at Winthrop University and taught school for a time before she married Vernon Eugene Hatchette, Jr., in 1933. The son of a prominent farmer and businessman in the tiny town of Chesnee, South Carolina, Hatchette worked in his father's car dealership. During World War II, Gene Hatchette became a full-time farmer because farmers were considered essential war workers and were exempt from the military draft. He tried his hand at raising chickens and working one of Cherokee County's first peach orchards on his family's land.

By the early 1920s, upstate South Carolina cotton farmers were suffering from the triple ravages of the boll weevil, low commodity prices, and severe erosion. Seeking to diversify their farming operations in order to remain on the land, several Spartanburg, Cherokee, and Greenville County farmers began to experiment with peach orchards. Encouraged by agricultural extension agents and by progressive farmers in their midst, they hoped that peaches would provide them with a more predictable and stable cash crop.[1]

Like many of their neighbors, by the early 1940s the Hatchettes had entered the peach-farming business. In addition to a packing shed that his father ran in Chesnee, Gene Hatchette built a large packing shed on the farm in 1945. Here, he planned to pack the harvest from his own orchards and those of neighbors with smaller operations. By this time, Ruth Hatchette and her brother co-owned another orchard, which the brother operated.

In 1947, Gene Hatchette died suddenly, and Ruth found that she was deeply in debt from the peach-shed operation and from the large, two-story, brick and Tudor-style home her husband had built for her. She set out to pay off his debts with proceeds from the orchard. She was successful. Within a few years, Ruth Hatchette was among the leading peach growers in the upstate.

In 1969, Hatchette remarried. Her second husband, Charles McBrayer, was a livestock dealer. She also raised a niece whose parents had died.

She farmed until the mid 1980s when she closed her packinghouse, rented much of her land, and retired. She still lives in the home her first husband built in a woodland on their farm in Cherokee County. I interviewed Mrs. McBrayer there on August 20, 1998. Books and family photos lined the comfortable den where we talked. Most of Mrs. McBrayer's interview focused on her years as a peach farmer, and her descriptions of learning the peach-farming business and of relations with her farmworkers are striking.

I was born on a farm in the State Line community, which is in Cherokee County. I was the baby of a family of seven. My mother died when I was seven.

I was in school [during the Depression], and of course, my daddy was a farmer and didn't make a lot of money. After mother died we moved into a smaller home. We had a big, two-story home with porches all around it, and we had a fire. The big old home burned, and we lived in a smaller home on the highway, which was built by my brother, who later moved to Florida. We occupied that.

I never felt that it [the Great Depression] was really hard because I was the baby of a family of seven, and I went to school in Spartanburg and came home on the weekends, and I was treated like a guest. I never felt the pressures of the Depression like most of the family might have. They tell me that I had never known how to work, but I learned how to work. I did learn how to work. I did work. Worked hard.

[During the Depression] the bank closed in Chesnee. My first husband's father was the president of the bank, I believe, at that time. And I didn't know much about that at the time; I was away in school. But I did hear things. I heard that I had an old great-uncle that had never been married and had a good bit of money and had it in the bank of Chesnee, and he carried a gun around, he was so infuriated about the bank closing.

But I didn't realize. I guess it was bad, but I guess I was happy as a youngster and growing up. I had two brothers that were just older than I, and I had lots of friends, so I didn't realize it was too much of a hardship. I know it was. My daddy didn't have a lot of money, but we had a good time.

My father farmed all of his life until he was old. He did a little bit of everything, I think. Cotton, corn, wheat, grains; he did a little bit of all kind of farming. And he had a sawmill. He helped saw the lumber for the first church around there, the State Line Baptist Church. And it [the lumber] was cut on his land, and you'd have it donated. You're not old enough to know about all that. That was hardship times. That's how you got your church. People donated the land and the wood and did the labor.

So Daddy worked hard. Mother died when I was seven, and that's why I was sent to Spartanburg to live. After my mother's death, I entered Spartanburg schools in the third grade and continued in Spartanburg schools until I was in high school. I lived with my older sister, who was living in Spartanburg. She had married the year my mother died, and I lived with her. I attended Southside Grammar School. I was very unhappy. But it was good for me because I learned to fend for myself and went to a better school than I would have if I had stayed home in the country.

I graduated [from high school] in 1930 and went to college [at Winthrop University in Rock Hill, South Carolina].

I taught in North Carolina, [then] married Vernon Eugene Hatchette, Jr. in 1933. He and his father were in the automobile business. A Ford business in Chesnee. After I stopped teaching, I worked there [at the car dealership]. I didn't know what I was doing, but I was there. Daddy Hatchette, my late husband's father, had the [peach] shed on the railroad in Chesnee.

During World War II, my first husband did not have to go into service, and we were fortunate there. Of course, nobody wanted to go, and he didn't want to go. But at that time, he and his father had the Ford business in Chesnee, and he disassociated himself with the Ford business and became a full-fledged farmer, and he really didn't know much about farming. We tried to grow chickens. We built a little chicken house, and actually we just almost heated those chickens so hot they died. We really didn't know. We had a man on the farm that did, though, and tried to help us, but still we didn't know much.

But we never had no trouble getting help. At that time I was not working in the peaches. I don't remember exactly. Well, we had local help, right here in this community. See people were poor at that time, very poor. I remember Mother Hatchette saying that there was a time when people would work for ten cents an hour, I believe.

But during the Second World War was a serious time in Daddy Hatchette's life. He was ill with cancer. And he was operated on twice at Duke and we had him to Richmond, Virginia, [to doctors] and stayed there with him a month. I was not working at all in the peaches at that time. And Daddy

Hatchette had made the remark that just about the time that [they] was in a position financially, it looked like he was going to be taken, and he was.[2] Gene's father died in 1944.

This would be a little interesting: one year—this was the first year that I ever worked at the peach shed. It was on the railroad tracks in Chesnee in an old fertilizer warehouse. And Daddy Hatchette had become quite ill, so Gene was put down here to look after the orchard, which he didn't know much about. I was put in the packinghouse to look after it, which I didn't know much about. We had a man from Florida to operate the shed. I was to sell the culls and keep the office.[3] As it happened that year, we were packing for ourselves and for a Mr. Deason, for my brother, and I think that was maybe all. And for some reason—we must have not done a good job growing peaches that year— and we had oodles and oodles of culls. And not very many customers [for culls]. They were packed from the floor to the ceiling. . . . It was cramped quarters. I knew that I couldn't do anything with those peaches. I just didn't know what to do. I don't know how I came to do this, but I got on the telephone calling people, and I called a winery in Charlotte. I do not know to this day how I did that. And my brother and I owned this orchard together, and he was a deacon in the church and very religious and really a good man.[4] [But] I called the Tennent Brothers Winery in Charlotte. And they were interested. And they came. One of the owners came talked with me. And I felt so inadequate. But I must have done a pretty good job. He sent barrels—big wooden barrels—and big trucks down. And I sold those culls to Tennent Brothers Winery. And then, see we were adjacent to the depot. I got permission from the depot officials to put those drums in a part of their depot, and we would fill those drums with our bad peaches, and Tennent Brothers would come pick them up. Why I did all these things I don't know, how I did them. I guess it was 'cause I was so young and venturesome. We made more money off of the culls than what we packed.[5] When I gave brother the money, he said, "Why, Ruth," he says, "I'm not going to do this anymore. Don't sell our peaches anymore to a winery." But that was a good sale that year. And I did buy some of the wine that Tennent Brothers sold. [laughs] It was good. Yes, it was good. I don't know whether they still make peach wine or not.

Gene, my late first husband, built a peach shed in 1945, but after Daddy Hatchette's death, the responsibility of all this was just too much for Gene. He had been protected for all his life. And he missed his father tremendously. And he had had a serious breakdown while I was at Winthrop, and he began to have troubles again after his father's death. And he had had some health problems and died in 1947.

And then the farm and everything was just dumped on me. He was an only child. An only child and an only grandchild, and so I was lost. I didn't know what to do really. But fortunately, I learned. And with a lot of good help, I paid his debts, which at that time seemed very, very large. Now in comparison to today, they wouldn't be so large. But I got those debts paid. And I decided that if I could make that much money—I was so discouraged and so grieved that I thought if I ever got his debts paid that I was just going to go somewhere else—and after I did that [paid off his debts], I thought, well, if I can make that much money, I'll make some for myself.

One thing that's nothing more than to prove how ignorant I was: [one year] we had a freeze. The peaches were killed, I thought. And I had a peach grower friend that came over [to look at my orchard]. We walked down through the Red Haven field, and they kept looking at the field and kept looking at the field and kept looking at the field.[6] And my mind was made up. They were all gone. They kept telling me that "No, you have a peach crop. This is a crop of peaches." Finally I said—this proves how ignorant I was—I said, "Well, I know peaches when I see them." And I had a beautiful crop of peaches that year. [laughs] The good Lord had thinned them exactly right.

So I became interested in my work. And I worked day and night for several years. I worked in the peach orchard and ran the packinghouse.

I had many challenges though. All the men in the community believed that I would fail, and they would own this property. And I had one friend who came to me and warned me that people were—his words were, "They are staying awake at night trying to figure out how they're going to get everything you have." That made me more determined, of course.

My late husband had a beautiful young orchard at the time of his death, which was just coming into a good bearing stage of peaches. So I was attributed with being extremely smart. I didn't deserve all that because the orchard was already planted, and the trees were good. But of course, I did have the desire to learn. I attended many Clemson meetings and all the peach meetings and conventions that were afforded me, and I studied.[7]

I worked with the men. I learned to prune. I learned to thin. I actually didn't know much. I had sat in the car when my husband would give directions to the men as we were maybe leaving to go someplace, but I didn't know I absorbed any of it. But actually I did. I had absorbed some.

I was fortunate to engage some good men to work here as foremen on the place and that I had two brothers that were retired that during harvest season would help oversee the harvesting. At first, I had a man from Florida, who was an experienced shed operator. After I learned all about the shed, I operated it myself. I had not worked in the shed very much. His father [Ruth's father-in-law] had become ill and had died of cancer, and I had begun to work in the shed, sort of in the office. But then I began to get to do a little bit of everything. I had said to my husband the year before he died, "I have learned to do everything in this shed except set those machines." And I said, "I'm going to learn to do that." So I would be standing on a peach box with maybe a sizer in my hands, setting those machines, in all the years that followed, those were the words that I remembered.[8] [laughs]

They were good years, hard years. At that time, we didn't have air conditioning in all of the house, and when we would have big refrigerated trucks running over at the shed, if the windows were up, I could hear if that truck went off, you know if the motor stopped running. Then I knew I had to get up and get somebody to start the motor or the peaches would go bad. So, of course my mind was fully on the operation. I dedicated myself to the operation.

I had an interesting experience with a man who was from Charlotte. He came by the office and wanted to buy a load of fruit. He offered me so much more money than I had been quoted that summer that I sold a little to him, which I should not have done, though I called my broker in Spartanburg and more or less asked and told at the same time that I had done it.[9] So when the returns came, I was paid considerably less [than I was promised] by this man from Charlotte, and of course, I would not cash the check. I called him, and he called me an impulsive woman. He said, "Lay the telephone down; I can hear you all the way from Chesnee." I was talking so loud. [laughs] I mailed the check back to him and threatened him. So he paid me the full amount. But he was testing me. Later he came to visit me at my home during the winter and wanted me to associate myself with him. And he would operate the shed, he would operate the orchard, he would furnish all the money that I needed.[10] And I looked at him. I was young, very young. I looked at him straight on, and I said, "I own this now. But if I did that, you would own me." I said, "I appreciate your offer, but no thanks." I guess the good Lord helped me. But later we were good friends. He's dead.

But it was hard. It was real hard. I would get up at five in the morning, sometimes even four in the morning. At one time, it was three straight days and two nights. I packed peaches for other people as well. We had one of the first sheds in this area. Every peach grower didn't have a shed of his own at that time. So we had lots of peaches to pack. We packed first in old-fashioned packing. We'd bring the peaches in and put the peaches in rings and kept them on bushel baskets and half-bushel baskets. And then there was cardboard boxes. And we also used wooden boxes.

I did pack for one of the men that became a big grower, Buck Price, before he got his packinghouse. I packed for his cousin, another Mr. Price. I packed for Mr. W. H. Gettys, who had real fine peaches. They had lumber-yards and such but they also farmed, but they stopped growing pretty soon after. . . . I packed for my brothers. I had two [brothers] that grew peaches for a little while. They didn't stay in it very long.

It was said one time a long time ago that next to Louis Caggiano, I put up the best pack in the area.[11] I thought that was a compliment. One year I had packed peaches in bushel baskets. They were shipped north in the area of Martha's Vineyard, and I got a letter from this person that wrote me—I had my own personal label and stamp on my packages. And my label was, of course, Hatchette.[12] And this lady wrote me a beautiful letter, which I appreciated very much, and . . . it [the letter] was read one time at one of the peach conventions. She only found one bad peach in our bushel. I really val-ued that letter, and I in return wrote her and thanked her.

I was most fortunate [with my help]. How this came about, my late hus-band had used a man from the Grassy Pond community to help him; he had acted as foreman for him [Gene Hatchette] during the harvesting season. And that man was most helpful in that he knew a black man by the name of Zero Ellis. And I could go down on Sunday evening and tell Uncle Zero that I needed fifty hands in the morning and [that] I would send a truck. And they would be standing on the side of the road [waiting for the truck to pick them up and take them to the peach orchard]. The best help that I've ever in my life seen, and they were dedicated to him. He was a wonderful black man.

Mr. Ellis was a real religious man. And he almost ran a black church by the name of Concord, and I would go before church time on Sunday [to tell him she would need workers on Monday]. And at Sunday service that night, he'd tell everybody to get ready. They lived in Grassy Pond community, which is between here and Gaffney. And the man, usually the foreman that I had, he lived near the peach shed. And we had a big truck that we used for a while to pick up the help. Then later we had a bus, just an old school bus that we used. At one time, I used a crew from Fort Valley, Georgia. And my nephew had a big, big old house that was a good old house, and I housed them, and they all stayed in one big house. We had fifty, maybe more, dif-ferent beds.

Then after he [Mr. Ellis] became incapacitated and the black people be-gan to get better jobs in the different areas of places of work, I used migrant help. And I had several crews of migrant people. One of them was by the name of Hernandez. He was from west Texas. And he would bring all the help that I needed. And we had some in houses on the place—at that time, they were not so strict about the housing for the workers. Later they did pass strict regulations. But all the growers didn't follow them.[13] And sometimes they were unruly. But they were good workers. They were real good workers.

I had said to my husband one time, when he was having a little bit of trouble—I thought he was doing too much for the help. I said, "I will be darned if I would haul them and beg them to work and haul them and pay them and loan them money and do all the things that you do. I just wouldn't do that." You know, I didn't have any experience. I didn't know.

I soon learned. I really soon learned that if they didn't like you, even if they were hungry, they would not work for you. So I went to the field when they went in the morning. I worked. Just any kind of clothes that I needed to wear. And if it were raining, the only way I could get them to pick peaches was to go and pick peaches with them or be in the field with them—I didn't do much picking—until time for the shed to start. It was all right when you had to leave when it was time to operate the shed, and they'd pick on, but I must go in the morning and pick with them until I had to leave. [laughs] So I worked with the people. And really I had respect. I had a lot of respect. They were kind; they were good. Some of them would come back to see me. I was really most fortunate. But I did change. *I* changed. Because I knew that if I didn't change—see, I didn't know the people. They lived down here all their lives, and I had, too. But I really didn't know the people that were going to work in the fields, so I had to learn them and they had to learn me, and they had to like me or they wouldn't bother working.

I had one [fore]man. And he was smart. He was real smart. He said, "Now about the time I get that so-and-so straightened out, you come in and they're not worth a ———— the rest of the day."[14] I began to get so when I'd go, I'd just walk quietly around the rest of the day. Do I think he was right? No doubt he was. But it was hard for me not to, if I saw something I didn't like, it was hard for me not to say that. And if the trees looked good, it was hard for me not to say that. I found this out. If you train somebody right in the beginning, they seldom deviate from that. They may leave off a little, but that was a lesson. I guess he was right.

So I tried hard to do the right thing. It was hard sometimes. It was frustrating. My older sister, who was a lovely lady, but had never worked anywhere. She taught school years ago. She worked in the peach shed. And she said to me one day, "I don't know how you do what you do." I said, "Well, every morning when I get up, I say a little prayer: 'Just please don't let me do anything or say anything today that I ought not to say.'" And it was hard to do the right thing always, and it's hard when things occur to not maybe offend someone. But I guess I had wonderful help, and the men who worked with me—they were very courteous and they would come to me daily to get instructions.

Many of my men were very, very kind and helped me. After the men in the community and around saw that . . . I had the determination and the courage and the ability, I guess, to do it, they began to try to help me.

At [Peach Growers Association] meetings at my peach shed, [the extension agent would come]. We would get chairs, and men would come speak. We'd have programs, and we'd have pruning demonstrations in my fields.[15]

Some years we were broke, you know, and didn't have a peach crop. . . . But I paid Gene's debts and, let's see, '47 wasn't a very good year. It was pretty good, I thought it was a lot of money when I got all the returns back, but I didn't finish paying all his debts off until '48. That year [we had a freeze]. Peaches all around me were killed, and mine were not killed. But I guess that was the Lord speaking to me because I had been so sad and so maybe resentful, I don't know what the word is. And then I was thankful; I was thankful that I was fortunate. I had a good year that year. And then I believe we had good years for a while after that.

But the years got leaner and leaner. I operated very frugally. I didn't buy a lot of new tractors like a lot of people did. I operated with as few spraying machines and equipment as I could get by. I did not buy a lot. I bought what was necessary and only what necessary. But I did buy the first air cooler. I bought the first irrigation system in this section, and people came from all around to see us out there in those fields, barefoot in our jeans and with our tractors waiting for the water to come on.

[The extension agent] encouraged me to buy this irrigation system, which was very profitable because you could irrigate in the evening and up into the night and you could increase the size of peaches by an one-eighth of an inch. But irrigation paid off. And I did get the first irrigation system in this section. I'm not talking about Caggianos. I'm talking about right in this section.[16] And then I put in the first air cooler. [Later] I did not get any new mechanical cooler like everyone else. But the orchard was getting smaller, and I was getting older. And everybody was encouraging me to quit work. So I did update with [peach] washers and new sizers. . . . I revamped the shed, but I did not put in mechanical coolers that I really did need to put in.

Clemson recommended that we plant vetch in the orchard, and whatever they would suggest, usually I tried it. And with my own two hands, I treated that vetch [seed] with something black to sterilize it, I believe. And then we planted it in the orchards. When that vetch came up, it was the most beautiful thing you've ever seen. It blooms a purple bloom. Are you familiar with it? It climbed into the trees. Of course, then Clemson recommended that it be destroyed. But it was a pretty vine, and I really do think it put nutrients of some sort into the soil. But I tried a lot of things that Clemson recommended.

We sold some peaches to my brother that I was in halves with. His wife's people were in the peach-canning business, Jones Canners. And we sold some peaches to the canneries. Not that particular time but later. I tried a little bit of everything. A little bit of everything. [laughs]

I had a good friend whose husband was a doctor. And they had a peach orchard. They had farms, and they had a peach orchard. And so after I became so active with the peach business, she was associated with the peach operation. She would take her Cadillac and go around and pick up help in the morning. And she would work with the harvesting. And they did have a peach shed. She and I went together to the peach meetings, which made it very nice. She was a lovely lady, and she would come back, of course, and she would subtly convince her husband [to adopt new technology in his operation]. Those were happy days, happy days, hard working days.

Then [I met] my second husband. His father was a livestock operator back when they had mules and horses for sale. They had big barns, and he would go and take his help—he had twenty-six tenants, I believe, on his farm—and he'd take them up on the train to some part of Tennessee and buy mules and horses, and they'd ride them back through the snow and ice back to his place, to his farm. And I have been told that when they would get back home, that their feet would be frozen to the stirrups. And then in later years, the senior Mr. McBrayer, they would bring them back by train. And people would gather to see them unload at the train station.

So Charles [her second husband] really had a background with animals. And he had a livestock barn in Shelby [North Carolina]. And he came over here looking for property to build a livestock barn.[17] He came, and someone recommended that he might buy some [property] from me. But before I met him, in the morning I would be out getting the help. I always had a station wagon, and I'd get the help, the local help, while the truck would go get the other help. I had a beautiful straw hat that I would wear to kind of keep my hair out of my eyes. And I would meet[18] this man with a Tennessee tag on his car every morning. He'd wave, and I'd wave. I had no idea who he was, but I thought he was a peach tree salesman, since he was from Tennessee.[19] So then, later, I met him when he wanted to buy property to build, he was over here looking around to buy property to build a livestock barn on. Mother Hatchette and I owned property in Chesnee called Chesnee Land Company, and he talked with both of us about buying property in town but later bought about one-fourth of a mile from my home from someone else. And that's how I met him.

When we had our first meeting with him, we didn't really have an office. And Mother Hatchette and I met him and these two men that were with him that we knew in this community at the city hall. I got out and went over to the car, and he immediately got out of the car and stood up, and I thought, "He has pretty nice manners." And I talked with him there about it briefly, that we didn't have any land to sell. So I was a little impressed, besides which he was handsome. And I inquired about him through my brother-in-law who was a banker, and I got a good report. So that's how I met him.

And through the years, we were friends. . . . He had never been married, and I was not wanting to be married; I had business on my mind. But we were real good friends always, and then we were married in 1969 at the home of his sister. We didn't want a church wedding, and I guess I didn't want to be married here at my home. We were planning to go the minister's home, but his sister insisted that we must have at least a home wedding.

He was a livestock operator. He operated the livestock sale barn [in Chesnee]. He used our pasture for steers, and his pastures near the sale barn he used for holding the cattle from the sale until the buyers could send their trucks and pick them up. And that way they could get grass. They could graze, and they could get water. He was a wonderful operator, a very good man, very good man. He died in 1995. I've been most fortunate to have two good husbands.

I had a little niece who had attended Lander [University] and who had graduated from art school in Sarasota, Florida, and was an artist. Her parents were dead, and she lived with me here. Beautiful little black-haired girl. She worked as an artist for Belk's in Charlotte for a while.[20] And I was here alone, and she was in Charlotte working alone. And so she came back home. She married, though, and went to Florida to live. Her husband died after five years, and she came back and worked with me in the peach shed and was a wonderful salesman. She could get a lot of money for the peaches [laughs], for the soft peaches, the ripe peaches, selling them to local reps. We had Georgia Belles near the shed. She could go out and just pick them and sell them right then and that was part of her duty, and she despised it [selling Georgia Belles]. She never ate a Georgia Belle, because she associated it with Georgia Belle sales. She said you could pick them off the tree green and by the time you got to the shed they were too ripe. She couldn't satisfy the customer [with Georgia Belle peaches].[21]

But my niece is dead. We've had lots of deaths in our family. She died in 1994, and Charles died in 1995. So I was lost two that were dear to me, really close together.

Through the years, I got smaller and smaller. I replanted several orchards. The first orchards were the best orchards we had. They were the famous old Elberta, Dixie Gems, Red Havens, Jubilees. Then later varieties were Redskins, Georgia Belles, don't forget Georgia Belles.[22] We planted some orchards, but I replanted them on old ground, some of them, and they do not do well on old ground. Even if you treat it and fumigate it and all that, they don't do well.[23] But after the older orchards began to get less productive, I became a smaller operator.

The heyday in peaches is over for this area. I haven't kept up with the actual prices, but the fertilizer and labor and necessary packaging that you would have to buy is all so expensive, and the freight and the marketability, the brokerage fee. If you want to do hard work, there'd be years that you'd make money. But the young people today, like if I had a son, he would not want to be in the peach business if he grew up in it, because he would know how hard it is. I think it's a wonderful business. And it's a beautiful operation to see the trees in full bloom and the beauty of the trees and the land when it's really growing and underneath the trees, it's real pretty, and when it's loaded with fruit. It's hard, but I don't think you can get the right kind of help. I don't believe you can.

I about stayed in peaches too long, because I didn't have enough good operating orchards to have big production, and then I was losing money. It was costing me too much. In the beginning, I counted 25 percent for expenses and 75 percent profit. Then it got to 50 [percent for expenses], then to 60, then it got to 75, then it was break even, and then it was going the other way, so it was time to quit. Past time to quit for me. Because it's too hard work. And there are other things.

[I still own] all my land. And I rented some for watermelons, and there's pastureland, of course. I don't have cattle anymore. I rent the pastures to people who mow for hay. It's grasses really. It's fescue, and I don't know all the different ones [grasses]. But they mow it and bale it. And I have some soybeans; I lease the land for soybeans. But I'm doing no farming. Well, that's about the history of my peach experience.

Notes

1. For more on peach farming in upstate South Carolina, see Mike Corbin, *Family Trees: The Peach Culture of the Piedmont* (Spartanburg, SC: Hub City Writers Project, 1998), and Walker, chap. 6 in *All We Knew Was to Farm*.

2. Mrs. McBrayer's father-in-law meant that he was finally in a stable financial position.

3. Culls are damaged peaches that cannot be sold for sale as fresh produce. Culls are often used for baby food, canning, and wine making, but they bring a much lower price than first-quality peaches.

4. She means that her brother felt uncomfortable selling his peaches for the production of an alcoholic beverage.

5. They made more revenue from the sale of culls than from the sale of first-quality peaches.

6. Red Havens are a variety of peaches.

7. The South Carolina Agricultural Extension Service was based at Clemson University, the state's land grant institution. South Carolina farm people refer to their extension agents as the "Clemson people."

8. A sizer set the machines to handle peaches of a particular size.

9. Mrs. McBrayer already had a contract to sell all her peaches through a particular agent at a particular price. She violated her agreement with her peach broker when she sold peaches to the Charlotte broker.

10. The broker was offering to serve as Mrs. McBrayer's operating lender, providing money for equipment and operations each year in return for the right to buy all her crop.

11. Louis Caggiano, the child of Italian immigrants, came to Cherokee County early in the twentieth century and became one of the region's top peach farmers. Although most of the Caggiano operation has been sold, a few of Mr. Caggiano's descendents still grow peaches. To "put up the best pack" was to pack peaches so carefully and so well that few spoiled or were damaged in transport.

12. She used a picture of a hatchet on her peach label.

13. By the late twentieth century, the federal government had established labor and housing standards for migrant farm workers, but many peach growers did not follow these standards.

14. In the interview, Mrs. McBrayer paused to indicate the expletive.

15. She hosted these educational opportunities for area peach farmers.

16. The area around Chesnee in Cherokee County. The Caggiano orchards were near Gaffney in Cherokee County.

17. Livestock sales agents ran auctions at which farmers from the surrounding area sold cattle to other farmers, to middlemen, and to meatpackers. The livestock agents needed barns in which to house the cattle until the auction, as well as facilities in which to hold the sale. Mr. McBrayer was looking for property on which to build a new livestock auction barn.

18. "Meet" was local parlance for passing a car going in the opposite direction.

19. Many of the nurseries that provided peach growers with young trees were in Tennessee.

20. The Belk department store chain, which was based in Charlotte.

21. Georgia Belles were a soft variety of peach. They were prized for their sweetness, and many people preferred Georgia Belles for eating raw. However, they bruised easily.

22. All varieties of peaches. Most of these varieties are rarely grown today because the old varieties did not ship well.

23. Peach orchards planted where orchards had previously been located would be susceptible to various plant diseases that might be harbored in the soil.

Mary Webb Quinn

MARY WEBB WAS born in Spartanburg County, South Carolina. She was one of nine surviving children of sharecropping parents, and she remembered a happy childhood focused on hard work on the farm. Like most farmers in the South Carolina piedmont, the Webbs grew cotton for the market and produced most of their own food as well. The years between the two world wars were difficult ones for Spartanburg area farmers. The average value of a Spartanburg County farm fell nearly 50 percent between 1920 and 1930, and nearly 70 percent of its farmers were tenants like the Webb family. In spite of hard times on the farm, Spartanburg County enjoyed a mixed agricultural economy that allowed many rural residents to supplement their incomes with jobs in local textile mills throughout the 1920s. Nonetheless, the Great Depression brought more hard times and reduced employment even in the textile mills. Mrs. Quinn remembered the financial struggles of her childhood, but her most vivid memories were of good times with her family.

Mary Webb Quinn's parents valued education and encouraged her to attend college, providing whatever financial support they could. Working in a shirt factory, Mrs. Webb managed to put herself through Textile Institute [later Spartanburg Methodist College], a two-year college in Spartanburg that offered students the opportunity to combine study with work. After she finished her two-year program, Mary Webb worked for a year to save money toward the rest of her college education. She received a scholarship and a work-study job at Winthrop University, which was then the state-supported women's college in Rock Hill, South Carolina. At Winthrop, she majored in home economics, and after graduation she began to teach school in Chester County.

Although Mrs. Quinn's husband, Eldred, grew up on a nearby farm, the two never met growing up. They, did, however, share relatives by marriage; Mary's aunt had married Eldred's uncle. After high school, Eldred sharecropped for a while and then went to work in a textile mill, working his way up to the skilled position of weaver. Later he worked in a shipyard in Charleston. After Pearl Harbor was bombed, Eldred enlisted in the navy and served in north Africa, participating in the invasion at Casablanca. While there, his parents wrote to tell him that the Webb family, including several single daughters, had moved in next door.

During World War II, writing letters to the "boys overseas" was considered a patriotic act, and young women often corresponded with soldiers whom they had never met. Soon Mary Webb began to write to Eldred Quinn, and they continued to correspond as he moved into the European theater. When Eldred Quinn returned home on leave in November 1944, the two met and became better acquainted. They continued to correspond, and they married two years after the war ended.

Mary Quinn taught school for several years after their marriage, while Eldred used his GI Bill educational benefits to earn an agricultural engineering degree at Clemson University. Then Eldred took a job in Alabama with Massey-Ferguson Tractor Company, setting up tractor dealerships in the southeast. Mrs. Webb taught school in Alabama and later in Atlanta when Eldred took a job with Case Tractor Company there. During these years, the Quinns had a daughter, Sheila, and a son, William.

In the mid 1960s, Eldred Quinn decided to leave the tractor distribution business because the travel was taking him away from his family too much. He entered public school teaching, and the couple moved home to Spartanburg County where they both took teaching jobs at Boiling Springs High School. They retired in 1986 and now devote their time to caring for their garden and spending time with their five grandchildren.

I interviewed Mrs. Quinn and her husband in their brick 1960s ranch home on land near the farms where they grew up in northern Spartanburg County, South Carolina. We spoke on October 18, 2000. Ever the hospitable homemaker, Mrs. Quinn served me a snack of homemade bread and jelly and sent me home with a small jar of her own preserves. In the summer of 2001, the Quinns corrected the interview transcript. I have included Mrs. Quinn's portion of the oral interview here, but the combined interview is available in the Kennedy Local History Room of the Spartanburg County Public Library.

I'll go first [before her husband] because he talks the most and the longest. [laughter] If I let him start, I may not get to come back. I was born in Spartanburg County, [and] spent most of my life here. I went to elementary school and high school at Boiling Springs. Of course, life was hard [during her childhood], and we were poor people, and we knew that we were. We didn't *really* know it because everybody was poor. And we had friends and they were in the same boat we were in. If somebody was a little bit better off, well, everybody helped each other. . . . But yet, we knew that there were other ways of making a living, that there was money out there and that some people had nicer clothes.

In the fourth grade, I can remember that Paul Dorman[1] came into my classroom; he was the superintendent of schools, and he had the teacher's checks, and he was paying the teachers. And I remember that he just opened my eyes, and I thought, "Well, for this you get paid, and this is what I want to do. I want to be a teacher." And from that moment on, my ambition was to be a teacher. And I didn't know how I was going to do it; I just knew it was going to happen.

Because my dad and mom had ten children, nine of which survived and the oldest one was lost when he was seven years old from typhoid fever. They were tenant farmers, living and paying half of our earnings to the landlord; [they] worked hard.

They [her parents] were always interested in our education and wanted us to go to school. One of the things that my dad always said was that he felt like he owed his children a high school education. He didn't have one. He was pretty much a self-educated man and knew a lot about a lot of things and did a lot of reading. And I think from him, I developed my love for reading, because as we worked and picked cotton and one thing and another, we would discuss books that we had read, and he would tell me how important it was that people learned to read and to discuss things that they had read, and it [the family discussion] was things that you would remember for a long time. So, what he said, he owed us a high school education, but he didn't owe us a college education. If we went to college, we were going to have to help ourselves. So I knew that I would have to help myself. But I also knew that I could depend on them to help in whatever way that they could.

And he was, I think, maybe and because of necessity, more conservative than my mother was, because I can remember that when I would want something that I felt like I might not be able to get—like a new dress for a special occasion or something—we would talk about it, and he would never be overly optimistic, but she would simply say, "Don't worry about it, we will get it if I have to sell an old hen." And I depended on that old hen for a lot of different things, and they usually would come through.

My grandmother was also conservative. She used to write to us. She lived in Boiling Springs, and she would write us ever once in a while. And she would either write on the back of a calendar sheet, or she would tear off a piece of a paper bag and write on that. I remember getting her letters. She had envelopes, but she would write her letters on that type of paper. I thought that was interesting to remember that she did that.

And talk about your pennies—my first job, I helped Miss Finch pull bitterweed out of her flowerbeds. She had a lot of bitterweed. You know how it gets in your pasture, and you don't want your cows to eat it. Yes, it ruins your milk.[2] And she would pay me to help her pull her bitterweed, and she paid me five cents an hour. And she would give me a glass of milk and sometimes a piece of fried chicken or something, and she paid me five cents an hour. [laughter]

Now we did have a little bit of envious feeling for our town cousins [growing up]. They had electric power and water running in the pipes, and we didn't have that at all out in the country. But I never realized at the time that they also were a little envious of all the food that we had. They liked to come out on weekends and sit down at Aunt Edna's table and enjoy the bounty of our big gardens. Well, it wasn't actually a garden; it was crops of sweet potatoes and okra and tomatoes and green beans and all that kind of stuff. And those women worked; oh, they canned. There was no such thing as a freezer for a long, long time, and they did a lot of canning. They canned green beans, and tomatoes, and even soup mixtures with corn in it. They made jellies and jams, pick blackberries and make jelly and jam with that. And some of us were fortunate enough to have peaches and apples and things of that nature; they put those up. But that was a big part of the wintertime supplies was all that canning they did in the summertime. And the city people, they didn't have that experience at all. I think that, too, having that type of knowledge, helped to develop a difference in [country and town] people, differences in their attitudes.

There was an Indian graveyard on the farm where we lived. It sat on top of a hill, and I remember that my dad always plowed around it. These were the circular rows; they went round and round and round that Indian graveyard. As a matter of fact, I remember my dad teaching me— I don't know whether it was biology or an ecology lesson at that time—he had me putting down nitrate of soda on the corn, to get it on the leaves. Well, I wasn't sure he knew what he was talking about, so I had to check. So I picked me out maybe a half dozen of the biggest stalks in the field, so I could identify them and put it right down the middle. You know how corn grows. So I didn't think anymore about it for a while.

He came in one day and he said, "Well your experiment worked." [laughter] I said, "What do you mean? I don't know what you're talking about." He said, "I told you, 'Don't get it on the corn.' Well, you got it on the corn, and it worked. You can go back and see now that it does kill the plant."

[laughter] He knew what I had done. He reported to me that my experiment had been successful.[3] Pretty smart old dad.

Let me tell you about one of the fun things that I didn't do. I was already out of school. Louise, one of my younger sisters, has told me about when they'd be working out in the fields—I guess they was hoeing in the hot summertime—said that she put her sunbonnet on the mule and had the mule walking round there with her sunbonnet on. And meanwhile the county agent—the farm agent—had come out to visit with my dad. And Dad was out walking and talking with him. And my sister said that Dad was *so* embarrassed when he saw that mule with the bonnet on. [laughs] But a few years later then we saw a picture in the paper where somebody had a mule out plowing in the garden. And a mule was kind of rarity by that time. And there they had a bonnet on that mule. That started a trend. [laughter] But they had fun; they *could* have fun.

When the threshers would come through, that was always a big day. Another thing that they did—not everybody had cane, but a lot of people had small patches of cane, and the people who owned the molasses mill would come to your house, and other people would bring it [their cane harvests] in, and they'd make molasses—squeeze out the juices and cook the syrup and made molasses.[4] That's a thing of the past. If they shared the work, it was more fun.

We had friends that lived over on the Valley Falls Road. We would [visit and] spend the night. That was a big thing, spending the night with each other. [We] played; [we] had a great big pasture, we played in the pasture and in the creeks. [We] played ball in the pasture; that was pretty much our entertainment growing up. Playing, having fun with our friends. And I played basketball; that was my big thing, I loved basketball in high school. And so I was tall enough and fortunate enough to make the team, because we had a lot of good times in basketball.

So when I finished high school, I went to Spartanburg Junior College for a year. It's the Methodist college now. It actually was Textile Institute, and it changed the name to Spartanburg Junior College. I don't know if it was while I was there or a year or so after I left there. But anyway, it became Spartanburg Junior College, and then it became Spartanburg Methodist College. And I went there for a year as a day [commuting] student, and the next year, my folks moved from off of number 9 [South Carolina Highway 9] from a big farm over there to here in what we call, what we called the Flat Woods section, right in this area. And it [the new farm] was a little too far for him to drive and take me over there [to college daily] like he had done the year before.

So this school [Textile Institute] had a program where you go to work two weeks and go to school for two weeks.[5] And I had a job at a shirt factory. We were making shirts for the war effort. We were making wool shirts to send to the soldiers, and I worked there during the summer. And while I was doing my registration at school for the next year, they were asking me about a job. They provided you with a job if you didn't have one; they helped you get one. So they said go over [to the shirt factory] and ask if they will work with our program—if they will allow you to work two weeks and let us provide them another work partner for the next two weeks. So I did, and this gentleman who was my supervisor was very understanding. And he said, "Well I've never heard of that. I never knew such a thing existed, but I certainly am in favor of it. I've never had the opportunity to go to college, but I think that's a wonderful idea. We'll try to work it out." So, fortunately, my work partner, Doris Dixon, was from a rural area up in West Virginia, and she also knew all about working hard—hard work. So she worked out fine; we just had a very good working relationship.

I finished the junior college that year and knew that Winthrop [College] was still a ways off and decided that I needed to work a year before attempting to go on to school.[6] So, I worked for one full year and brought my check in and handed it to my mom, and they put the money away.[7]

I used to think that the nicest job would be to work in a dime store. My daddy said, "Absolutely not. No way are you going into town and working in a dime store." [laughter] The Blackwood girls, they all the time worked in a dime store, but my dad thought evil was in town, and he did not want me in that evil down there.

I worked at the shirt factory [after finishing at Textile Institute]. I kept working right there at the shirt factory the entire time. I got about fifty cents an hour. And the year went by, and I was able to enroll at Winthrop. In the fall then, Dad picked me up in his pickup truck and put me in the dormitory, and somehow or other between what I had saved and what he and mom were able to send to me [I managed].

Mama sewed day and night on her treadle sewing machine [to make Mary's college clothes]. That was back in the days when Winthrop was all navy blue and white. And we had a few uniform pieces that we had to buy there, but she made most of my navy blue and white things. I remember a younger sister asking me not too long ago if I was ever envious of some of my friends who could wear store-bought clothes, and I said, "Why no. I was always even proud of my clothes." My mom was a wonderful seamstress. She said, "Well, I was [envious], and my friend was always showing me what I thought was the cutest things that she had just bought." But she says, "I think back on it, but I think it's [the envy] because she was so tiny and I was so big." [laughter] And, too, she's [the sister] twenty years younger than I am, so that may have something to do with it.

And so they [her parents] would send me things; it wasn't like running home every weekend whenever you want to, like it is now. I think I came home Thanksgiving and Christmas. I'd ride the bus home.

Now when I was at Winthrop, I had a part-time scholarship. Well, I worked in the teacher's dining room. It didn't pay full-time—like if you worked in the student dining room—but it was educational. I majored in home economics, and it [the dining hall job] was great experience, because that's where the teachers did their entertaining. Of course, they weren't married, and that's where they did their parties. We would be invited over to assist them in getting ready and set up the tables and serve. One of the things I remember about this *old* man. I've forgotten who he was, but he was fragile-looking. He was very elderly. And he was hosting. The dessert was block ice cream. And he got down to the dessert, and after it was served, he said, "Well, folks, I don't know which one of these tools you use with it." Said, "Just use whatever you wound up with. I notice some of you's got a fork, but I got a spoon. So just use whatever you wound up with." [laughter] And I remember that our foods professor told us after that, "Now did you see how doctor so-and-so handled that? He handled it with such ease. He knew exactly what to use. He was just putting everybody at ease. The important thing is not what you use, but that you know what you're supposed to use." [laughter] But it was an interesting situation. I really enjoyed that work in the dining room.

So, after I finished Winthrop, then I went right into teaching, not a problem. I taught for one year down at Blackstock, which is right below Chester. I taught for a year there, and then that is the year we decided to get married, and I came home and taught here at Boiling Springs for a year, and we got married at Christmastime then. My husband was going to Clemson at the time, so I finished the semester in Boiling Springs, and we moved to Clemson. We lived in our little pre-fab, and I taught over at Keowee until he finished Clemson.[8]

At Keowee, they were country children, and they were wonderful children. One of the cutest things that happened there was—I taught some of seventh grade history, and I remember asking a question: where a treaty [negotiation] was held between the Indians and the white men at one time, they were talking peace, and we had talked about them meeting at Keowee.[9] So one little boy had written [that the treaty was signed] "right here in the high school." The high school that I worked in. [laughter] He thought the high school had always been here. I thought that was really cute.

On my first job teaching home ec, I coached the girls' basketball. He [her husband] always makes my coaching sound a lot better than it was. [laughter] I coached at Keowee, too.

I mostly taught home economics. Whenever I would make a change [to a new school], sometimes I'd have to do science, and I've even had a little math. I've had to come home and have Eldred [her husband] help with my homework at night. [laughs] I did teach chemistry a few times. I was fortunate at Keowee. They put me to teaching chemistry up there, and Eldred was a student, and he'd have to do my chemistry problems until I got Sam Perry.[10] He was my student teacher. And he was wonderful. I just retired [from teaching chemistry] after that and sat back and listened to Sam. [laughter] It was great having him. And then he taught there at Keowee and was the principal for a number of years. Then he came over here and taught out at district six.[11] But he has recently died. Cancer took him away. He was a good old boy. I remember his help in the class, in the chemistry class.

And after he started his work, I taught in different places. We moved to Alabama, and I taught there. I taught in Atlanta two years. And then we were on our way back here after about six or seven years spent out of the state, I guess. [We] came back here and moved downtown [in Spartanburg] in a rented house for about a year. And then we built right here, and we have been right here ever since. I went back to Boiling Springs [High School] and started teaching home economics.

I really loved my home economics, because most of the time it was girls, until we integrated with the male population. And most of those boys, when they started coming in, it was because they thought it was a cook-and-eat situation. And so when they would come in, there would usually be maybe half a dozen or so of 'em. And I would start my food classes with nutrition, and I mean I would beat them to death with nutrition like it was the most important thing in the world, and you don't cook nothing till you get nutrition. And they'd be tripping off down to guidance and changing their schedules. [laughter] So I got rid of a few undesirables like that. But then I got a few good boys that I enjoyed.

But I really enjoyed it when it was all girls, and we had a very active FHA.[12] We had state officers, and we had district officers. And it was just good leadership training. After we got into the state and district officers, and it got to be popular, our department got to drawing in the better students. And we have a little girl that works in the bank over here—and she's told me many times, she'd come down to my room with our FHA officers. And she said, "Mrs. Quinn, you all do such fun things in there." Said, "I didn't do anything in high school that was fun. I just took all those old hard courses. I wish I had done something that was fun." [laughs] And you know, they need to. They really do. They need to have something that's fun. And we did have [fun]; we'd hear it all. You'd hear everything in home ec. And it was just wonderful. You'd meet so many wonderful girls, from wonderful families. Sheila said, "Mama, I just can't believe how many girls I meet out there that tell me how much they loved you." And I said, "Well, it worked both ways; I loved them too. I really loved my girls."

I taught there [at Boiling Springs High] until 1986. By that time, my husband had decided education was not such a bad idea after all, and he had joined me in the education field and was in it about twenty years, wasn't it? So, we retired together in 1986. [We] had a wonderful party, great [retirement] party. That was the nice thing about retiring together: all the friends, family decided it was a great big deal, so let's party. [laughter]

The biggest thing that has happened to us since then, I guess, is our fiftieth anniversary party and the enjoyment of our grandchildren. We have enjoyed them and spoiled them. Put one in the University of South Carolina last year, and one is in high school here in Boiling Springs. And I'm sorry to tell you that we have lost our three little granddaughters to the state of Virginia. They're up there now. And of course, all three cried and screamed and yelled when they left, but they have settled down. And they really have wonderful programs for children and families [in Virginia]. They are much better at furnishing athletics for them. And they have too much to do—soccer and softball and basketball and cheerleading.

I was telling you about my daddy felt he owed his children a high school education, so I added to that, and I said, "I feel like I owe you a college education," I told Sheila. And when Sheila finished Carolina,[13] she had a friend that was going on to get her master's. I said, "Sheila, we've got Billy coming out of high school. He's going on to school, and we need to help him, too." And I told her what my dad had said. I said, "Now I feel like we owed you a college education, but now you're going to have to help yourself with, and I feel like it would be better for you to get your masters' after you've come out and worked anyway." She went back and got her masters' after she had worked two years. I felt like she needed that experience.

We have good genes that have been passed on from hard working on down the line. We had grandparents who went through the rough times and they survived and had a good life and passed on their attitudes to all of us. I think all of that plays a part in a good attitude.

Farming changed after World War II. And the crops changed, too. King Cotton left, and peaches came in. This area was the largest peach area. As a matter of fact, they said Spartanburg County had more peaches than Georgia at one time. But weather took care of that.[14]

I didn't tell you much about the hazards of growing up back then. I don't . . . you know, you don't dwell on those times. You know that you have been fortunate to have lived long enough to see the advent of the modern transportation, the modern telephone systems, and TV with their little things that you have to program with. [laughter] My grandchildren have to come in and do it for us. Yeah, and the computer. We have a computer and use E-mail.

NOTES

1. A superintendent of schools in one of Spartanburg County's school districts.

2. When a cow eats bitterweed, her milk takes on the taste of the bitterweed.

3. Nitrate of soda was a common fertilizer. The compound contained 16 percent nitrogen, an essential plant nutrient. In order to make the most efficient use of this expensive product, many farmers applied it when the crop was about knee-high by broadcasting it on the soil around the plant. However, farmers had to be careful not to get the nitrate of soda on the corn plant. If Mary had accidentally dusted specks of nitrate of soda on the corn, the fertilizer would simply have left white or brown spots on the leaves. She apparently applied it liberally to some of the plants, killing them.

4. At threshing time, the threshing machine went to each farm, and neighbors came to that farm to help with the work. At cane-grinding time, families would go to one farm where they all used the molasses mill at once.

5. This innovative program might be seen as a combination of modern cooperative education and job sharing. Two students shared a job. They alternately went to class two weeks and worked two weeks. Classes were scheduled to accommodate this pattern. In this way, students could earn enough money to pay for tuition, room, and board while obtaining their education.

6. Now Winthrop University.

7. Her parents held on to her earnings, saving them for her college education.

8. The educational opportunities created by the GI Bill caused massive overcrowding at most of the nation's higher educational institutions. In addition, most colleges did not have the facilities to house massive numbers of older, married students. Like many institutions, Clemson University coped with its housing shortage by bringing in some small, pre-fabricated dwellings as a temporary measure. The Quinns lived in one of these.

9. During the Anglo-Cherokee conflicts of the 1750s and 1760s, a series of negotiations was held near Keowee, in present-day Oconee County. For more information, see John Oliphant, *Peace and War on the Anglo-Cherokee Frontier, 1756–63* (Baton Rouge: Louisiana State University Press, 2001).

10. Eldred made up chemistry problems for Mary to use as examples in class.

11. Spartanburg School District Six.

12. Future Homemakers of America.

13. University of South Carolina at Columbia.

14. See Ruth Hatchette McBrayer interview for more on upstate peach farming. In recent years, erratic weather, including a series of unpredictable late spring freezes, have helped lead to the decline of the local peach economy.

Dorothy Skinner and Virginia Skinner Harris

Dorothy Skinner and Virginia Skinner Harris were sisters, born on a cotton farm in Lee County, South Carolina. Lee County, in the South Carolina sandhills region, was rich farming country. First settled in the 1840s by English and Scots-Irish settlers moving south from Virginia and north from the lowcountry, the county had a population that was, by 1920, over 65 percent African American. Before the Civil War the area had been dominated by large plantations, but after Reconstruction, partible inheritance patterns gradually fragmented the land. By 1920, landowning farmers with large holdings, like the Skinner sisters' father, were rare. The average farm size was 46.7 acres, hardly large enough to support a family, and 78 percent of the county's farmers were tenants. Three-quarters of those tenants were African American. Cotton and tobacco accounted for over 70 percent of the value of crops raised in the area, and the boll weevil's impact was severe.

The fifth and sixth children of a family with a long tradition of local leadership, the sisters paint an unusually detailed picture of daily life on an early-twentieth-century farm. With the help of several African American families who lived and worked on the farm, the Skinner family raised cotton for the market, as well as most of their livestock feed and food for the family's use. The sisters describe a largely self-sufficient family that may have occasionally found itself strapped for cash during the lean years between the world wars but a family that was nonetheless much better off than most of its neighbors.

Dorothy Skinner and Virginia Skinner Harris left the farm when they became adults and built successful careers, Dorothy as an independent insurance agent and Virginia as a hairdresser. Virginia was married briefly and had a daughter. The sisters lived together in Columbia, South Carolina, for most of their adult lives.

Although Lee County is slightly outside the southern upcountry where the rest of these women lived, the story of the Skinner family's life on the farm is very similar to other stories of prosperous families included in this volume.

I met the Skinner sisters in 2001 when I spoke to a group of retirees who lived at Summit Hills Retirement Center in Spartanburg, South Carolina. My topic was rural life during the Depression, and at the end of my talk, a number of audience members shared stories of their own rural childhoods. One of them was Virginia Harris. After the group broke up and Virginia Harris disappeared, another resident, Frances Amidon, urged me to talk with the sisters, because she believed their memories would be so interesting to me. She was right.

The interview was conducted in the ladies' apartment on May 31, 2001. This particular interview is noteworthy because of the way each sister's personality comes through. Dorothy Skinner's mind was beginning to fail, but her memories of childhood on the farm were vivid and nostalgic. She was the idealist of the pair, and her sunny outlook comes through in nearly every line. By contrast, Virginia Harris was more realistic, perhaps because she had experienced more disillusioning life events. She remembered unhappy experiences as well as happy ones. Her memory was also sharper and clearer, and her approach to life was marked by a strong Christian faith. On September 27, 2001, in consultation with Miss Skinner, Mrs. Harris annotated and corrected the interview text, filling in blanks where the tape was inaudible. I made the corrections in the transcript.

VIRGINIA SKINNER HARRIS: Yeah. Well, she's older than I am [laughter], so she knew things before I came along.

DOROTHY SKINNER: Well, I hardly know how to start. [laughs] I was born in Oswego, South Carolina. It is about halfway between Bishopville, South Carolina, and Sumter, South Carolina. I was born on January 19, 1914, during World War I. Those were hard days. I must have been the fifth [child in the family]. Let's see. There was Ila, Ernestine, Emily . . .

VH: Leslie, Dorothy, Virginia, Kathleen, and Jimmy.

DS: There were eight [children in all]. I thought eight was enough. [laughter] But we had a good father and mother. They supplied all of our needs and a lot of our wants, and at Christmas, it was so special. And our father just loved Christmas. He loved to see that we got the things that we wanted. He was precious. And mother was, too. Mama was always busy in the kitchen, preparing meals. Seems to me she cooked all of her life. [laughter]

VH: She did.

DS: And our mother went to Lander College. I'm telling you, Mama had good English, and she wrote well. They were taught then. They need the books that they had back then. I think they'd [children] learn more. Our father didn't [go to college]. The parents [Dorothy's grandparents] were well-to-do on either side, so they [her parents] never lacked for anything.

Papa brought us a pony, a little Shetland pony, and he brought her in the house to see us when we had the flu. Her name was Patsy.

VH: Can you imagine bringing a pony in the house? And what did the pony do?

DS: She just [makes pony noises]. She'd speak to us.

VH: Patsy played with them like a dog would do. I think she was like a dog. They said she used to step on their toes and make them sore because she'd run around the haystack like a dog.

DS: I think we had one of the happiest childhoods that anybody could ever have. I can think about it at night, and just enjoy thinking about it.

Papa had a buggy specially made to fit the pony. And when the days were pretty, we would drive her to school sometimes. And the children would ooh and aah over her. And they wanted to ride her. And our next to oldest sister [Ernestine], she could ride her standing on her back. [laughter] And she would illustrate to the other children how she could ride standing up. And they would just be enthused to death over it. [laughter]

VH: She was a tomboy.

DS: She saw that in a circus, and she went home and tried it. I thought she must have had some special gift. She had to do something with it. There was nothing, in my opinion, that she couldn't do. And I'd go to school, and I'd tell all the children what my sister could do; you know how children brag about what they can do. I said, "Well, my sister Ernestine could do anything." And I began to tell them what she could do. [laughter] And she could. She was just one of a kind. She was special.

Ernestine always told me things that I would need to know. You know, the facts of life and things like that. Ernestine would always take special time to tell me.

VH: She was a very sweet sister.

DS: And the children couldn't believe that my sister could stand up on that pony and ride. So I said, "You come over to our house some Saturday, and I'll show you." [laughter]

VH: You were going to prove it, weren't you?

DS: I have a picture of our pony. Papa had a little buggy made for her. [She displays a picture of four children in a cart pulled by a pony.] Ah, that is our oldest sister, Ila. This is the next sister, Ernestine. And there I am. And I think our brother is back there somewhere. And I think that must have been Virginia.

VH: No, I was not in the picture.

DS: That wasn't you?

VH: Huh-uh. I wasn't in there. Dick had to be in there. Maybe you were the baby. Because that was before my time. I've just heard them talk about it.

DS: Maybe I was the baby [in the picture]. That must have been Dick back on there.

VH: Well, it probably was.

DS: Our brother was named Leslie, but a colored man on the place started calling him Dick, so everybody started calling him Dick. And everybody said, "Well, was his name Richard?" No. Well, how did he get Dick? [laughter] You know, they usually say that Richard is Dick. But we don't know how that happened.

VH: Well, you know people do that in the family. They give them little nick-names. And lots of times, children themselves, sisters and brothers, they can't say it [the name of a sibling] and then the name sticks.

DS: Both of them [both parents disciplined them], but when we really were bad, our father. And when he gave you a talking to, you didn't forget it.

VH: I don't remember him ever whipping me. Did he whip me?

DS: I don't know, but he whipped me.

VH: Well, you all came up all together, and it was just the three of us. And I was the oldest, I guess.

DS: I was the baby of the first family.[1]

VH: And I was the oldest of the second. But you remember how children used to have fits?[2] When he [brother Jimmy] was born, what did the doctor say about him? He had a pressure on the brain, didn't he? And he [the doctor] said, "He'll either be smart or he won't have any mind at all." He was a very smart and brilliant person.

DS: In fact, I don't see how he retains all that he does. You can ask him about anything, and he can come up with something.

VH: But when he was a little boy, he'd have those spells, if he couldn't have his way, or if you wake him up, he would jump up and down. And I saw Papa put him out in the smokehouse one night to get him quiet.

DS: And I'll tell you, our father loved to tell ghost stories. And he'd get us around a big fire, and he'd start telling us. Oh, and they were so exciting. We'd just get closer and closer to the fire. And then sometimes he would just stop. We'd say, "Papa, what happened then?" He's say, "I left about that time." [laughter] He'd run out of something to say. But he and our mother, they were always there for us.

VH: They were. It's not like the children today. It's a different world. It's a lot different. The children have so much that they can see to buy. They have so much that they can get into, entertainment that's not good. The entertainment that we had was what we made up ourselves, playing around the farm or going swimming in the branch or, you know, like that. Visiting friends or going fishing. It didn't cost a thing. And we had oak trees, and oh, you talk about leaves.[3] [laughter]

DS: We had tremendous oak trees, and I've been to the top of every one of them. [laughter] And sometimes I couldn't come down. So my next-to-my-oldest sister, she said, just stay right there; I'll come get you. She would always come get me and bring me down. [laughter] You know, that was frightening to be up in a real tall tree, and you look down, and everything just began to look so far down, impossible. Going up was fine, but that coming down. Oh land.

VH: But you know, Mama didn't worry about us. Our mother didn't seem to worry about us. She trusted the Lord Jesus.

DS: No, she didn't. Good thing she didn't.

VH: She didn't say "be careful" or anything.

DS: We don't know what was going in her mind. She was probably praying. [laughs] "Take care of them, Lord," I reckon she said.

VH: Let the oldest take care of the younger ones. That's the way it comes up.
But you know, living on the farm, you learn to live with what you have. If you don't have it, you substitute with something else you know. Because I've seen my mother substitute things in food.[4] We had a lot of food, and we

canned. We girls had to . . . Oh, I hated it when pear time came. Those hard pears, you know, were hard to peel and made your hands so sore. But we'd do our part, and everybody did their part. And we had a big pantry filled with shelves filled with food, and we had everything that we could can in it, you know. So we lived at home except for sugar, and salt, and the things that you could not grow.[5]

DS: You name it, we farmed it.

VH: I wrote it down. Cotton, corn, . . .

DS: Peanuts . . .

VH: Wheat and oats, soybeans and peas in the fall. You know, back then you dried food for the winter and canned vegetables and also fruits and cured meat in the smokehouse.

DS: And sweet potatoes and Irish potatoes.[6] And we had a big garden.

VH: Oh yes, we always had plenty to eat. We had a sweet potato bank. You ever heard of a sweet potato bank? They had to make a potato bank by putting a layer of soil and then a layer of straw. When finished, you would dig a hole in the middle and place sweet potatoes in the bank.

DS: They kept all winter long.

VH: I can remember Mama would say, "Go get some potatoes," and I'd dig . . .

DS: You'd dig out a little bit and get some, and you'd cover it back up, you know.

VH: I remember I was wearing my high school ring—that's when I was in eleventh grade. I realized when I finished getting the potatoes I didn't have it. And I started feeling around and found it and that made me happy. I found it. I didn't get excited, because I said, "It has to be there."

DS: Do you remember the year it rained so much?

VH: Oh, do I!

DS: And over 150 acres of cotton made three bales. And our father was just, he was so worried, so upset. It was in the '30s—'31, I believe.

VH: Yeah, it was away in there. 'Cause I remember, that's when we had so much rain one year, you remember, we had to get out of the school bus and into a boat to get to the school. The bottom was close to the school.[7] And the ground was so wet you couldn't walk. And it had rained so much one year that one oak tree in the front yard—you remember that one tree—was ready to fall over, the ground was so saturated.

All the lowland had water standing where we were in Lee County, but that was the best farming land in the state. The government in the late 1930s bought land for the needy people, gave them so many acres apiece.[8] We didn't sell our land. There's no farming land here [in Spartanburg County]. It was the best in the state. Because the government bought it up, you know, back when they brought the government in. The government project people needed homes; the people were needy. And they didn't buy my daddy's farm, because he says, "I'm not going to sell it to the government." But a lot of them did.[9] But it's good farming land.

DS: We had pecan trees, and we had pear trees, and we had, what, one apple tree?

VH: I think you all had apples before I planted some apple seeds when I was in high school. They were Winesap apples. And I planted them. And they gave good apples. About three trees. We had peach trees, too, but peach trees don't last.

DS: Peaches, apples, and pears.

VH: Our grandfather knew how to bud and—what's the other?

DS: Graft.

VH: Graft. He had a peach tree had three different kinds of peaches on it. He did pecans that way too. And we had to pick up pecans and oh. And [when] it rained and the wind blew, it would scatter pecans all around the ground. You always had to get them off the ground. We sold them, but they didn't bring as much as they do now. We had I don't know how many different kinds of pecans. They all had a different flavor. We had two walnut trees. We had that one out there at the front. We had one in the lawn, that little hard one that you had to get a hammer to break.[10] We had one in back of the house, right at the porch.

But now for one thing, a reason they don't make anything is the insects eat them.[11] Now this is something to think about. When you have chickens, they eat the insects. We had chickens that ate the insects and kept them from getting into the pecans. They destroyed the insects. You didn't have to spray the ground at the base of the tree. Yeah, they don't get in it. And we don't have the rain we used to have. They used to be loaded, didn't they?[12] Oh, they were just loaded.

DS: [Our house had] two big porches, one across the front and a long porch on back. We had a big, screened porch [in the back] with a big table, and we would sit out there in the summertime, we'd eat on the back porch, and it was so pleasant. It was near the kitchen.

Oh, I remember those meals, and mama was such a good cook. Ohhh.

VH: Sometimes at Christmas we enjoyed eating on the porch. If the weather permitted. That was pretty unusual. But our weather now is not like it was back then. It'd turn cold in October, and you had cold weather till, I would say, March, wouldn't you? But now it kind of messes around.

The house had a big front porch, and you'd go into a hall. There was a bedroom on the left and the living room on the right, and we had so many girls, he [their father] put all the girls in one big room. [laughter]

There were six girls and two boys. And then there was their [their parents'] bedroom. And that's where they had the fire all the time. And it was so cold back there. And then there was a little room that they put the small children in. And the hall was L-shaped. It was cool in the summer.

DS: A long back porch went all the way across the back.

VH: It had a nice dining room next to the kitchen. And the dining room was where the hall came in. There was the dining room and then the kitchen and the pantry, and then the bathroom was on the end. You know, the bathroom wasn't built until the remodeling was done. You know, the only way you could do it was to cut it off [the porch].[13]

DS: And we had an inside bathroom, which a lot of the people around didn't have, which we were grateful for.

VH: We had a generator; I think the Alamo plant was the first one. I was a child, but I do remember it. And then we had a Delco plant that supplied lights for use.[14]

DS: Then the kerosene lamp was there for emergencies.

VH: We had an Aladdin lamp that we could use. And, you know what an Aladdin lamp is? You have to wash those lamps. And you had to be very careful when handling it because of the delicate mantle, and you also had to be careful washing the glass shade. When the mantle turned black in a spot, you have to turn the light down and let it burn out. And when you all left, I did it.[15] I was the oldest girl [of the younger group of children]. But you know what I told them; I told my sister and brother, "You go in there and put your clothes up. You can help me wash dishes. I'm not doing it all, 'cause

I won't be here forever." [laughter] I think my mother got tired of trying to get them to obey. She didn't say anything but really did.

DS: And she [their mother] made all of our clothes. She was a beautiful seamstress. You just wouldn't believe the clothes that she'd make.

VH: She was so particular.

DS: Everything had to just perfect. [laughter] She French-filled [French seams] everything that she made.

VH: Well, back then, they did. But see, they don't do that now because it's too . . . I know when my youngest brother got married, I made our mother's dress. She thought it had to have French-filled seams, a thing of the past.

DS: I remember they let Santa Claus come to me early 'cause I had double pneumonia, and they didn't expect me to live. So they let Santa Claus come to me, course I was sick, but my eyes got big when I saw his face. [laughter] He brought me a doll and little doll carriage, and I don't know what else.

VH: You know, back then, pneumonia was dangerous. It killed people.

DS: They didn't think I was going to live. That's why they let me have Christmas early.

VH: Our daddy lost his baby sister and baby brother with pneumonia, but the mother lived. [The mother had pneumonia at the same time.] But the younger boy and Aunt Jenny, the one I was named for, died. Our doctor used mustard plasters to treat his patients. The other doctor experimented with shots that had just become available. You ever heard of mustard plasters? It works, provided you mix it with equal amounts of flour and mustard, then water, to make a paste and spread it on a flannel cloth. It [the skin] would turn pink, and you'd have to take it off.

DS: They'd put oil or grease on you before applying the plaster, and when you started getting pink. . .

VH: They'd take it off.

DS: You had to watch it so it would not blister.

VH: And then you could put it back. I've seen it done where Mama put a kerosene plaster on. They made a plaster with a few drops of kerosene and melted tallow. Have it warm and apply it to the chest or back. You didn't use much kerosene, but whatever it did, it loosened up that [chest congestion]. . . . It worked.

I don't see how my mother stood it, because I don't think I could have, because our house always had children—friends—coming in to visit. All of us had friends, and they'd come in, and well, she'd just fix [for the friends]. She wouldn't say anything. Our mother always managed to handle the situation.

DS: But we always had somebody extra in our house all the time. But Mama and Papa enjoyed having them as much as we did.

VH: In fact, we had a cousin down the road—his mother was our daddy's sister. And he stayed at our house more than he did at home. And she [their mother] would say, "William, when you coming home?"

DS: Said, "Don't you know where your home is?"

VH: He said Dorothy was just like a sister to him because . . .

DS: Yeah, William and I were like brother and sister. When one hurt, the other hurt. I wouldn't take anything for our childhood life. It was so happy.

VH: And if we had a party or they [their parents would] come in, they always sat there, and they chaperoned, and they enjoyed it as much as we did. I mean, they didn't just turn us loose. They never left us alone.

DS: Our father could make anyone feel welcome. He was so hospitable.

VH: And you know, he always helped when anyone on the street would come to him asking for help. He'd said, "Now if you're hungry, we'll go get something to eat," because he would never give them money.

DS: We'd say, "Papa, how many people did you feed today?" [laughter]

VH: We children had to take care of the garden—pick the vegetables and carry them to the house. The black people—we had hands on our place—worked on the farm. [They worked] in the fields and helped harvest the crops grown. They were day hands. There were five or six houses for the workers to live in.

DS: And we had our black mammy. She was the sweetest thing. Never went to school a day in her life, but she had more common sense; you just wouldn't believe the sense she had. And she used to tell Papa and Mama what to do. [laughter] And if one was sick, she knew exactly what to do. She was better than any doctor I ever saw.

VH: Well, she experienced it. That's why you learn. God made her that way; you learn from experience. Well, anyway, we'd have to help Mama in the garden, pick the butter beans, tomatoes, peas, anything that needed to be gathered. You remember, our daddy always planted his watermelon and cantaloupe away from the garden, and the hands would bring them in the house on a cart. It was up in a certain special place, because it grew better.

And we always took a nap after the midday meal. Everybody took a siesta. That is what's missing today; that's what wrong with people. Maybe people today need to slow down to rest like the old-timers did. And when we got up, he'd always have a watermelon or cantaloupe to eat. That was our evening dish.

And back then, we didn't have electric refrigerators, we had an icebox.

ds: And it always had room enough to put a watermelon in it. [laughter]

vh: I'll tell you about that story [about milking the cow]. My youngest brother wanted to go to a party. The older children had moved out, so the three younger ones were left. And I said, "Well, Jimmy, go on, and I'll milk for you." Well, I want you to know I started to milking, and it was the hardest job I had ever tried. I got a cramp in my hands, so I turned the calf and cow together and let the calf do the milking. I didn't volunteer [to milk] any more.

ds: You know, I never could milk.

vh: I just couldn't, I can't tell you how bad it hurt me. You know some people can do it, and some can't. Huh-uh. I'll tell you what I didn't like. Churning butter. Churning, churning, churning. You had a churn that turned this way [she indicates a crank]. It wasn't one like that [she indicates an up and down movement].

ds: Yeah, it was one that, I reckon you call them a crank.

vh: And I can remember in the afternoons when the farmhands would come in, the ones that picked cotton, usually the women picked too. But they would rest from twelve to one, depending on how hot it got. At the end of the day, they would bring the cotton to our yard next to the barn, and they'd weigh it. And our daddy kept a record and paid each one according to the amount they picked. He paid them at the end of the week. And I remember that if I wanted some spending money, I'd pick some cotton. But I wasn't a cotton picker. Hard and backbreaking work. When I thought I had to have a little something [I would pick to earn money]. And you know it's good for children to have something to do. And now it's just handed out to them.

Our oldest brother was away so much of the time going to school and a mechanic. He could work on our Delco plant that provided our lights. He worked on cars and . . . When we were in school, he was the one kept the buses up [repaired].

DS: And people were calling him all the time. He could do anything.

VH: He can now. He can carpenter, he can masonry, he just . . .

DS: He was like our grandfather, our mother's father. He was like that. Just could do anything. Nothing ever fazed them. They just went into it and started doing it.

VH: It was so nice to hear the black people in their church singing. It was so pretty, wasn't it, Dorothy?

DS: Oh, it was beautiful. They'd start off with asking Sister Thomas to sing and lead the music.

VH: It was one of the oldest churches in South Carolina. It's still there.

DS: Said "Sister Thomas, you find us a tune." Well, she'd start off [hums]. The congregation would join the singing. It would give you chill bumps. It was so pretty I will never forget it.

VH: And they'd always march us up to the front.

DS: Yeah, we had to sit on the front seat.

VH: We were the guests.

DS: And they loved us, and we loved them.

VH: We went whenever they invited us. Seems like I remember going twice. But they would invite us.

DS: We went to one of the oldest Methodist churches in South Carolina.

VH: Rembert Church.[16] It was one of the oldest. It's still there.

DS: I don't think they have services there, or do they?

VH: No, they don't have services. I think they have special meetings there.

DS: I remember we used to drive our pony and buggy to Sunday school and church. If we were early, we'd go under the church and play with doodles [a small insect which makes a little mound with a hole in the middle]. You know those doodles you played with? [laughter]

VH: If they didn't drive the pony, they would drive a Model T Ford. Sometimes if it rained the bottom would be full of water, and the car would choke down. And our sister Ernestine, the one that was a tomboy—she'd have to take shoes and socks off and pull her dress up and get out and crank it. [laughter] See, she was the tomboy in the crowd. It was funny.

DS: She was precious. I think we had one of the most enjoyable, pleasant childhoods that anyone could have had. Oh, I wouldn't take anything for my child life that I had.

VH: And you know, we had a nice community and nice people there. In fact there was about three or four big mansions in that community. And you didn't have the trashy people that [you have now], you know . . . And it was a good community. We all fit into the community.

DS: And Papa belonged to the Masonic order. And Mama belonged to Eastern Star. They met, I think, once a month.

VH: And you know, we'd get out and walk for entertainment and walk when we visited. It was a long walk. There was three large tracts of land. There was the Manning plantation, Governor Manning of South Carolina, about three miles away from us. And then there was the big Rose Hill Plantation that covered acres of ground. There was another big mansion, Uncle Burl's home.

DS: A plantation mansion. And I started school right in front of it in a little two-room schoolhouse. And I had the sweetest first-grade teacher that ever was. Oh, she was just.

VH: Miss Vaughn?

DS: Miss Vaughn. And I loved her to death. I just couldn't keep my hands off of her. I just wanted to hug her neck all the time.

VH: Not all of them are that way, are they?

DS: The schoolteachers lived in Uncle Burl's [house]. It was a big place. I tell you the hall was a big as some rooms. It was a mansion.

VH: That was where they stayed. Teachers lived up in Uncle Burl's home. He had help to do the work like cooking, cleaning, and taking care of the teachers' rooms. They boarded with him. They had a cook there, and they stayed there.

When I was five years old, a tornado came through our community and did lots of destruction.[17] It was a big tornado. And the colored girls on the farm had just washed our clothing. They had hung out Mama's linen tablecloths. And it was hot. And I remember a feeling like I had never experienced before. I felt like there was a pressure. I felt like I just couldn't breath. When I got older I realized that [feeling] goes with the storm. And we all stood in the hall and watched the storm move very fast. One of the girls said, "Miss Mary, it's not going to hit this house." They kept comforting her. The Bible says that you have what you say or confess what you want God to do for you. And if you believe in your heart, and you doubt not, you will have it.

DS: It changed its course completely, just like somebody was doing it.

VH: That's right. The storm changed its course as if God's hand told it to go another route. And it turned and hit, our aunt had a big two-story house, too; it wasn't a mansion, but a big two-story house. And she had bought a brand new automobile. And it was in the garage. And it took the top off [the garage] and turned that car over and didn't even hurt it. The storm killed people. It was a feeling that when you looked out, you wondered what could happen because the trees looked as if . . .

DS: An entirely different country.

VH: You can't explain it. [The trees] were just gone. You see, it just mowed them [the trees] down. I mean it went in there, and it [the tornado] just tore everything up. And in the house [her aunt's house], I remember getting the most eerie feeling, because the sides and the top were not together because it had twisted it.

DS: The tornado blew a man out of his house, and he hit a bell post and severed his head from his body.

VH: You see, there were no telephones, some [were] miles away. And at school, the teacher didn't know what was happening. Papa was on his way back from Bishopville, but he managed to miss it. A man in the neighborhood had got in it; he had to get out of the car. He held on to roots of a big oak tree. It kept it from taking him. His clothes were tattered, almost torn off by the wind. Well, people helped people that didn't have any place to stay.[18] People just had to make a way.

DS: Back then, people helped people.

VH: You didn't have any help from the government.

DS: Where they found a need is where they'd all get together.

VH: The Bible teaches to help one another. I think it was more informal [than churches organizing help for people], because the churches were so small. The pastors usually had more than one church to minister. The church we went to, we had a minister, and I think he had several other churches. People simply came to the rescue. People didn't have money to give. A lot of times they had to give potatoes or maybe chickens or something. Whatever they had.

When the banks closed in the Depression, people lost their money, couldn't get it out [of the banks]. People lost their money.

During the Depression, the black people came to the house to receive what the government was giving, flour, sugar, lard, things to keep them from starving. Our daddy was one of the men selected to handle it.[19]

DS: Sugar.

VH: Whatever. And he took care of that. And different places they had it, you know. And the colored people would come in cold weather, sacks tied around their feet, because they didn't have any shoes.

DS: Old bags around their feet, couldn't buy shoes.

VH: We had shoes, a Sunday dress, and several dresses for school. But we didn't have a lot. Not like they have today.

DS: I hope I *never* have to go through another Depression.

VH: Papa also had the hands to plow up what the government required [for New Deal acreage reduction programs].[20] I remember they plowed it up. I don't think he thought much of it. I don't think he did. I think my daddy thought it was crazy.

DS: And I remember in this big barn that we had . . .

VH: It was a big one.

DS: It had a long hallway; oh, I reckon it was long as from there to the end of that wall (indicates a distance of forty to fifty feet.) In the wintertime, the skates would roll on the wooden floors, so we could skate any time, even when it was raining. And we used to skate the passageway. Yeah. I had more fun. This was skates on the cement on the floor. And we'd invite our friends over. We'd all skate.

VH: Well, on one side of the hall were bins to hold different produce, like peas, cotton—long staple and short staple, we grew both kinds—beans, wheat, oats. The hay was upstairs and . . .

DS: And it had different stalls in it, almost as big as this room, that they put short-staple cotton, long-staple cotton, ah, hay, and beans.

We had one big ditch, I know our land was low, with lots of bottom, and it took drainage ditches to take the water off. And I and somebody else in the family used to slide down it in our britches. [laughter]

VH: Mama didn't like that.

DS: Red clay.

VH: But it's not like this clay [the heavy clay soil around Spartanburg]. . . . The land here is almost all clay. We had nice topsoil with clay underneath. It was easy to plow or work. This clay is like a brick. I'm telling you. If you fall in it, it'll about kill you; you may as well fall on the cement. [laughter] I couldn't handle it. I don't know what to do with this clay. When my daughter and her husband bought that land, I said, "Why in the world can't you all find something besides this clay land?"[21]

DS: That land that we had, it was real good for farming, because it did have topsoil, and then you'd get the clay, and that's what kept the moisture was the clay.

VH: And Papa had certain types of soil that he used. He liked to plant his watermelons and cantaloupes in a certain type of soil.

DS: In fact, it was known as some of the best land in the county.

VH: He learned that [about good soil] from his parents. His father was a farmer, so he learned living on the farm with his brothers and his father. His father was in the Civil War. The land didn't sell for much in those days, not like today.

DS: He [their grandfather] was injured in his back and never able to work too much. But he had a big farm, too. In fact, they had a lot of land, but they had more land than they could farm. And the land didn't bring anything, so you farmed.

VH: But we all came out all right, didn't we? God made a way. He makes a way when people are willing.

Our daddy didn't grow tobacco. I think Uncle Luther grew tobacco, his uncle. You see they bought a tract of land and the sister—oldest sister—bought a tract, my daddy bought a tract, and the youngest brother bought a tract. Together. That land must have belonged to the Kings, all of it.

DS: And they divided it; each took a third of it. Oh, but we did have a wonderful childhood. I can think back, sometimes I wake up at night, and I can't go to sleep, and I start thinking about it, you know, the beautiful days we had when we were children. And I said, Lord, you were so good to us. [laughs]

VH: We would go to town maybe once a month or when something special came up, someone would go and do the shopping. Most of the time, we went to Bishopville, because my daddy had the money in Bishopville bank. But of course, they'd go to Sumter, and they [the merchants] would honor the checks.

DS: When we wanted to do real shopping, we'd go to Sumter. It was bigger. And we children could go in and get anything. We'd say "I want so and so."

VH: That was in Bishopville.

DS: That was in Sumter, too. Yeah. They would honor us. We'd say we were Jim Skinner's children, and that's all they wanted to know. And they would send the bill to Papa. And next time do the same thing over.

They [the older children] bought Santa Claus, after Mama got where she'd let them go buy it.[22]

VH: When the oldest boy weren't there, and Jimmy was too young, we girls pitched in. Washed dishes, pumped water with a hand pump, anything around the house that needed attention. The youngest brother was too young to do much. I remember our mother always wanted the porches scrubbed on the weekend. Every Saturday the kitchen had to be scrubbed. That's the way you did it, you kept it clean. And we brought wood in, and we brought coal in. And what else did we do? You had to wash the lampshades. And that sweeping the big yard was a real chore. It had to be done on the weekend.

DS: We had grass in the front. There was this big front.

VH: We had Bermuda grass. When our daddy died, we had to take care of Mama. When we carried her back to the farm, we decided to plant grass. My oldest sister and I put out lots of centipede grass, and it outgrew the weeds. But it was beautiful. When you go over in a plane, it looked like an oasis. But, you know, the land is so pretty there. And that doesn't affect people in the city, because they don't know how pretty it is. When it's plowed, it's like a cake that has just been freshly covered with icing. It's so pretty.

DS: You could look down a road and see way up. Because the plots were big, you know.

VH: Back then they plowed with mules. But during the war, my daddy bought tractors, because the hands, some of them went to war, and he couldn't do it. So they bought the tractors, and it didn't take as many hands to do the work.

DS: And all the mules had names. When you talked to them [called] to their names, they knew their names.

VH: Well, I was afraid of them.

DS: Sometimes they would kick.

VH: We had one that learned how to open the gate, and she would push the latch up, and the gate would swing open. She was a mean thing.

DS: Georganna. That was her name. And then she'd get all the other mules to go behind her. She wasn't satisfied. Papa used to say, "That's the meanest mule."

VH: But you know what Papa did?

DS: He shot her one time.

VH: Shot her in the rump. It was a, not a big shotgun. It didn't hurt her.

DS: It taught her not to open the gate any more. And I remember we all had the flu and survived. Later I had pneumonia, and I got over it.

VH: It was hard at times, don't think it wasn't. It was so cold back then. I remember heating an iron and wrapping something around it to put in the bed to warm up. You know, you get your feet warm and you stay warm. And the cover was so heavy you could hardly turn over.

DS: And those mattresses had to be put out and sunned ever so often.

VH: That's right, at least once a month.

DS: We'd wipe off the banisters so the mattress would not get dirty.

VH: Our brother wasn't there to lift the heavy mattresses, so we girls did it. We did what our mother asked us to do. Our daddy had hurt his back, so he could not lift. But you do what you have to do. Mother was so clean, that's what you did.

Mama had our mammy to help in the house. She was so good to help, so humble. And she was real black. She had other black girls to come and wash once a week.

DS: We'd fight over who was going to sleep with her, when Mama and Papa went off. They always had Anakie to come [babysit].

And she wore a white cloth on her head all the time.

vh: And we didn't have a telephone, so Anakie would tell Mama to put a white sheet on the clothesline at a certain place, and that was the way we got the message. And she'd say, "Miss Mary, if you want me to come cook Sunday, you just put a white sheet on the line." We had a clothesline, and she could see it. And that was our telephone. If we wanted her and she'd see it, she'd come see what we wanted. That's the way it was. Does that give you a picture?

Anakie was the only help Mama had. Well, the girls that washed the clothes were different. They came to our house. Anakie didn't wash clothes. And you had the big pot that you boiled your clothes in. And they were sterilized when you got them out of there.

ds: We had two black iron pots to boil in. The clothes were sterilized.

vh: We had a pile of clothes to iron. The older girls did it. And we'd get the ironing done. We learned to do the ironing.

ds: And Anakie taught me how to iron a shirt. And I could do a shirt as good as any laundry you've ever seen. I think I could do better. And I love to do a good shirt, so clean and starched.

vh: Well, I didn't learn [to iron shirts]. When the older girls moved out, that left me and my younger brother Jimmy and our older brother. I told my brothers—I didn't get any complaints—I said, "Now, if you don't like it, you can do it."

Papa let my brother help him farm after all the children left. When the older children moved away to take jobs, our youngest sister was left, Kathleen. Jimmy volunteered for the navy. That left him [their father] and Mother by themselves. And my oldest brother, Leslie, lived about four miles away, and he helped him farm.

Our father became ill so we had to close the home and bring them to live with us in Columbia. He died in 1955. They lived with us two years before he died.

ds: He had so many friends. And he had one of the biggest, longest funeral processions. He was loved. Friends called him Mr. Jim.

vh: Yes, he loved everybody. Then our brother farmed it for a while, and then after Mama died, the girls—Dorothy and I—decided we'd rather sell our part. If you can't farm it and take care of it, it doesn't mean anything. Those who didn't want to sell kept their part, and the others sold except for the house. We let our youngest sister and her husband have it. We have enjoyed going back to visit, just getting together.

DS: Our mother's father was a pretty wealthy man. And at Christmas, I remember, he would give Mama never less than five hundred or a thousand dollars for a Christmas present. And he would always give.

VH: He just seemed to know how to invest his money.

DS: He knew a bargain when he saw it. And I don't know, he had something up here [indicates her head] that I wish I had. He farmed.

VH: Well, I don't think any of the children had what he had. We didn't have the know-how as he did.

DS: And he was good to everybody. He would give, I reckon, everything away if he hadn't had a family. He farmed. And he made investments. He knew what to invest in, you know. His name was Willis Josey Woodham. His mother, she was a Josey. He was a very prosperous farmer. And he was so good to us. Oh, he was precious to us.

VH: Well, he had so many grandchildren.

DS: And sometimes he'd reach in his pocket and say, "Gert, take them swimming."[23] And he'd put his hand in his pocket and pull out a dollar bill. And you know, that was a lot of money back then to give a child. [laughs] Because there were too many of us for Papa to put money in our hands. And he'd give me a dollar bill, and he'd give the other one a dollar bill. My head must have been big. Grandmother was brought up by the rich Cokers in Hartsville.[24] Her father and mother died during the Civil War.

VH: Her father was killed when he went to see her. Peter Dalrymple went to see his baby girl. On the way back [to the front], he was shot by the enemy while hiding behind a tree.[25]

DS: We used to spend Christmas with our grandparents.

VH: Yeah, Christmas Day. Before we got the car, now, you all went in the buggy; that was a long trip in a buggy.

DS: We'd get up early in the morning.

VH: Well, they lived between Hartsville and Bishopville.

DS: They lived on one side of Bishopville, and we lived on the other. We lived between Sumter and Bishopville.

vh: They had to go over Lynch's River [Lynch's Creek], if you've heard of Lynch's River. That was an all-day trip.

ds: All our people are buried at old Hebrew Church.

vh: Yeah, we'll be buried there. That church used to be Skinner's Church, according to the history.

ds: The Skinner house, our old grandparents' house, is still there. It's right funny. Our mother's people lived on one side of the church, and our father's people lived on the other. [laughs] So they oughta know each other, didn't they? And grandfather, our mother's father, he was always so good to us.

vh: Yeah, he was. He'd give us a nickel or something. But you know, you didn't expect it, because you didn't have it. And people now spending money they don't have because they can charge it. And they don't know what's coming up. We don't know what's coming. This world can't go on like it's going on. Because when times get bad, it will be worse than anything we have ever seen.

ds: It was during the Depression when I graduated from high school. And I had put my application in to the university.[26] But I got to thinking about it. And I said, "That's going to be so expensive. And I just don't believe I'm going." So I took a business course at Bowen's business college. The president gave me a job. He said, "I want you to work for me." I said, "Oh, that's the answer to prayer."

vh: Well, he saw your ability.

ds: Yeah, I'd do anything, anything he asked me to do. Got my graduation from that [business college], and I had a job before I finished. And from there I just kept on.

vh: You worked at the highway department, and then you went to work with Mr. Wilson. And that's where she stayed until her boss, Mr. Wilson, died and then she opened up her own company in Columbia. In insurance.

ds: I had four girls working for me. And they were the sweetest things. They just couldn't do enough for me. Sometimes I wake up at night and think what good workers I have.

vh: All the girls were Christians, so that makes a difference.

ds: I had agents all over Columbia, South Carolina, to call me and ask me what was covered, how could you get such and such a thing covered by insurance. And ask me questions that if they had—I said, "If you get your manual and read it and study it, you'll find out." They said, "But it's easier for you to tell us." [laughs] They'd say, "Well, after I read it, I don't know what I've read." What do you do with people like that? You just help them.

VH: They wanted to use her mind.

DS: I'd always tell them, "You stupid thing, find out like I found out."

VH: We worked on the corner of Taylor and Bull in Columbia, South Carolina. Of course she moved from different places, and I did, too. I worked by myself. I had a beauty shop, and I worked by myself. My oldest sister and I bought a beauty shop in 1945. We worked together until her husband got a job in Sumter.

My little girl was born. So Ila [an older sister] had been working with her [the owner of a beauty shop], and she [the owner] decided she wanted to sell out, and we bought the shop. And then she went to Sumter. Her husband moved to Sumter, and it left me holding it, and I didn't want to be with any-body. I got to thinking, "Well, I think I can do it myself." And I had so many nice customers. I had them for years and years. And some of them that I had when I was young, well, none of them are living now. Most were older than I. Well, I loved them. And they loved me. And they gave me some of the nicest gifts at Christmas.

I had the shop until I retired when I was sixty. And I'm eighty-one now. I got so tired. The last place I had was in the office [office building] where she [Dorothy] had her business. Well, they [the landlords] had sold out. And I had a contract, so they couldn't do anything about it. I kept asking the Lord to give me a place,[27] and he said, "I want you to retire. You can do on what you have." Of course, Dorothy and I lived together, you know.

Dorothy never married. She was married to a business.

DS: I was married to a business. [laughs]

VH: I married. I married a soldier during the war. But it didn't work out. I think the army changes them.

DS: I was too busy to get married. No man would live with me, because I was always up and doing. Oh, but I enjoyed it. And the harder the job was, the better I liked it. It brought out something in me, that I wanted to do some-thing I'd never done before, you know. The challenge. I liked everything about running the business. [laughs]

I think I bought our home in August 1955.

vH: The brick home, the one you bought? When did you buy it? Papa died in August, and you started building it in November. We lived there until we came here.

We enjoyed [our home] when we could, but we got where it was too much for us. It's off of Hardscrabble Road [in Columbia]. The house was a well-built house. It was a warm house, easy to cool and easy to heat. It was two lots to keep. We had a garden on half of the second lot. The house was on one, and on the other we had, half of it was azaleas and half of it was a garden.

DS: And did she tell you we had a stream by the house? We had a small stream that ran along the side of the house. And we'd have azaleas all over. We had the bank fixed with big rocks to keep it from washing. We put dog-woods and azaleas on the bank. It really made a beautiful picture when it bloomed. It looked like a fairyland. Virginia's bedroom was on the back of the house, so the flowers gave a pink reflection in the room.

vH: It was so pretty.

DS: It was the prettiest thing in the spring you ever laid your eyes on.

vH: We had this dear friend, a Christian girl from Florida, who visited us. Dorothy's room was up to the front and mine was in the back, and I always had my room in white because I liked to sew, and I could see well.[28] And when there was pink shining, and I had a mirror over here and a mirror over here, that pink was just [shining], and she commented, "Honey, if I slept in this room, I'd think I was waking up in heaven." It was so pretty.

The stream didn't overflow. We were able to grow some pretty flowers, because the rain came down the hill and kept us damp. She had big rocks put on the bank. But we did have trouble with children wanting to climb up on the banks.

DS: I'd say, "Now, boys, girls, let's don't play on the rocks, because they might fall on you, and they are big, and they will hurt you." "Yes, ma'am, we'll get off them."

You'd put the window up, and you could hear the water trickling down.

vH: Oh, we had a bullfrog. You know the sound they make, they don't make it too much. And he was right there near my window. My window was as close as that [she indicates the far side of the room] to the water. And for a long time, we didn't have one [bullfrog]. The children killed it. And I noticed before we left, we had one; I guess he wasn't grown yet. He kind of made a little noise; I said, "There's a bullfrog." But it was good to hear him. We had the prettiest, what are those trees that bloom in the spring that look like gardenias but they're not? Bays. We had three bay trees along the stream. They were kind of crooked, but there was an interesting shape that they had. They had beautiful, nice-smelling blooms. The bay, it must be from the magnolia [family], because it kind of has an odor similar to that. We didn't have a magnolia. Not enough room for a magnolia. I think one came up in the back, and I chopped it down. They need to be in big spaces.

DS: We had two good fig trees.

VH: We had more than that. We had two big ones. Then we had another one. And then we had one that came from my daddy's farm.

DS: Three fig trees.

VH: Yeah, we had three. I hope those people [who bought the house] like figs. But you know what? The last two summers before we left, they did not produce anything. They came on, but we didn't get rain, and they dropped off.[29] Oh, I used to have figs to make fig preserves, and I'd give people figs.

DS: And I suppose those pecan trees are there now, because they were big trees. Two of them.

VH: They volunteered [came up from seed that had dropped on the ground]. You know, how things will grow better [when they volunteer] than when you plant them? Well, they volunteered. The squirrels put them in the garden. You know, I don't like squirrels. A lot of people likes them, but I don't. We had the most beautiful plum tree next to our clothesline. It was so pretty. And you know, they'd get up in that tree, and they would just fight, and they was so sassy. They didn't want us to get the fruit.

DS: I'd get a stick, and they'd fuss at me. It was like boxing. Oh, I couldn't stand them.

VH: I had a funny thing [to happen]. We were taking a nap one day. And I happened to look up, and I saw a squirrel on my chest of drawers. At first I thought I was dreaming. I thought, "Well, my word, I saw a squirrel." We got up and closed the door to the hall so he couldn't get away. I picked up a bath mat and grabbed him by the neck [through the bath mat], and when I got him out he was dead. They're really a nuisance. You plant things, and they come and dig it up. And they'll come in your house, and they will damage your curtains and draperies.

DS: I can see my mother in the kitchen now. Getting her meals ready.

VH: When we'd come home from Columbia [to the farm] on the weekend—she [their mother] usually had fish for Friday or Saturday—so she was in the kitchen working, and he [their father] was standing waiting for us to come. He always gave us a big hug.

DS: He'd just hug us and love us.

VH: See, Mama always stayed busy cooking.

DS: I always said we had two of the best parents that anybody could have.

VH: Jimmy [their younger brother] went to Clemson College for a year and decided to go in the navy. And when the war was over, he was located in a hospital and gave shots to boys coming back from the war. After he got out of the navy, he went to the University of South Carolina in Columbia. And he finished in pre-med. He wanted to be a doctor. But then he could not get in med school. And he would have made a good one, very smart. He got a job working in the government lab in Columbia. Dr. Penny, who taught at the university, got the job for him. I did Mrs. Penny's hair. When the lab moved to Atlanta, he made his home there. He lives in Doraville, but he works down there on malarial fever and viruses. He had two things he worked on. They sent him to Malaysia; he had to manage a lab in Malaysia. I think that was a good experience for him, but he said the weather stayed the same, and it was not good, because he likes cool weather. But I think he enjoyed it. He had his own amah—what is that, is that his maid?—to keep his house for him.

DS: Our teachers used to say that Jimmy was one of the smartest students they ever taught. He would read till three o'clock in the morning.

VH: That's when he lived with us.[30] He did lots of reading; when he got sleepy, he put his books up under the bed. [laughter]

DS: He could talk on any subject.

VH: But he doesn't have a whole lot to say.

DS: No, he's very quiet.

VH: He's received several medals from the government. We don't know, two or three. He just never says anything.

DS: You'd think he never knew anything [because he says so little].

VH: [He finished pre-med] at University of South Carolina. My son-in-law and two grandchildren finished college there also.

And my granddaughter, Jill, is a computer whiz. She didn't lack, I don't know, but just a little bit, being cum laude. And she studied, and she carried two jobs and finished in three years. And she went into computers, and so does her husband. She was in Jacksonville, Florida, and they sent her to Illinois and sent her to another place, and now she's in Raleigh. And she has a little boy, and she works for them from her computer at home. Do you remember Ross Perot? She works for the company that Ross Perot owned.[31] He sold it.

We came to Spartanburg because my daughter lives in Landrum. My daughter and her family moved from Lancaster to Inman, and from Inman to Landrum. And that's where they settled; they bought land there. And we just got where we had more house than we could keep in Columbia. It was getting me down. It was more than we could handle. And Dorothy had a hip operation, and she couldn't do much. It took a lot out of me, trying to do. And she said, "Mother, it's too far." It was killing her, going back and forth to Columbia, see that's two hours there and two hours back, and she said, "I don't even have time to look at you."[32] Because she had to go get groceries for us. And so Julie just said, "Mother, you're just going to have to make a decision now." And I knew it, and it wasn't easy. And it was kind of traumatic. Because we had so much stuff in the attic and in the house, you know. It wasn't easy. But I like it here. It's still not like having your own home, because it's small, but it's nice.

ds: We owned the house and a lot next to it. And we had a vegetable garden 'cause we'd always had a vegetable garden, you know. And I just couldn't see it without one. That's what I bought that land for.

vh: So she [Julie] said, "We'll see what we can do. You're going to have to start getting things together." And I had had one of my eyes operated on, and you're not supposed to lift. Well, I couldn't do much, but I did what could and tried to throw out things that needed to be thrown out. She moved us up here; she found this place. We had prayed. We had come and looked at it, and we knew and we'd told them that we wanted it, and we prayed and asked the Lord for a place, because we needed a place. And you know somebody canceled.[33] It was answered just like that. And I told Julie, "I don't think she needs to climb stairs. We're going to need a downstairs apartment." And the Lord must have changed her mind; [laughs] she decided she didn't want it. But that's the way it happens.

But she [Julie] works here [in Spartanburg County]. She's in real estate, and she comes in to see us, and if we need something, she's here. And we'll go spend the weekend [with Julie].

But it's good to have her [Dorothy] here, because I knew it was bothering her.[34] And, you know, that house sold. Because she never put it on the market, because she knew a lady in Columbia, and she never put it on the market. And she didn't want people going through. The couple decided they would take it as is. She didn't have to do any painting.

DS: We had so many things I would like to have but couldn't bring them. Especially some of the tools.

VH: Tools and stuff. My son-in-law and my grandson got some of those tools. When you're the woman around the house and the man, too, we had to have something to work with.

DS: I hated to leave that place. I loved it.

VH: Well, it's a blessing. I just say, let it be a blessing for them. I pray the home is a blessing to the people who bought it. There's an old saying, you can't cry over spilled milk, can you?

In the country, you learned where food came from and how it was grown. You only bought what you could not grow. You learned that God sends rain and sunshine, and only God can make a seed grow and produce and make a harvest. You learn to trust God. I think a farmer has to have faith in God. You can't put your money in something if you don't have faith that it's going to grow. And I think when people go into farming, don't you think so, they have to have faith that God's going to give them rain, and he's going to multiply, give them a good crop. Well, I think really, living in the country, it makes you humble, because you've got to depend on the Lord so much, now haven't you?

We thank God for our life on the farm. We learned to cope with situations when we were young—circumstances help to make you stronger. We thank God for living on the farm. The experiences we had as children, enjoying one another, seeing God in nature, how he created this earth for man to enjoy and give him glory for protection and supplying every need we might have for life.

NOTES

1. In the Skinner family, there was a gap of several years between the first group of five children and the second group of three. They thought of it as almost being two different families. Dorothy referred to herself as the baby, or the youngest, of the first family, while Virginia saw herself as the eldest of the second.

2. Apparently their youngest brother, Jimmy, had seizures as an infant.

3. A favorite pastime of farm children in the autumn was to turn the chore of raking leaves into a game. Children would rake the leaves into piles and then take

turns jumping into the piles, either from ground level or from a higher surface nearby.

4. Substitute ingredients she did have for those that she did not.

5. "Live at home" was a common expression, popularized by the Agricultural Extension Service. It referred to the practice of raising as many of the goods the family needed on the farm to minimize the need for cash.

6. Rural southerners usually referred to white potatoes as Irish potatoes in order to distinguish them from sweet potatoes.

7. "Bottom" or "bottomland" referred to low-lying ground that was prone to flooding in times of heavy rain.

8. During the Franklin Roosevelt administration's New Deal, the federal government's Resettlement Administration established a subsistence homestead resettlement project in Lee County. These projects were designed to settle displaced farm workers and tenants, miners, and other unemployed people on small subsistence farms in communities that also ran cooperative workshops or factories such as canneries and furniture-making operations. Residents purchased their new homes through long-term, low-interest federal loans. The Lee County project was known as Ashwood Plantation and was designated for white farmers. A subsistence homestead project at Allendale, South Carolina, was designated for black farmers, and one at Orangeburg included farmers of both races.

9. A number of Lee County landowners did sell their farms to the Resettlement Administration.

10. You needed a hammer to crack the nuts. The hard nuts Virginia Harris refers to probably came from a black walnut tree, while the other tree was probably an English walnut.

11. "Make anything" refers to the per-tree yield.

12. Loaded with walnuts.

13. When adding indoor toilets to farmhouses, families often enclosed a portion of a back porch to accommodate the room.

14. Alamo and Delco were brands of generators that charged storage batteries that could then power lights and small appliances using direct current.

15. When the older children left home, cleaning the Aladdin lamps became Virginia's responsibility.

16. Rembert Methodist Church was founded in 1786 and was one of the oldest Methodist churches in the nation.

17. I was unable to determine the exact date of this tornado, but given Mrs. Harris's age, it was probably in the early 1920s.

18. Neighbors helped neighbors whose homes were damaged or destroyed by the tornado.

19. The federal government purchased staple food items and distributed them to the poor during the Great Depression. Usually local men were selected to handle the commodities distribution.

20. The Agricultural Adjustment Administration paid farmers to reduce their production of certain agricultural commodities in an effort to reduce a market glut of those products and thus raise wholesale prices. The program was first implemented

in the spring of 1933, after most farmers had planted their spring crops. In order to reduce acreage and receive federal payments, farmers had to plow up crops that were already well established. In later years, farmers simply planted fewer acres in order to qualify for payments.

21. Mrs. Harris's daughter and son-in-law purchased some acreage in Landrum where they now live. Apparently the soil on their land is also clay.

22. The older children would shop for the younger children's "Santa Claus" gifts.

23. Gert was the sisters' aunt.

24. The Cokers were an old and influential South Carolina family. Most likely, Dorothy Skinner's grandmother was raised by Major James Lide Coker, a Hartsville merchant.

25. The family story explained that the sisters' great-grandfather Peter Dalrymple was killed by the enemy as he returned to the front lines after a visit home to see his newborn daughter.

26. The University of South Carolina.

27. She knew that when her lease expired, the new landlords would either raise the rent or ask her to move.

28. The white walls reflected the maximum amount of light, making it easier for Mrs. Harris to see her sewing.

29. The blooms fell off.

30. Jimmy lived with the sisters in Columbia while he attended the University of South Carolina.

31. EDS, Inc.

32. Virginia's daughter, Julie, found that it was difficult for her to make frequent trips to Columbia to assist her aging mother and aunt.

33. Someone who had leased a first-floor apartment canceled, freeing up a first-floor apartment for the sisters.

34. Not being able to maintain the Columbia house properly was bothering Dorothy.

Afterword

Reflections on Interpreting Oral History

> All human beings are practicing historians. As we go through life
> we present ourselves to others through our life story; as we grow and
> mature we change that story through different interpretations and
> different emphasis. We stress different events as having been decisive
> at different times in our life history and, as we do so, we give those
> events new meanings. People do not think of this as "doing history";
> they engage in it often without special awareness. We live our lives;
> we tell our stories; it is as natural as breathing.
>
> Gerda Lerner

As I said at the outset, oral histories are really stories—stories about the way
individuals and groups lived in the past. We are all familiar with stories.
Stories are the narrative devices people use to describe significant experiences and explain their meanings. We grow up listening to stories—about
Little Red Riding Hood and the Wizard of Oz, for example. We read stories in books. We know that some stories are true—in the sense that they
describe actual events—and others are "made up"—that is, they are narratives about events created in someone's imagination. We quickly learn that
stories are ways of embedding details about events in an interpretive framework. Using stories, we make sense of events that might otherwise seem random to a listener or a reader. By telling stories, we pass our individual and
family histories on to others.[1]

Thinking of oral histories as stories reminds us of some of the challenges
inherent in studying the past through oral history. We would prefer to think
of oral narratives as pure recall—an accurate retelling of exactly what happened in the past. But upon reflection, we realize that Alessandro Portelli's
conception of oral history as a set of stories embedded in the "knot of memory and imagination that turns material facts into cultural meanings" is
more useful.[2] For memory is *not* pure recall. Memories contain distortions,

omissions, rearrangements, and occasionally outright fabrications. As any police officer will tell you, memory is fickle, and the longer the time span between witnessing an event and recounting it, the more likely a narrator will distort that event. Since oral history accounts are usually given years after the event, it stands to reason that oral historical accounts will not be simple verbal reproductions of that event.

Even a beginning student of oral history senses that narrators' accounts are often flawed. For example, in our interview, French Clark told me that her son Kenneth was born in Maryville, Tennessee, but in the family history questionnaire she later completed with her daughter's help, she noted Kenneth's birthplace as Detroit, Michigan. I was subsequently able to confirm that Kenneth was born in Michigan by checking with the family. Mrs. Clark was mistaken in her interview. This is a minor example of a factual error in oral history interviews but a useful one in drawing our attention to some of the challenges of using oral history as a historical source.

In order to understand why oral histories contain inaccuracies, it is useful to examine psychologists' most recent theories about the ways human beings construct memories. Neuropsychologists studying the way the brain receives memory have found that the brain does not receive memories passively but rather interprets the incoming data.[3] In other words, rather than merely recording the events perceived by a person's senses, the brain seeks to make sense of those events by connecting them with things the individual already knows. Thus, memories are being assigned meaning as they arrive in the brain, and the brain stores those memories in an organized fashion by connecting them with similar knowledge and memories already stored in the brain. The brain also does not organize the memory of a single event as a unified whole; rather, discrete pieces of that memory are stored in the brain and may be connected to disparate series of other memories.[4]

When the brain is asked to recall a particular memory, it does not recall an exact recording of the event. Instead, it recalls the interpreted event and some of the related knowledge or memories to which it was connected in the brain. As psychologist John Kotre put it, "When we recollect, the brain literally *re-collects* [emphasis his] all neural events that took place on a prior occasion." To make matters more complicated, as the memory of an event is retrieved, the brain may reinterpret the event in light of new information or subsequent memories. Alterations in memory can occur for several other reasons. First, memories can be reshaped by the circumstances of their recall. We recover memories by using retrieval cues—old letters, smells, contact with a place where the memory was made. We also recover memories in response to questions or cues from others. The type of trigger to recall may influence the shape of the recall. For example, cognitive psychologists have found that the thoughts produced by random, unbidden recall of events are always structurally different from conscious, deliberate recall. Information received from others can alter memories.[5]

The shape and content of oral history narratives are also determined in part by the way the brain organizes memory, and a historian who wants to understand why narrators include some stories and not others must understand this organization. Autobiographical memory is organized hierarchically. Over time, our sense of chronology fades. We lose our sense of "when" events happened as we begin to organize the content of memory—the "what" —according to the meaning we assign to that memory.[6]

We take the repetitive events of everyday life and arrange them hierarchically. At the lowest level of hierarchy are single events. Over time, single events will be forgotten or incorporated into memories at a higher level of the hierarchy unless the single events were particularly noteworthy for some reason. Gradually, recollections become more thematic, pulling more activities together. These thematic memories become "generic" memories. For example, farm women did not remember every time they canned tomatoes or cooked for threshers or milked cows. They remembered these things generically.[7] We also remember—or think we remember—specific events in some detail if they are unique enough or life changing enough.[8] Happy events and painful events are likely to be remembered in more detail. For example, French Clark vividly recalled the occasion when one of the children ironed a garish patch on her husband's only good work shirt. Although the event was funny in retrospect, at the time her husband was embarrassed by his poverty in not being able to afford to replace the damaged shirt. Virginia Harris remembered losing her class ring in the sweet potato bank and then finding it. These were unusual events, and so the women remembered them.

Sometimes people have both generic memories and specific memories about particular types of events. For example, Korola Lee spoke in some detail about her generic memories of the peddler coming to her parents' home in his buggy, exchanging manufactured goods with neighborhood women in return for their butter and eggs. The story of the peddler was constructed from dozens, perhaps hundreds, of peddlers' visits over the course of her childhood and early adulthood. Miss Lee also had a specific memory of a particular visit by the peddler. She spoke of the time the peddler's horses became spooked and ran away, turning the wagon over and dumping the butter, eggs, and other cargo all over the ground. Korola was a small child when this event occurred, but it was memorable enough for her to recall it in great detail nearly seventy years later.

Like Korola Lee, we remember some events in great detail, but others are more vague in our memories. For example, we are more likely to remember personal events than national events. Psychologists have found that the information that people store about public events includes facts about the event itself, facts which relate the event to other events, and facts about the event's personal context.[9] People remember facts about the event's personal context in more detail than the larger event. Korola Lee never mentioned the Great Depression or even World War II as discrete events. She mentioned cuts in her salary in the 1930s, and she remembered that a male teacher was offered a higher salary for the teaching position than Korola herself subsequently received, but she never mentioned the Great Depression as being the context for this salary cut. Similarly, when I asked farm women to talk about New Deal programs, most responded with vague answers. They remembered that these programs were implemented during the Depression and that the government's efforts were designed to help people who were suffering from the economic downturn, but only in cases where women had direct contact with a program did they have much to say about the program's details. One example was Mary Evelyn Lane's description of her husband hauling surplus cotton to federally sponsored mattress-making projects for poor women. She did not remember which New Deal agency organized the mattress-making project nor much about how it operated, but she did remember that her family quilted with scraps from broken bales of the cotton her husband hauled. Similarly, Virginia Harris remembered that "people lost their money" when "the banks closed in the Depression." She also remembered that her father was one of the agents commissioned by "the government" to give out surplus commodities to poor people in her own community, but she said nothing about the specific federal agency that distributed the commodities or the way needy people qualified for such aid. In part, the vagueness of her memory may be attributed to the fact that Mrs. Harris was a child during the early years of the Depression, but the event of the Depression itself was significant only in the ways in which it touched her own life.

Psychologists have found that people tend to remember best the things that happened between eighteen and thirty-five. Many significant events happen to most people during these young adult years, including financial independence, marriage, and the formation of careers and families. This is also the period of time when major historical events have their greatest impact on memory, perhaps because this is the period of time when national events have their greatest impact on individuals.[10] Mary Evelyn Lane's memories of the Great Depression were intertwined with the fact that her father lost his farm during those years and that the economic downturn forced her and her husband to live with his parents. Ruth Hatchette McBrayer remembered World War II more vividly than many of the women whose stories are told here, because the structure of wartime draft laws encouraged her husband to leave his father's business in order to become a full-time farmer and thus avoid the draft.

Most of these women were telling their life stories during old age, and this fact shaped their stories, too. Late in life, we become aware that we are among the last living witnesses to a time period or particular way of life. This knowledge stimulates many memories. We may engage in "life reviews" at this point, and as John Kotre noted, "The feeling of satisfaction from a life review may be augmented by seeing your life as part of a larger drama, as a variant of some archetypal tale. You may come to see your place in history." Indeed, many older people become acutely aware that their own generation witnessed events or experienced a way of life that subsequent generations did not. These older people have a sense of being "memory bearers." Many of these women understood that they had lived through a period of remarkable transformation, and this self-consciousness helped shape the way they told their life stories. Virginia Harris's eloquent conclusion to her interview, in which she sums up the significance of her farm childhood for her life, provides one example of this self-consciousness of the significance or uniqueness of a life story.[11]

Other factors shape the way we recount our life histories. We have occasion to repeat some memories over and over, while we rarely need to recall other events. Historian Alice Hoffman and psychologist Howard Hoffman, in their joint work on the accuracy of memory, have called the frequently repeated memories "archival memory." Archival memories are those "recollections that are rehearsed, readily available for recall, and selected for preservation over the lifetime of the individual." The life events stored in archival memory tend to be those that are most salient to a person's life. If an event provided a turning point in an individual's life, such as the outbreak of World War II, or if it dominated daily life, such as the struggle to provide food and clothing in the face of grinding poverty, that event will be stored in archival memory.[12] Life events stored in archival memory will usually be rehearsed internally or in conversation. The more a memory is rehearsed, the more quickly and easily it will be recalled.[13] Frequently rehearsed stories are perfected and, to paraphrase one historian, can be moved further from reality. Often with rehearsed stories "events are telescoped, chronology tightened, order rearranged and edited. Rehearsed stories tend to omit negative events and concentrate on triumphs." Oral historians have to listen carefully to distinguish rehearsed stories from more spontaneous retellings.[14]

Not only are memories reconstructed, but they are also socially constructed. As French sociologist Maurice Halbwachs argued long ago, people acquire memories in society, and they also recall, recognize, and localize their memories in society. Individuals remember, but they do so in a specific group context, drawing on that context to recreate the past. Even stories about one's own life are shaped by others—by the expectations of one's family, one's community, and one's culture. Halbwachs noted that "[i]ndividual memory is . . . a part or an aspect of group memory, since each impression and each fact, even if it apparently concerns a particular person exclusively, leaves a lasting memory only to the extent that one has thought it over—to the extent that it is connected with the thoughts that come to us from the social milieu."[15]

Historian Alistair Thomson has noted that "[f]rom the moment we experience an event we use the meanings of our culture to make sense of it. Over time we remember our experiences, as those public meanings change. There is a constant negotiation between experience and sense, public and private memory. . . . Our memories are risky and painful if they do not conform with the public norms or versions of the past. We construct and contain our memories so that they will fit with what is publicly acceptable; or we find safety in smaller 'publics' or peer groups, which may be socially or politically marginal." Historians can use the knowledge that oral history is a social act, influenced by social forces, to better understand the function that stories about the past serve for the narrator. For example, individuals tend not to include details in their oral histories if they are not acceptable to the larger society, or if they do include them, they tend to explain them. Historians who use oral history must be attuned to this social construction of memory.[16]

Narrators also construct stories that portray themselves in a flattering light. Historians Raphael Samuel and Paul Thompson have argued that all life stories, written or oral, are by their nature "a personal mythology, a self-justification." Other scholars have noted that narrators rarely share accounts of their own failings with interviewers. Few of the women here mentioned their moments of personal failure or disappointment. They did not talk about children who disappointed them or their own shortcomings as wives, mothers, or farmers. They might laughingly refer to their dislike of housework or their failure to be good housekeepers, but they usually made these references in the context of asserting some other personal strength. They often glossed over personal events that they perhaps considered personal failures.

For example, Virginia Harris mentioned her brief marriage only in passing and probably only to explain how she came to have a daughter. She blamed the marriage's failure on the way World War II "changed" her husband, and then she moved on to another topic. Korola Lee told the obviously painful story of the day she ran over and killed a small child, and she told that story to defend herself. I suspect that she assumed that I had heard the story from my family (I had not) and that she therefore wanted to state for the record that she did not intentionally run over the child (something I would never have assumed). As evidence that the event was a terrible accident, she offered her insurance agent's defense of her and the fact that the child's father chose not to sue her.[17]

Women are particularly likely to shape their stories around society's expectations for women's lives. As scholars Alexander Freund and Laura Quilici put it, "Women may mute their own thoughts and feelings by describing their lives in ways that outwardly conform to acceptable behavior." Women may shape their stories around the mythic ideal of womanhood, the idea of the hardworking, self-sacrificing wife and mother, always acting in the best interests of her family. Similarly, she may deny having done work that violates notions about the work appropriate for women.[18] When I asked Mabel Love about her work on the family's dairy in the 1930s, she talked about housework, caring for chickens and cows, and selling eggs. She readily admitted her participation in milking. Finally I pressed her: "Did you work in the fields?" "Yes," she admitted, seeming reluctant. She did sometimes work in the fields. Then she changed the subject and returned to stories about feeding men at threshing time. This exchange was revealing. Mabel Love had been a partner in the family farm. She spoke of decisions to buy land or invest in new equipment as joint decisions. Clearly she considered herself a driving force in her family's farming operation. Her reluctance to talk about her fieldwork suggests to me that she was uncomfortable with having worked in the fields. Perhaps she believed that I would not approve or that my readers would not. Or perhaps fieldwork violated her own notions about the work a prosperous farm woman of her status should do. Her telling and retelling of the story of cooking for threshing parties, while it may be indicative of the importance of that experience in her life, also seems to be a way of avoiding talking about her fieldwork.[19]

Not only do people shape their memories around the expectations of the larger society, but they also shape their stories around their interaction with the interviewer. Oral history is a dialogue, a conversation between an interviewer and the narrator. The interviewer plays a huge role in creating and shaping memory as it is expressed in an oral history. The questions an interviewer asks shape the story. Leading, suggestive, or repeated questions all tend to distort memories and answers. Open-ended questions may elicit more accurate memories, because the narrator is not trying to direct an answer to the interviewer's specific agenda, but open-ended questions may also elicit less information than more detailed questions. An interviewer who says "tell me your life story" will get a far different set of recollections than an interviewer who says "tell me about life in the Great Depression." An interviewer who fails to listen and ask follow-up questions may not obtain significant details or explanations of complex family sagas.

Narrators respond to different interviewers and audiences in various ways. They will often shape their stories based on what they perceive to be the expectations of the interviewer. For example, an older narrator who maintains racial beliefs that have become unpopular in our twenty-first-century world may not share them with a young interviewer. African American subjects are often not forthcoming with white interviewers and vice versa. A southerner may not provide certain details of southern life to a "Yankee" interviewer. Women will not share some intimate details of childbearing or marital relationships with male interviewers. In short, the narrator will share information he believes is appropriate for sharing with that particular researcher. The way a narrator tells a story is based in "assumptions about the audience to which a performance is directed, so that narratives always exist through a web of social relationships."[20]

The way people tell a story is also shaped by who is listening or might listen in the future. My interviews with Loudon County, Tennessee, farm women are a case in point. The interviews were arranged by another prominent farm woman in the community, a woman somewhat younger than the women I was interviewing. My local contact accompanied me to the interviews, hoping to help break the ice with my narrators. My contact believed that she was making the process easier for me; at the time, so did I. Only later did I realize that my contact's presence might have caused my narrators to censor themselves. The Loudon County interviews were shorter and often less richly detailed than most of my other interviews. They contained less information about other people in the community than some of my other interviews. The Loudon County women understood that they were not simply talking with a young scholar who would disappear after the interview; they were also talking with a community member who might disapprove of certain interpretations of the rural past or might spread the word if they shared some unflattering story about a neighbor.[21]

A final factor that shapes oral history narrators' stories about the past is the present. As folklorist Elizabeth Tonkin has noted, "People talk of 'the past' so as to distinguish 'now' from a different 'then.'"[22] It is important for historians to understand this and to understand how this moment in the narrator's life and current experience shapes their stories about past events. Their stories tell us much about the way these people view the world they live in today and the things they feel have been lost in the wake of modernization. When Dorothy Skinner complains that today's children "need the books they had back then. . . . I think they'd learn more," she is not only criticizing the way children are educated today, but she is also reinterpreting the past in light of her opinion about the world she lives in now. Often, stories about the past are cautionary or moral tales told to educate the young. Sometimes narrators tell stories about the past in an attempt to shape the future. The fact that the story is being told for a didactic purpose also shapes the story.[23] By the same token, people interpret the present based on their memories, on their previous knowledge of the world around them.

To sum up then, an oral history is a story—the story of one person's life and the way that life intersected the larger past. The autobiographical memories that are expressed in that story are reconstructions and interpretations of events in the life of the narrator. These reconstructions are shaped by subsequent events in the narrator's life, by the society in which the narrator lives, by the interaction with the interviewer, by concerns about who might be listening, and by the narrator's perceptions of the world in which she lives today.[24]

If oral history is so problematic, if it contains inaccuracies, omissions, and distortions, if it is murky and challenging to interpret, why should historians use it at all? It is important to remember that these problems are not unique to oral historical sources. All historical sources are subject to inaccuracies, omissions, distortions, and differing interpretations. A simple comparison of various diary accounts by Civil War soldiers and officers who all witnessed the same battle illustrates the distortions that are possible in the written historical record. Moreover, the ways historical records are structured reflects power relations in the larger society. Traditional historical accounts are shaped largely by the memoirs of elite citizens, by the incomplete accounts of journalists, and by the limits of records kept by government officials who had their own biases. For example, a scholar might never know that most early-twentieth-century farm women engaged in fieldwork by looking at the records of the United States Department of Agriculture.[25]

Oral histories may be less important for what they add to our store of knowledge about the "facts" of the past than for what these narratives tell us about what the past meant to the people who lived it. As Italian historian Alessandro Portelli has put it, "oral sources tell us not just what people did, but what they wanted to do, what they believed they were doing, and what they now think they did."[26] In short, oral histories are valuable for helping us understand the mindset of historical actors. They help us understand how people interpreted the past and how that interpretation of the past may have shaped their past (and their present) choices.

Oral history can provide us with the opportunity to understand the past from the point of view of people who lived it. In the process of recreating the past, narrators provide us with a level of information and knowledge that goes beyond the dry facts that are conveyed in documentary evidence. The narrators try to convey a sense of what it was like to live in the past. They also stress the events that were most important to their lives, especially giving texture to our sense of what daily life was like in the past. A dry description of a farm family's efforts to raise most of its own food and make most of the things it needs can never be as vivid as Wilma Williamson's descriptions of her grandmother's life.

Oral history can perform other important functions. Historian Paul Thompson points out that "one of the great advantages of oral history is that it enabled the historian to counteract the bias present in normal historical sources. . . ." In other words, oral history is most useful in giving voice to the voiceless, all those ordinary people who rarely keep diaries, write letters, or preserve the details of their lives in written form. Oral history has become an invaluable tool for understanding the perspectives of ordinary people from the past. In the process, it can provide a more complete picture of the past and a corrective to the elite bias of histories written from traditional written sources. The historian's job is to use oral history carefully, to use it in conjunction with other types of sources, and to make some effort to read between the lines.[27]

So, what can we learn from the stories of the rural women contained in this volume? First, I think we learn that farm women saw themselves as in integral part of the family economy. They described their work in great detail, and they understood that their work—whether it was child-rearing, preserving food, caring for livestock, or earning wages at an off-farm job—was essential to the family's well-being.

Second, the orientation of these women's lives is profoundly local. They knew and understood what was happening on the national and international scene; indeed several of them mentioned late-twentieth-century political events in their interviews. But the women who tell their stories here centered their lives around their families and communities. Even as they were being buffeted by economic and political forces beyond their control, forces such as the Great Depression and World War II, these farm women were focused on the daily needs of their families. Wilma Williamson could not accurately remember the dates of World War II, but she was very clear on the year her daughter was born, suggesting that the birth of her daughter was far more significant in her universe. These ordinary women remembered details of larger historical events only when those events touched their individual lives. They forged their identities in a local world.

Third, these southern farm women were part of a transitional generation. During their lives, the upcountry farm economy underwent a profound shift. At the beginning of the century, most farmers in the region were engaged in commercial agriculture, producing for the world market, but they combined commercial farming activities with subsistence production and diversified production for local exchange. By the 1950s and 1960s, many rural southerners were pushed out of farming and even off the land. Those who left agriculture moved into industrial and service jobs in and out of the South. The few farmers who remained became specialized commercial farmers, producing few goods to fill their own needs, instead focusing most of their efforts on producing for world commodities markets.

Farm women were inevitably part of this transition, and we can trace the changes in the lives of the women in this volume. While some of the oldest women remained traditional farmwives, most of the younger women in this volume carved out new niches for themselves. Mabel Love became a farming partner with her husband, building a commercial dairy-farming operation. Ruth Hatchette McBrayer took over the peach-farming operation after her husband's death, and she farmed successfully on her own for four decades. Other women carved out careers off the farm. Mary Evelyn Lane and Peggy Delozier Jones's parents were prosperous enough to provide them with college educations, enabling them to return to careers after their children were older. Their salaries helped educate their own children, and in a sense, they subsidized the farming operation by earning money off the farm to meet some of the family's financial goals. Korola Lee's parents provided her with enough college courses to earn a teaching certificate, and then she put herself through the last two years of college, one summer school term at a time. Mary Quinn managed to put herself through college by combining on-campus jobs with work in a local shirt factory. She went on to a long career as a high school teacher. Dorothy Skinner was truly a self-made woman, working for another insurance agent until she learned the ropes. Then she became an independent insurance agent, a feat quite unusual for a southern woman in the 1950s. The youngest woman in this collection, LaVerne Farmer, attended college and became a home extension agent, but she continued to help on her parents' farm and indeed retired to the farm to care for her aging mother. These career women spent much of their adult lives engaged in work off the farm, and they expressed great pride in their accomplishments—in the students they had taught, the employees they had known, and the contributions they made to their communities through their work.

Some of the rural women in this collection did not live on farms as adults. French Clark, the daughter of a farmer, married a man who made his living working at the Aluminum Company of America (ALCOA). She clung to rural folkways and rejected town living, choosing to raise her children in the country. Like many rural southerners of the mid-twentieth century, Mrs. Clark and her husband combined traditional rural survival strategies, like planting a large garden for the family's food supply and running a crossroads general store, with less-traditional industrial wage labor. Evelyn Lewellyn grew up in the city of Knoxville but spent two long periods of her childhood on an east Tennessee farm where housing was free, if substandard. She took an industrial job at ALCOA during World War II, and there she met her husband, a machinist. Bill Lewellyn spent his life as an ALCOA machinist, but he bought land as soon as he saved enough money. While Bill Lewellyn worked at ALCOA and engaged in part-time farming, Evelyn Lewellyn used rural subsistence strategies to stretch the family's resources.

In the end, these stories tell us that the women in this collection valued hard work, community, and family. Their lives show us how ordinary rural women coped with rural transformation, how they felt about their daily lives, and how very local and personal were their concerns.

A few final observations on the stories contained in this volume are in order. These farm women constructed their stories about early-twentieth-century rural life around their notions about the flaws in contemporary life. Their recollections present yesterday's strong, hardworking communities of farm folk in sharp contrast to what they perceive as the disconnected neighborhoods of soft and materialistic young people in which their children and grandchildren live. To say that they idealize the past through the sentimental lens of old age is perhaps too harsh. While they are grateful that their children and grandchildren did not have to struggle so much, they recognize that their own struggles developed strength of character. Their stories turn again and again to hardship, and none expressed any interest in returning to that earlier time and standard of living. Still, they share a sense of loss. The women who tell their stories in this volume believe that people's inability to survive outside the market economy leaves them vulnerable and weak. They lament the loss of community networks that sustained them in mutual support. Their nostalgia for a world in which "everybody helped each other" in times of sickness and hardship grows out of their sense that they must face sickness and hardship alone in today's world, a feeling that is probably particularly acute because they are now elderly. Narrators believe that, most of all, modern America has lost a type of psychic strength, an emotional stamina that they believe allowed them to outlast hard times. This sense of loss—these notions about what is missing in the world they inhabit today—shapes their stories about the past.

NOTES

Epigraph: Gerda Lerner, *Why History Matters: Life and Thought* (New York: Oxford University Press, 1997), 199.

1. See Barbara Allen, "Story in Oral History: Clues to Historical Consciousness," *Journal of American History,* 79 (September 1992): 606–11.

2. Alessandro Portelli, *The Battle of Valle Giulia: Oral History and the Art of Dialogue* (Madison: University of Wisconsin Press, 1997), 42.

3. Daniel L. Schacter, ed., *Memory Distortion: How Minds, Brains, and Societies Reconstruct the Past* (Cambridge, Mass.: Harvard University Press, 1995), x.

4. John N. Kotre, chaps. 1 and 2 in *White Gloves: How We Create Ourselves Through Memory* (New York: The Free Press, 1995).

5. Kotre, *White Gloves,* 43; Marigold Linton, "Phoenix and Chimera: The Changing Face of Memory," in *Memory and History: Essays on Recalling and Interpreting Experience,* ed. Jaclyn Jeffrey and Glenace Edwall (New York: University Press of America, 1994), 69–84; Elizabeth Loftus, "Tricked By Memory," in *Memory and History,* ed. Jeffrey and Edwall, 17–29.

6. Kotre, *White Gloves,* 85–96.

7. Ibid.

8. Psychologists use the term "flashbulb memories" to describe memories of high-impact events. There is controversy among psychologists about the accuracy of these memories and some evidence that flashbulb memories are less accurate in older adults than younger ones. See Martin A. Conway, *Flashbulb Memories: Essays in Cognitive Psychology* (Hillsdale, N.J.: Lawrence Erlbaum Associates, Inc., 1995) and Gillian Cohen, Martin A. Conway, and Elizabeth A. Maylor, "Flashbulb Memories in Older Adults," *Psychology and Aging* 9 (September 1994): 454–63. I am indebted to Monica McCoy for teaching me about flashbulb memories.

9. Martin A. Conway, "Failures of Autobiographical Remembering," in *Basic and Applied Memory Research Theory in Context,* ed. Douglas J. Herrmann et al., vol. 1 (Mahwah, N.J.: Lawrence Erlbaum Associates, Publishers, 1996), 295–315; Norman R. Brown, Steven K. Shevell, and Lance J. Rips, "Public Memories and Their Personal Context," in *Autobiographical Memory,* ed. David C. Rubin (Cambridge: Cambridge University Press, 1986), 137–57.

10. Kotre, *White Gloves,* 172.

11. Ibid., 173–76; Barbara Myerhoff, "Life History Among the Elderly: Performance, Visibility, and Re-Membering," in *A Look in the Mirror,* ed. Jay Ruby (Philadelphia: University of Pennsylvania Press, 1982), 99–117. I am indebted to John Theilmann for referring me to the Myerhoff article.

12. Alice M. Hoffman and Howard S. Hoffman, "Reliability and Validity in Oral History: The Case for Memory," in *Memory and History,* ed. Jeffrey and Edwall, 107–30.

13. Jerome Sehulster, "Individual Differences in Memory Style and Autobiographical Memory," in *Basic and Applied Memory Research: Practical Applications,* ed. Douglas J. Herrmann et al., vol. 2 (Mahwah, N.J.: Lawrence Erlbaum Associates, Publishers, 1996), 209–29.

14. Donald A. Ritchie, foreword to *Memory and History,* ed. Jeffrey and Edwall, vii.

15. Maurice Halbwachs, *On Collective Memory,* edited, translated, and with an introduction by Lewis A. Coser (Chicago: University of Chicago Press, 1992), 38, 22, 53; Joseph E. Davis, ed., *Stories of Change: Narrative and Social Movements* (Albany: State University of New York Press, 2002), 20–21.

16. Alistair Thomson, "The Anzac Legend: Exploring National Myth and Memory in Australia," in *The Myths We Live By,* ed. Raphael Samuel and Paul Thompson (London: Routledge, 1990), 73–82, quote on 78; Naomi Norquay, "Identity and Forgetting," *The Oral History Review* 26 (winter 1999): 1, 9. See also Elizabeth Tonkin, *Narrating Our Pasts: The Social Construction of Oral History* (Cambridge: Cambridge University Press, 1992) and Karen E. Fields, "What One Cannot Remember Mistakenly," in *Memory and History,* ed. Jeffrey and Edwall, 89–104.

17. For examples of psychological studies which suggest that people portray themselves in flattering ways, see Michael Ross and Sicoly Fiore, "Egocentric Biases in Availability and Attribution," *Journal of Personality and Social Psychology* 37 (March 1979) 322–36; Anthony G. Greenwald, "The Totalitarian Ego: Fabrication and Revision of Personal History," *American Psychologist* 35 (June 1980): 603–18. Historians and sociologists who have noted the tendency of oral history narrators to portray themselves in a flattering light include Samuel and Thompson, *The Myths We Live By,* 10 and Jean Peneff, "Myths in Life Stories," in *The Myths We Live By,* ed. Samuel and Thompson, 36–48.

18. Alexander Freund and Laura Quilici, "Exploring Myths in Women's Narratives: Italian and German Immigrant Women in Vancouver, 1947–1961," *The Oral History Review* 23 (winter 1996): 19–25, quote on 10; Samuel and Thompson, *The Myths We Live By,* 17.

19. Alessandro Portelli notes that velocity of storytelling is important. Narrators dwell on some stories and gloss over others. Sometimes the narrator accelerates the pace of a story because it is not important, but at other times narrators hurry through a story or change the subject because of "a wish to glide over certain points." See *The Death of Luigi Trastulli and Other Stories: Form and Meaning in Oral History* (Albany: State University of New York Press, 1991), 48.

20. Tonkin, *Narrating Our Pasts,* 38, 48–49.

21. Ibid. See also Portelli, *The Death of Luigi Trastulli,* 31–39.

22. Tonkin, *Narrating Our Pasts,* 9, 66–67; Michael Frisch, *A Shared Authority: Essays on the Craft and Meaning of Oral and Public History* (Albany: State University of New York Press, 1990), 12.

23. David Thelen, ed., *Memory and American History* (Bloomington: Indiana University Press, 1989), xi, xv; Iwona Irwin-Zarecka, *Frames of Remembrances: The*

Dynamics of Collective Memory (New Brunswick: Transaction Publishers, 1994), 101, 107; Fields, "What One Cannot Remember Mistakenly," in *Memory and History,* ed. Jeffrey and Edwall, 10; Frisch, *A Shared Authority,* xxiii.

24. Davis, *Stories of Change,* 12.

25. For a cogent discussion of the potential biases in various written historical sources, see Paul Thompson, chap. 4 in *The Voice of the Past: Oral History* (Oxford: Oxford University Press, 1978).

26. Portelli, *The Death of Luigi Trastulli,* 50.

27. Barbara Allen, "Re-Creating the Past: The Narrator's Perspective in Oral History," *The Oral History Review* 12 (1984): 1–12; Mary Anglin, "Toward a Workable Past: Dangerous Memories and Feminist Perspectives," *Journal of Appalachian Studies* 6 (2000): 71–99; Paul Thompson, *The Voice of the Past,* 123.

Suggestions for Further Reading

On the Southern Agricultural Economy in the Twentieth Century

Corbin, Mike. *Family Trees: The Peach Culture of the Piedmont.* Spartanburg, S.C.: Hub City Writers Project, 1998.

Daniel, Pete. *Breaking the Land: The Transformation of Cotton, Tobacco, and Rice Cultures since 1880.* Urbana: University of Illinois Press, 1980.

————. *Standing at the Crossroads: Southern Life in the Twentieth Century.* New York: Hill and Wang, 1986.

Kirby, Jack Temple. *Rural Worlds Lost: The American South, 1920–1960.* Baton Rouge: Louisiana State University Press, 1987.

On Southern Farm Women

Hagood, Margaret Jarman. *Mothers of the South: Portraiture of the White Tenant Farm Women.* 1939. Reprint, New York: Arno Press, 1972.

Jones, Jacqueline. *Labor of Love, Labor of Sorrow: Black Women, Work, and the Family from Slavery to the Present.* New York: Vintage Books, 1985.

Jones, Lu Ann. *Mama Learned Us to Work: Farm Women in the New South.* Chapel Hill: University of North Carolina Press, 2002.

Sharpless, M. Rebecca. *Fertile Ground, Narrow Choices: Women on Texas Cotton Farms, 1900–1940.* Chapel Hill: University of North Carolina Press, 1999.

Walker, Melissa. *All We Knew Was to Farm: Rural Women in the Upcountry South, 1919–1941.* Baltimore: Johns Hopkins University Press, 2000.

On the Nature of Memory

Engel, Susan. *Context Is Everything: The Nature of Memory.* New York: W. H. Freeman and Company, 1999.

Halbwachs, Maurice. *On Collective Memory.* Edited, translated, and with an introduction by Lewis A. Coser. Chicago: University of Chicago Press, 1992.

Kotre, John N. *White Gloves: How We Create Ourselves through Memory.* New York: The Free Press, 1995.

ON MEMORY AND ORAL HISTORY:

Frisch, Michael. *A Shared Authority: Essays on the Craft and Meaning of Oral and Public History.* Albany: State University of New York Press, 1990.

Grele, Ron, et al. *Envelopes of Sound: The Art of Oral History.* 2d ed. New York: Praeger, 1991.

Jeffrey, Jaclyn and Glenace Edwall, eds. *Memory and History: Essays on Recalling and Interpreting Experience.* New York: University Press of America, 1994.

Portelli, Alessandro. *The Battle of Valle Giulia: Oral History and the Art of Dialogue.* Madison: University of Wisconsin Press, 1997.

Thelen, David, ed. *Memory and American History.* Bloomington: Indiana University Press, 1989.

Index